2004

Parker,

Thank you so much for all of your help and morale support. You really were a lighthouse for me when I was in the middle of the ocean.

Much, much love,

Bryan

LESBIAN BUDDHA IN HOLLYWOOD
An Autobiographical Trilogy

Part One : HUNGRY GHOSTS

(1979 - 1985)

ROXANNE REAVER

Part One

HUNGRY GHOSTS

(1979 - 1985)

Copyright © 2003 by Roxanne Reaver.

Library of Congress Number: 2003098119
ISBN: Hardcover 1-4134-3620-X
Softcover 1-4134-3619-6

All rights reserved. No part of this book may be reproduced or transmitted in any form or by any means, electronic or mechanical, including photocopying, recording, or by any information storage and retrieval system, without permission in writing from the copyright owner.

This book was printed in the United States of America.

To order additional copies of this book, contact:
Xlibris Corporation
1-888-795-4274
www.Xlibris.com
Orders@Xlibris.com

This book is dedicated to my teacher and spiritual mother, JoAnne—the one with the Bodhicitta heart. You taught me how to breathe and to smile. You saved my life. Thank you. I would not be who I am today without all those years of your unconditional love and support. Harry, Kensho, Dump and Matahari, I bow to you with immense love and gratitude.

This book is also dedicated to all the wonderful, dynamic women and men and other sentient beings who have helped to shape the fabric of my life. My heart overflows with love and gratitude at the mere idea of each of you.

This book is dedicated to the ultimate happiness of all beings.

"There's a life-affirming teaching in Buddhism, which is that Buddha, which means 'awake' is not someone you worship. Buddha is not someone you aspire to; Buddha is not somebody that was born more than two thousand years ago and was smarter than you'll ever be. Buddha is our inherent nature—our buddha nature—and what that means is that if you're going to grow up fully, the way that it happens is that you begin to connect with the intelligence that you already have . . . you allow it to grow, you allow it to come out . . .

"'When you feel afraid, that's "fearful buddha."' . . . If you feel jealous, that's 'jealous buddha.' If you have indigestion, that's 'buddha with heartburn.' If you're happy, 'happy buddha'; if bored, 'bored buddha.' In other words, anything that you can experience or think is worthy of compassion; anything you could think or feel is worthy of appreciation."

(from *Start Where You Are* by Pema Chodron, Shambala Publications, pp 98-99.)

This story is one small thread in the larger fabric of 'lesbian buddha.'

First we are asleep.

Then we are in pain.

Eventually the pain wakes us up.

PREFACE

It is only in hindsight that we can discern the gossamer fingerprints of the Divine on the pattern of our lives. It is so obvious when we are awake and so elusive when we are asleep. And so it is only now when I am forty-five and have reached the halfway point in my life that I can look back over the last twenty-years and sit with an open heart for the tortured young woman that I had been, for the fantasies of my youth, for the delusions from my abuse.

The road of the spiritual warrior is not an easy one. But if you persist and survive, you will be amazed at the magnificent clarity of freedom.

The story I am about to tell you is a true one. I have changed people's names to protect their privacy. The facts and the circumstances are the truth to the best of my memory. But please remember that all memory is subjective, having been filtered first by the mind we were looking through when we experienced the reality and then again by the mind we are in when we remember the past. Add to that the truth that everyone involved in my life has his or her own "true" version of what took place. Every version is true. They are all beautiful threads in a much greater Divine fabric that sustains us all. Mine is simply my truth to share.

You see, I am an incest survivor. I did not know that until I was thirty-four years old. But my story begins when I was twenty-four, struggling to assert myself as a writer in the harsh world of Hollywood. That was when I first heard the Voice.

NATASHA

It was a hot L.A. night in May 1979. I was sitting at a table in the Blah Blah Cafe with Bree and Cricket. We had just come from a night of dancing at the Dummy Up, an upscale women's club in Studio City. The Blah Blah was an after-hours coffee house, a blast from a past that I never really experienced. A '60s sort of place that showcased live bands and encouraged artistic people to congregate there for intellectual discussions. Well, that's what it hoped for anyway. The truth was it was the only after-hours place in Studio City so it drew in most of the gay crowd tumbling out of the Dummy Up, Oil Can Harry's and any other clubs in the nearby vicinity.

Bree was a wildcat from St. Louis. A curly brown mop of hair, chic and trés classé glasses, always stylishly dressed. Bree could wear anything and it looked good on her. I always felt like a big clod in clothes no matter what my body weight. A geeky energy clung to me like sweat on a clammy night.

"It's an attitude," Bree explained to me one night. "You have to have a come fuck me attitude to wear clothes well."

"But I don't want people to come fuck me," I mumbled.

"It's an attitude," Bree insisted. "If you don't feel like you look hot, you won't, no matter what you wear."

"Well, that's true," I conceded. I certainly had had days

when I felt hot and I looked great. But more times than not, I felt invisible.

Cricket, on the other hand, was a stocky Polynesian woman who looked like she could beat the crap out of anybody.

"It's an attitude," she explained one day. "You have to feel like you can beat the crap out of anyone and then people respect you."

"But I don't want to beat the crap out of anyone," I complained.

"It's an attitude. If you don't have that then people will mow right over you."

Is this what being a lesbian was all about? Wearing Joan Crawford come fuck me pumps and then beating the crap out of someone when they made a pass at you? I don't think so.

I decided to continue in my normal mode—invisibility. After all, if no one noticed me, then I couldn't get hurt. Right?

Possibly. But that's not how the big 'L' of Life generally tends to go. At least not mine.

So there I was sitting at a table at the Blah Blah with wildcat Come-Fuck-me-Bree and Watch-It-Or-I'll-Beat-The-Crap-Out-Of-You-Cricket. I felt secure.

But I also felt very, very lonely. For all the disco music and sensuously swaying feminine forms in the Dummy Up, for all the glittering lights and booze, for all the eyes that met mine and ignited my soul, for all the arms that held me fast as our bodies crushed together on the crowded floor, I always ended up here at the Blah Blah alone with Bree and Cricket. Why?

I told myself I just did not believe I could have a meaningful relationship with a woman I met in a bar. But that was just a pompous intellectual cover-up for a very deep fear of intimacy. Nine months had gone by since I broke up with Karole. We had been together for nearly five years. I had thought it would last forever, my one and only heart's desire, together we would change the world. Now I couldn't even remember the sound of her voice or the color of her eyes.

How could life be so cruel? Or was I really that cold inside? I did not know. I could not stay long enough with myself to find out. Instead I threw myself into my work.

I got up at one o'clock in the morning to do my workout, drink my protein shake, take a shower and get dressed for my three a.m. job as a stock clerk at Ralph's Market in Canoga Park. I lost weight on that job. It was like being in a gym for six hours a day.

I worked there until about eight a.m. and then I would drive to Topanga Plaza where I worked at B. Dalton Bookstore, receiving books until one-thirty in the afternoon. Then I would return to my bachelorette apartment on Dickens Street in Sherman Oaks and wonder what the hell to do with my life. When was I supposed to go to sleep?

After three months of graveyard confusions, Bree rescued me.

"Come on," she cooed to me over the phone. "You need to go out and dance. You're turning into a mushroom."

She was right. I certainly did not think that becoming a toadstool was part of my destiny. It was my night off. And I loved going to the bar, having a beer and watching all those wonderful women dance. On this night in particular, I was hoping to fill that hole in my soul, that aching need to feel wanted and loved by someone. I felt lost and alone in a desert wasteland, parched and arid with no hope of rain in sight.

Bree and Cricket were discussing the monotony of life. They sounded like a scene out of a Rod Steiger play.

"What do you want to do tonight, Marty?"
"I don't know. What do you want to do?"
"I don't know. What do you want to do?"

I began to spiral into a pit inside myself.

"Would you like some coffee?" A sultry woman's voice filled my ears. I awoke from my despair and gazed up at my waitress, Natasha. Her blue eyes sparkled at me.

This was not the first time I had met Natasha. She had been a waitress at the Blah Blah long before I began going there. For six months I had watched her elfin form move about her business, wondering who she was, never having the nerve to ask, certain she would reject me.

And then something happened. It was New Year's Eve. I sat at a long communal table in the darkened smoke-filled room where the bands played. The house was packed with men and women, gays and straights. We swayed and sang in drunken unison to the music, imbued with a primal animalistic energy that arises with youth, alcohol and drugs.

Natasha had been bustling back and forth all evening, handling the crowd with the finesse of Ginger Rogers dancing backwards in high heels. Customers had been buying her drinks.

The clock struck twelve. Everyone began kissing everyone else. We were all pretty wasted, myself included. I watched as a couple of men kissed Natasha. I rose from my seat. This was my opportunity, I told myself. I would probably never get this chance again.

"Happy New Year, Natasha," my low voice rumbled in her ear. She turned, intoxicated and smiled at me. Our lips met one another as we merged into a deep, passionate kiss.

"Happy New Year," she smiled sexily.

I stepped away, sinking back into the anonymity of the crowd. She would not remember that kiss, I told myself. She would not know who I was. She only did that because she was drunk. But I would never forget that moment.

In that kiss, there was such a longing in me, crying out in every cell, "save me from this incessant pain; I cannot bear it anymore; just give me a few moments of relief; I can disappear in an embrace." I did not know then of the unspeakable horror that lurked within me. I could not hear it moaning in the darkness of my soul, crying out for the caress of my consciousness. I could only hear the band blaring and feel that familiar loneliness settle into my stomach as I slipped back into invisibility.

"I want coffee," Bree's drill sergeant voice bounced me back to reality.

"I want coffee too," Cricket stated.

Natasha looked at me and smiled. "Would you like coffee?"

I nodded. "Yes, I would, thank you."

She left the table. Bree and Cricket returned to their discussion. I tried to appear interested but my ears could not hear what they were saying. A powerful movement of energy began to swell up inside of me. Suddenly I heard a deep baritone voice reverberating within me.

"Ask Natasha out," the Voice commanded.

Terror overwhelmed me. I felt like Moses talking to the burning bush. 'Oh, no, I couldn't do that,' I told the Voice internally. 'She'd never go out with me.' The voice was so real, it never occurred to me to doubt its authenticity.

"Ask Natasha out!" the Voice increased its volume and intensity.

Thoughts raced wildly through my mind. What would Bree think? She'd kill me. What if Natasha said no? What if she laughed in my face? I could not bear the rejection.

"ASK HER OUT!" the Voice bellowed.

The fear of rejection was great but it could not match my fear of being destroyed by some bizarre Primal Force that had taken up residence within me and had somehow gained control of my auditory faculties.

What harm could it do? I reasoned with myself, hoping that Natasha would politely turn me down and I could thus prove to this unseen Voice that I was right to begin with.

I stood up at the table.

"Excuse me," I told Bree and Cricket, "I have to go to the bathroom."

They looked at me like I was crazy then returned to their discussion.

Turning, I spotted Natasha in the sunken kitchen. The kitchen sat at the back of the restaurant, a level down from the main floor. A ramp with a rail separated the kitchen from the dining area. This ramp also led into the adjoining room where the bands performed.

I approached the rail, bracing myself for the rejection that I was certain would accompany my request. Natasha was busy preparing an order. The room vibrated with the sound of conversations and music.

I took a deep breath and called out "Natasha!"

She turned. Seeing me, she stopped what she was doing and approached the rail. My body collapsed with weakness as I got down on one knee and leaned through the railing to speak with her.

Her face softened into a smile at my posture. I'm quite sure I looked like I was going to propose. A lump formed in my throat. My heart melted as I gazed into her eyes.

"Do you ever go out with customers?" I asked meekly.

Her blue eyes sparked at me. "I make it a policy not to date the clientele," she said matter-of-factly.

I nodded sadly, my gaze dropping to the floor.

"But in your case, I'd make an exception," I heard her voice say.

My eyes shot up at her. "Really?!" I nearly screamed.

She grinned and nodded.

"Oh, my God," I mumbled.

My head raced with logistics. I hadn't anticipated being accepted. What was I supposed to do now? But as Primal Voices are wont to do, mine had disappeared without bothering to give further instructions.

"Well, um," I stumbled, "ah, what time do you get off work?"

"Tomorrow, I get off at one-thirty," she said.

"Great," I responded. I would have said 'great' to

anything at that point. She gave me her phone number and then graciously turned to continue her work.

In a state of complete euphoria, I returned to my table. In the short walk back, I attempted to hide all my emotions and to appear quite casual. I was terrified that my dating Natasha would upset or hurt Bree and that Bree would retaliate against me. I had no real basis for these paranoid fears but they fit perfectly into the emotional landscape I was living in at twenty-four years old.

"What were you doing?" Bree asked, her voice tight and controlling.

"Oh, I was just asking Natasha to bring us some more coffee," I replied as I sat down at the table.

I awoke the next morning and realized that I wasn't sure if Natasha meant one-thirty in the morning or one-thirty in the afternoon. My bizarre work schedule had completely screwed up my ability to make a date. I felt humiliated. She'll think I'm a complete fool, I berated myself. There was nothing to do but call her to straighten it out.

"I get off at one-thirty in the morning," she said.

"Oh, no," I cried, "that won't work. I have to be at work at three a.m. We'd only have an hour together."

There was a pregnant pause. "How about seven-thirty Friday evening?" she asked.

I tried to rapidly calculate if that would fit my schedule then thought 'To hell with the whole thing. I don't care if I'm asleep at this damn job.'

"Friday at seven-thirty would be perfect," I assured her calmly.

I was anything but calm on Friday at seven-thirty as I walked up the flight of stairs to Natasha's apartment. She lived on a quiet street in the Hollywood Hills. Her apartment comprised the top floor of a large two-story house. It had a private entrance.

I knocked at the door. The moment waiting expanded like a hot air balloon. I stared at the large elm tree shading the front lawn from the ninety-degree sunset. My armpits perspired. I inspected the bouquet of carnations I held in my hands. The door swung open. I looked into Natasha's blue eyes.

"Hi," she said.

"Hi." I smiled, mesmerized. Her eyes darted to the flowers. "Oh, these are for you," I said, handing her the bouquet.

"They're gorgeous . . . Come on in."

I followed her up the stairs. She wore loose white cotton pants with a wide, brown leather belt. Her translucent black silk blouse billowed gently with the breeze coming from the windows. My hormones danced euphorically up and down my spine. In the back of my mind, I could hear a lecture droning automatically.

For Christ's sake, get hold of yourself. Don't act like a man. It's been a long time since you dated anybody. Women don't cruise like men do. You're getting too aroused. Just cool it. Let her get to know you first. You don't just want her for sex. You're not that shallow. This is just dinner. Remember that. You don't have to do anything. You shouldn't do anything anyway. She'd just reject you and you'd feel like a fool. Nobody thinks you're physically attractive. And she's a knockout. Okay, okay. Look, I'm not going to do anything. I just want to get to know this woman. I'm going home afterwards. Besides, I can't have sex tonight. I have to be at work at three a.m.

We reached the top of the stairs and stepped into the living room.

"Have a seat," Natasha said. "I'll put these in some water."

She went into the kitchen. I made a beeline to the large cushioned chair and ottoman in the far corner of the living room. By this time, I was quite numb and experiencing the entire drama from the safety of my head.

"These are so pretty," Natasha said as she placed the vase on the coffee table. "I love the colors you chose."

"Thank you," I replied. We stared at the flowers for a minute. "I tried to figure out where to go to dinner but I'm not very familiar with the restaurants around here," I explained. "Do you have any suggestions?"

Natasha turned around, the last rays of the sunset cascading through the window, creating a halo of auburn light around her golden hair. It took my breath away.

"There's a Denny's at Gower Gulch. Do you want to go there?"

"Sure."

Denny's was a traditional straight, middle class coffee shop, the kind of place you took your visiting grandmother to for a piece of apple pie. Natasha and I sat in the smoking section. The booth sported orange vinyl seats and dark walnut wood. Not a terribly romantic atmosphere for a first date but definitely within my budgetary restrictions.

Natasha ordered a tuna melt. I ordered a French Dip sandwich. I tried to make sure that my feet did not touch hers beneath the table.

Natasha was twenty-six and an aspiring film director. She had begun her studies at UC Santa Cruz. I had spent my freshman and sophomore years at that campus. Same campus, different years. I had been there when three mass murderers, independent of one another, were killing Santa Cruz students and residents and burying the bodies in the redwood wilderness. According to one theory, there were particularly bad sunspots that year and Santa Cruz was the focal point of where that radiation hit the earth. I also had to contend with a suicidal maniac on my own dorm floor. One of my dorm mates had been dating a paroled convict. He did not take kindly to her breaking up with him. Instead, he broke her jaw in three places, then locked himself in her dorm room and proceeded to slash his wrists in such a way that he would not actually bleed to death but that he would in fact soak the carpets with his blood and terrorize the women on the floor as he fled into the night. So much for an idyllic college experience.

"Would you care for dessert?" our waitress asked cheerily as she popped by to refill our coffee cups.

Natasha and I grinned wickedly at one another. She ordered apple pie a la mode. I ordered a hot fudge sundae.

"Well, my years at Santa Cruz were not nearly so dramatic," Natasha said. "I got my bachelor's in drama then I moved down here to study film directing at Antioch."

The waitress returned with our dessert.

"Are you working on any particular film project right now?" I asked, taking my first sumptuous bite of cool rich vanilla ice cream surrounded by thick hot fudge.

"I'm working on a piece about a young girl who falls in love with her drama teacher," Natasha explained, stabbing a piece of her apple pie. "The teacher is an incredibly dynamic woman who is really a closet lesbian. She uses the girl for her own purposes but in the process, the girl discovers her own sexual identity. It's sort of a lesbian rite of passage story."

"You're kidding," I gasped. "I had that exact experience with my high school English teacher. I've been playing around with that concept for a script for over a year now."

"I knew it!" Natasha exclaimed. "I've always felt like this was some sort of archetypal thing when it happened to me in high school. Now you're telling me that it happened to you too." She stared at me intently as she ate her apple pie. "Maybe we should collaborate."

A sliver of me hesitated at the idea of going into a writing partnership with a stranger. My libido dominated the rest of me as my mind raced into sensuous possibilities. The two of us making passionate love on the couch in her living room, the script strewn across the floor. The two of us making passionate love on the living room table covered with script notes. The two of us making passionate love on the—

"Maybe," I replied. A voice rose up inside my head. She's not interested in you that way. She just wants a professional relationship. I tried to squelch the raging passion building in my stomach. I took another bite of my sundae.

After dinner, we returned to her apartment. It was late. I sat in the chair in the corner. She sat on the couch across the room. Silence filled the space around us. Suddenly, Natasha bounded off the couch and began pacing back and forth like a caged animal. Her hands played with latching and unlatching her belt buckle. I had never seen anyone behave this way. My eyes were mesmerized by the movement of her hands. Latch. Unlatch. Latch. Unlatch. Latch. Unlatch. Latch—

"Are you always this nervous?" I asked quietly.

She collapsed on the couch and in the voice of a very little girl said, "You're a stranger."

Every cell in my body softened as my heart opened wide. This I understood. "Oh," I nodded. I wanted her to know that she could trust me. After a few moments, I stood up. "I should probably go. I need to get some sleep before I go to work."

"Don't go!" she nearly shouted. I stared at her, surprised by her intensity. Her eyes dropped to the floor. "You can sleep here," she offered casually, pointing to the bedroom. "In there."

"In there?" I stammered. "Gee, I don't know. I really have to get up by one-thirty. I have to be at work by three."

"I'll make sure you don't oversleep," she insisted. Then noticing my hesitation, she said firmly, in a husky woman's voice, "I really don't think you should go home tonight."

Now I was the little girl standing in this stranger's apartment. Did I want to stay here? The long freeway drive flashed up in my mind. I looked at the clock on the table next to the cushioned chair. It was eleven forty-five. An image of my apartment crossed my mind. Dark. Empty. Silent. Then I looked at Natasha sitting on the couch. Her blue eyes sparkled at me.

"Okay," I said quietly.

She led me into the bedroom. The light from the hallway spilled through the doorway, illuminating the bed.

"You can sleep here," she said.

I nodded. We both stared at the bed for a few moments. Then I realized I needed to get undressed.

"Thank you," I said as I turned my back to her and began undressing. I pulled off my maroon suede boots and sat them next to the chair by the nightstand. I unzipped my French cut designer jeans, pulled them off, folded them and placed them on the chair. As I began unbuttoning my soft, chocolate-brown rayon blouse, I turned. Natasha was staring at me. I stopped, cocking my head slightly, raising my eyebrows and giving her a shy grin.

"Oh," she shook off her reverie as she recognized my message. "I'll just leave you alone then."

"Thank you," I smiled.

"I'll be right out there," she mumbled as she left the room.

I got undressed and crawled into bed. The sheets felt cool against my nakedness. I rolled over on my side, my back facing the wall and the doorway. She doesn't want to make love, I told myself. I felt safe. My eyes closed as I heard my breathing sinking softly into a somnambulistic rhythm.

Suddenly, there were two light bounces on the bed. Natasha lithely slipped beneath the covers. She was nude. Her body pressed up against my back as she wrapped her leg around mine, filling me with wondrous heat. Every cell in me ignited with sexual fire, an electrical rainbow pulsating through my beingness. My head spun with the intoxication of my senses.

"Can you sleep?" Natasha's voice rumbled in my ear.

Every syllable of her voice sent waves of eroticism through me.

"Not if my body keeps doing what it's doing right now," I replied.

"I never make love on a first date," she said quietly.

"Oh," I said. Determined to let her know that she could trust me, I steeled myself to my fate—burning up with sexual fire. I knew if I could just go to sleep, I would be fine.

"Do you want me to leave?" she asked. Her voice sounded so vulnerable.

"No," I replied. "But I really do have to get up at one-thirty."

"I'll wake you up," she said happily as she curled up into my back and we fell asleep.

I awoke at one-thirty with a start. Natasha was snoring gently at my side. Who was this woman and why did she have such an effect on me? I felt like I had fallen into an endless ocean without a life preserver. I carefully rolled out of bed and got dressed.

"You going now?" a groggy little girl voice called out from the bed.

I leaned over and kissed her softly on the lips. "Yes. Go back to sleep."

"I'll fix you some coffee."

"No. I'm fine. Go back to sleep." We kissed again. "I'll call you later this afternoon."

"Mnn."

"What time do you go to work?"

"Six."

"I'll call you before then."

One last sweet sensuous kiss and I mustered all my willpower to leave her.

That night at the market, the load was unusually large. I cut through my boxes like a hot knife in butter. Before I knew it, it was break time.

"What's got into her?" Tim asked Mac as they ate their microwaved burritos on break. "She's whipping through her load like a wild banshee."

"I don't know. Must be those protein shakes she drinks."

Tim nodded. "Must be."

*   *   *

We made love for the first time on a balmy afternoon. Our bodies stretched out across the cool sheets as our mouths and hands eagerly explored one another. God, I loved Natasha's mouth. She kissed me as if she were savoring some incredible food, as if she wanted the flavor to last forever. Luxurious lesbian kisses.

She moved like a wild stallion in slow motion beneath my body, every muscle rippling beneath the touch of my hands, my lips, my tongue. Backs arching, torsos twisting in an erotic dance of energy and desire, becoming one energy, one desire as my lips moved sweetly down her stomach, kissing her hips, her legs, her inner thighs. Her hands clasped my head.

"No." A little girl's voice rose out of the mist.

I looked out through the haze of my satiated senses. "What?"

"I can't," she whispered, embarrassment rising to her cheeks.

I kissed my way back up to her face and looked longingly into her eyes, my body pulsating with uncontrollable desire. "I want you," my breathless voice reverberated in her ear.

"I think I have a yeast infection," she blurted out guiltily. "I'm not sure."

Every cell in my body paused. "Oh." This was my first encounter with a yeast infection. My entire attention shifted to her well-being. "Do you want to stop?"

"No, no," she kissed me again, igniting my passion.

"Can I go inside you? Would that hurt you at all?"

"No, no. It wouldn't hurt."

My hands moved down her side and along her buttocks. She moaned and opened her legs. The hot, wet heat inside of her shot up my arm and neck and made my head spin. She felt so good inside. In that place where there are no words, no form but only sensation and sound, rocking back and forth, up and down, gyrating in a wondrous, ever—tightening spiral of tension and release, tension and release, each time the energy tightening, tightening inside both of us until ultimately exploding into sound as her body convulsed in ecstasy beneath my hands and her release rushed up through my body, exciting me even more.

She pulled me up on top of her, kissing me furiously and rolling me onto my back.

Her mouth moved across my breasts and down my side, my stomach, my hips, swirling onto my most intimate parts. I could feel a powerful energy rising from my feet, rushing up through my legs. My breathing quickened. Something was happening inside of me that my mind could not comprehend. My hands began to vibrate with energy, transforming somehow. Not visually. To my eyes, they still looked like my hands gently placed on top of Natasha's soft, blonde hair. But inside of me, these did not feel like hands. The energy building within them was transmuting them into something non-human. Alien. Primeval. Panic ceased me.

"Wait," I said breathlessly, gently patting Natasha's head. "Wait a minute."

She stopped immediately, raising her head, her eyes looking like an injured doe. "I was kissing you too hard, wasn't I?" she said, like a little girl guilty of some wrongdoing.

"No," I panted, trying to slow down.

"Jane said I always kissed too hard down there," she confessed.

"No," I said again. "Something's happening to my hands," I managed to explain. "They feel like lobster claws."

"Oh." Like an emergency paramedic, Natasha bolted up and began massaging my legs. "You have too much energy building up. It's locking up in your hands."

My hands felt triple their normal size, seemingly ready to explode.

"You need to regulate your breathing."

"I feel like I'm hyperventilating." The energy was tightening inside me.

"You're okay," she said firmly, pulling the energy down my legs. "Just slow down. Relax. You're okay."

"I don't usually do this," I apologized. "This has never happened to me before." I could not believe my body was doing this to me. My mind raced to figure out what I had done wrong.

"Just begin breathing in and out more slowly," Natasha said quietly as she massaged my feet. "Let your body relax."

I nodded, trying to consciously regulate my breathing. The lobster claws shrunk and then subsided, sinking back into the primordial abyss from which they rose inside of me.

"I was afraid I was kissing you too hard," Natasha repeated as she rubbed my arms.

"No, not at all," I assured her.

She relaxed.

"How are your hands now?"

"Much better."

She curled up next to me, a soft kitten nuzzling into my chest.

"Thank you," I sighed.

She kissed me gently. A warm breeze from the open window caressed our bodies. The afternoon sun cast shadows of the tree next door onto the rug. We fell asleep.

* * *

"How long were you with Jane?"

The dishes clattered in the kitchen sink as I sudsed-up the water. Natasha moved about the living room, collecting our wine glasses and plates from the night before. After our catnap, we had made love on and off all night long. The infamous lobster claws had remained dormant in the primordial goo.

"Four years," she called back.

"When did you break up?"

"Six months ago."

I could feel the presence of this absent lover as a potential threat to my relationship with this woman. I pushed the threat out of my mind.

"What about you and Karole?" Natasha asked, piling the dishes into the sink. The kitchen was very narrow. Natasha squeezed in behind me to grab for a dishtowel.

"We broke up nine months ago," I responded. "We were together for five years. I haven't been with anyone since."

"Oh," she said sexily as she placed her hands on my hips and pulled herself up against my butt. "No wonder you were so wet."

I blushed. She ran her hands up my spine, igniting my passion once more. I turned and kissed her.

"You have a particularly strong effect on me," I replied.

She laughed sexily and kissed me again. I handed her a dishtowel.

"I'll wash. You dry."

I returned to the task at hand. Natasha quietly dried a wine glass, considering what she was about to confess.

"I dated a man after I left Jane."

"Really?"

"I'm bisexual," she said firmly. "I want you to know that from the start."

"Okay." While this information did not surprise me, I felt uncomfortable talking about it, like I was walking down a dark alley in a bad part of town.

"Jane knew that when we got together," she continued.

"Is that why you broke up?"

"No. We had other problems." She picked up a clean wet plate. "I told Carl about Jane when he and I started dating. He didn't care. Actually I think the idea excited him. He thought a threesome might be fun. Men, they have such big egos. But you know, I don't think any of them can handle the depth of a woman's sexual power. After four years with Jane, I was so attuned to my feminine energies that I blew Carl out of bed the first time we had sex. I felt like I had to hold myself back or he'd completely wig out. Well, then when he walked in on me and Jane making love—"

"What?" I stopped washing and stared at her.

"It was his own fault," she defended herself. "Just because he had a key to this apartment doesn't mean he can just come over without calling."

My mind went numb. Something about this conversation did not feel good but I could not grasp what it was. "What was Jane doing here? I thought you said you had broken up."

"Oh," Natasha stumbled. "Well, Jane and I have been dating on and off since I moved out. Carl knew that. But the reality of seeing it was a bit too much for his masculinity to bear. I haven't heard from him since that night."

"Oh." I quietly began washing the dishes. My mind leapt to an image of me walking in and finding Natasha with someone else. My heart hurt. I could not bear the idea of investing myself into another relationship that would only end in pain. Yet I could not deny my incredible attraction to this woman. Unable to tolerate contradictions, my mind immediately chose door number three, behind which were hidden fantasies of a marvelously happy, lifelong relationship with this wild and wacky blonde. Our film was a mega success, much to the chagrin of Christian fundamentalists. We became renowned throughout the world as the lesbian moguls who helped educate the world out of its insidious homophobia. Of course, we got a standing ovation as we accepted our Oscars for Best Picture, Best Writer, Best Director.

Natasha put her dishtowel down. She reached past me and turned off the water. "I won't go out with Jane while you and I are together," she said quietly.

A lump formed in my throat. I looked into her eyes. She touched my cheek with her hand. I pulled her into my arms, consuming her with kisses.

The next few weeks were spent in that gossamer wonderland known as falling in love, that magnificent time when all dietary and health rules are cast to the wind as the two lovers devour everything in sight, including each other. Oral ecstasy. It's incredible. Love and chocolate. Who needs anything else?

We talked about everything in the universe, our childhood memories, our favorite films, our passionate issues. I told her all about the spiritual quest I had been on since I was twelve years old. How my mother had dragged our family to the Sherman Oaks La Reina Theatre to hear Dr. Donald Curtis (a retired actor turned minister) teach the doctrines of the Science of Mind. The Science of Mind was one of the first American religions to establish a connection between the premises of science and the teachings of religion. It was during the sixties when books like *Psycho Cybernetics* and *The Power of Positive Thinking* were best sellers. My mother gobbled those types of books up with the ferocity of a starved beggar. She exposed us to Transcendental Meditation and Edgar Cayce. At the Science of Mind Church, we made friends with other non-traditional thinkers. It was at one of the youth group meetings where I was first exposed to *The Seth Materials* and other Jane Roberts' books. Seth was a non-corporeal being who spoke through Jane Roberts when she went into trance. He discussed and described the nature of personal reality, how our thoughts and beliefs form the threads that create the fabric of our physical experience. It was here that the seeds of my own desire to understand my life were nurtured and watered.

I told Natasha about an experience I had had while driving home from her apartment one morning. I was heading west on the Ventura Freeway, driving towards Sherman Oaks. It was a clear day in the Valley. The foothills looked beautiful. And then it happened. The energy kind of went boom—boom and the mountains went from a two-dimensional image like a painting and they became a three dimensional image like a holograph. In other words, everything became more real. At the time, I thought that the outside had become more real. But the deeper truth was that *I* was becoming more real. My soul was stirring inside my body—a sleeping giant beginning the powerful process of waking up. When I told my sister Susan about what happened, she discussed it with a psychology teacher at her college. He became very excited. He said it was highly unusual for a person to have that kind of experience without being on drugs. That pleased me. Natasha was not impressed.

Natasha thought my metaphysical beliefs were faulty. She introduced me to the Church of Spiritual Science, a religious organization that applied scientific knowledge to spiritual growth. I had heard rumors about this church. Most people thought it was a cult. I was not concerned that Natasha was involved in this group; but I was not interested in exploring it. I told her that I did not have the money required to take classes at the church center. It was very expensive. Personally, I always felt that spiritual services should be freely given. After all, Jesus didn't charge admission to any of his sermons. Natasha insisted that the church did conduct free services on Sundays but that the classes offered were like any other class in self-improvement and the instructors deserved to be paid. I would have to think about that one. I was content with following my own metaphysical pursuits in my own fashion.

We began collaborating on a script. We decided that she would get sole directing credit and I would get sole screenwriting credit but we would allow one another unrestricted input. Natasha bragged that she knew Jon Voight, that they had gone to acting school together, that he loved experimental projects, that he would gladly produce this script once we completed it.

Jon Voight. "The Champ." "Coming Home." My ears rang with excitement. He was a sensitive man. He would understand the importance of the lesbian voice in film. This was my once in a lifetime chance, my crack in the wall of Hollywood. This would get me out of the rat race of working at the bookstore and the market. This would make me a real writer, recognized and respected.

For the next month, I spent every waking moment thinking about the script, working on the back-story, taking screenwriting workshops and brainstorming with Natasha. By the end of June, I was ready to begin writing the script.

Then the next thunderbolt struck in my soul. I was driving home from the Blah Blah Cafe. It was three o'clock in the morning. I was driving along Ventura Boulevard coming to the dip in the road at the intersection with Riverside Drive. As my car bounced in and out of the dip, I heard words coming out of my mouth.

"You want me to quit my job?!"

I looked around the car. I was alone. I was the person who spoke the words but I could not fathom where they had originated inside of me. Usually, my mind was filled with thinking, carefully constructed logics that lead to an ultimate conclusion. This statement, however, did not derive from a logical train of thoughts. This statement simply came unexpectedly out of my mouth. When I looked inside of my mind, I could only see blackness and silence. The silence of the Void. I waited for more information. Only a crystalline silence that told me I was completely awake. This was not a dream. This was another message from my Primal Source. I lit a cigarette and began to analyze the situation.

"This can't be right," I said to the blackness as I continued my journey home. "You can't expect me to quit my job on blind faith. How the hell am I going to pay the rent?"

The blackness did not answer. I took another drag off my cigarette.

"Okay, look," I said, using my best negotiating voice, "if you're the Supreme Being and you want me to do this, then you're going to have to give me a dream tonight to tell me if I should quit my job and what the hell I'm supposed to do after that. Okay?"

I paused. Nothing.

"Well, that's my final offer," I said emphatically as I pulled into my driveway and parked my car. If Gideon and Moses could make demands, then so can I, I thought as I entered my apartment and went to bed.

I awoke hours later to daylight. My eyes opened. I felt a heavenly calm inside me. Then my nocturnal commandment crashed into my mind. I checked for more information. Nothing. No dreams. Nothing. I was empty inside. I bolted out of bed and fled into the shower, hoping I could somehow wash away this horrible knowingness sitting calmly inside my stomach. No matter how hard I tried to stuff it, shove it aside, or run away from it, it just sat there staring at me. Finally I could not bear it anymore. I called Natasha.

"Can we go to lunch today?"

The urgency in my voice jolted her. "Well, sure. Are you okay?"

"No. Something's happened. We have to talk."

We drove out to the Moon Shadows restaurant on the beach in Malibu. It was a quiet Wednesday afternoon. We ate crab salad and hot sour dough bread. The ocean stretched out to the horizon like a painted movie-backdrop.

"Okay," Natasha began after hearing my story. "Let's look at this logically. What is it you really need right now?"

I thought for a moment. "Two weeks. I need one week to lock myself up and write the script and the second week for rewrites."

"Good. Is there a way that you can get that?"

"God, I don't know. The market won't let me take that much time off. I've only been working there for three months." I stared out at the ocean. A cluster of seagulls hovered over the beach in front of the restaurant, waiting for food scraps. "But, you know, I do have two weeks of paid vacation coming to me from the bookstore ... I hate my job at Ralph's. I feel like it's killing me."

Natasha finished her salad. "How much money would you need to survive if you quit your job at Ralph's and take that time off to write the script?" She handed me a clean napkin. "Figure it out on paper. Then think about it. I'm going to wait for you down on the beach. This is something you have to come to on your own. I don't want any responsibility for it."

With that Natasha got up and walked away.

I felt completely abandoned. Why did she leave me alone with this? I thought we were partners. Aren't lovers supposed to make joint decisions together? I stared at the blank white napkin. I pulled a pen out of my purse and wrote down my monthly expenses, my savings and my income from the bookstore. Surprised, I lit a cigarette. I had enough money to last for two months. That would give me two weeks to write and revise the first draft. Natasha would have those two months to round up the financing. I could start looking for another part-time job to replace the market job if Natasha ran into any trouble getting the backing after the first month. This could work. It was risky. But it could work. I stared at the figures on the napkin.

"Okay," I muttered to myself. "What if everything falls apart? I'm letting go of all my security. What happens if the project fails?" I took a drag on my cigarette. "Well, I'm twenty-four years old. I can find another job." The idea terrified me. I pushed it out of my mind. It's simple, I told myself, we just won't fail.

The night before my lock up, Natasha snuggled up to me in my bed.

"I've decided to quit my job at the Blah Blah," she whispered in my ear.

"Really?" I was surprised.

"It's time for me to get out of that hell hole," she muttered dramatically. "There're too many drugs. It's too easy for me to fall back into old habits. Besides, I'm sick of being a waitress. This way, I can get in touch with Jon Voight and get the production rolling while you're in here writing."

I sat up on my elbow and stared down into the passion burning in her eyes. I grinned.

"So when I'm on Johnny Carson, do I say I got my first big break by sleeping with the director?"

She laughed sexily and pulled me down on top of her, consuming me once more with her sensuous mouth. She made love like a tiger stalking its prey, moving in powerful, slow undulations, carrying both of us into ecstasy.

Morning came too soon. I walked Natasha down the stairs and out to the interior garden of this Frank Lloyd Wright apartment building.

"Good luck with the script," Natasha said. "I'm really proud of you."

"Oh," I smiled. "Thanks."

"Good luck with Jon Voight," I called after her.

Natasha paused, turned back towards me and waved goodbye.

I felt a horrible sinking feeling in my stomach. In that moment, I saw the delusion. She was a lost little girl. She was not going to quit her job. She was not going to call Jon Voight. I stood frozen like a doe in a headlight of truth. I had just banked my life's security on a delusion. Instantly, the feelings were gone. I put a fake smile on my face and waved back at Natasha. What else could I do?

Natasha disappeared around the side of the building.

I returned to the sanctity of my apartment. I locked the door, unplugged the phone, covered the clocks and pulled all the blinds. I checked the refrigerator to ensure that I had all the supplies necessary for this journey into another world—the world of my characters. Then I began taping blank sheets of typing paper on the walls surrounding the main room. Each paper on the wall contained a brief scene description in bold, black lettering. The movie was laid out perfectly before me. Now I had to encapsulate it into words on paper. I sat down in front of my manual Smith Corona typewriter and inserted a crisp, clean blank page. I typed the words "FADE IN:". My odyssey had begun.

Drinking tons of coffee, smoking packs of cigarettes and munching bags of Doritos, I danced, acted, laughed, cried and fought my way through the first draft. When I finally typed "FADE OUT. THE END.", I sat back in my chair and lit a final cigarette. I was vaguely aware that seven days had passed. It was pitch black outside. I ceremoniously uncovered the clock. The white numbers stood out against the black flip cards. It was three o'clock in the morning. There was something holy about this moment. I picked up the script and held it in the palm of my right hand, feeling the wondrous weight of my words filling one hundred and twenty pages.

I finished my cigarette, turned out the lights and stretched out on my couch that was also a single bed. The darkness surrounded me like black velvet. And then I heard it. The silence. It was awesome. An electrical aliveness resonated all around and through me. Suddenly I understood. For seven days, my apartment had been alive with the cacophony of voices. The life force of the characters had been filling this space, dancing with my soul as we created something material out of the ethers. This was not some mental device. This was as real and as tangible as the furniture in the room. I basked in this afterglow of birth until I gently drifted into sleep.

When I awoke the next day, I could feel a residue of that magical energy. It was as if reality were solidifying into what was supposed to be my 'normal' real world. I opened the curtains and discovered that I had a new neighbor. Interesting. I had not been aware that the old one was moving out. What else had happened while I was gone? I turned on the portable TV that my gay Uncle Rob had given me. Skylab had fallen out of the heavens and landed somewhere in the Western hemisphere. How bizarre. I wondered how a satellite could fall out of orbit. I knew it had to do with the gravitational pull of the earth. But where do these things land? Could you be walking down a quiet residential street one evening and suddenly be struck dead by a falling satellite? Like Dorothy's house killing the wicked witch in "The Wizard of Oz"?

I called Natasha, eager to tell her the good news and to hear about what she had accomplished on the producing side of the line.

"I haven't quit my job," Natasha snapped matter-of-factly.

My heart froze as I strained to listen to her.

"I realized it would be stupid for both of us to be out of work. Besides, I can't do anything until I have a finished script to market."

"Oh," I mumbled. "Did you talk with Jon Voight?"

"No," she snapped. "I wanted to see if you could really finish the script first."

Everything inside me went numb. Now I knew where Skylab had landed. It had landed on me.

"Well, I did finish the script," I replied in a monotone.

"Good," she snapped. "I'll come over in an hour and read it."

"Great," I replied, trying to sound enthusiastic but feeling dead.

Natasha sat on the couch and smoked while she nervously read. I paced about the kitchen, doing dishes, reorganizing cabinets, anything to keep from feeling the horrendous knot of anxiety in my stomach or hearing the incessant drone of my mind. You know you can't write worth shit. She'll hate it. Who wants to read a script about lesbians anyway? I imagined that I was Jane Fonda in "Julia," waiting for Dashell Hammet to render a verdict on the script. Isn't this what all great writers are supposed to do when their work is being read? By the time I wandered into my walk-in closet, sat down in a fetal position and began crying softly, I was already miles away from myself, thinking about how dramatic this scene would play in a film—the tortured young screenwriter saved by her compassionate and understanding lover.

Natasha opened the closet door and stared at me. I was sobbing uncontrollably.

"Who stole your spiritual integrity?" she demanded.

I was so shocked by the question that I stopped crying. "What?"

"Who stole your spiritual integrity?"

"I don't know."

"Well, you need to take it back."

I began to relax. "I was afraid you didn't like the script."

Natasha's tiny frame towered over me. "I was expecting a professional script," she said gleefully. "This script isn't professional quality."

I felt like I had been kicked in the stomach.

"But at least this is something I can sink my teeth into," she continued, rubbing her hands together. "Of course, we'll have to renegotiate the credits. I'll want co-writing credit since you obviously can't write it by yourself."

Another kick to the groin.

"Okay," I whispered in the voice of a five-year-old girl.

"We have to do something about your spirituality problem," Natasha said, the disgust dripping off her words. "I know just what you need." She wanted me to join the Church.

I could not afford it. But I trusted in All That Is to provide me with whatever I needed.

We began the painful process of rewriting. I had never collaborated on a writing project before and Natasha's directorial bombasticness bowled me over. I lacked the self-esteem required to disagree with her.

One evening, I was particularly daunted by the task of finishing the script and the idea of trying to somehow get it through the maze of Hollywood. I called out to God for help. "I need an angel who can guide me through Hollywood," I asked boldly.

The following morning, Natasha pounded on my door excitedly. She had done the impossible. She had gotten me some free counseling at the Church of Spiritual Science. The synchronicity astounded me. I was willing to try anything to finish the script.

Interestingly, when I walked into the large Church of Spiritual Science to meet my counselor, I felt something very familiar inside of me. I felt like I had come home. One of the first questions I asked my counselor was how the Church of Spiritual Science felt about homosexuality? I was tired of dealing with religious prejudices in this area.

"I'm gay," I told her. "So if the Church of Spiritual Science teaches that homosexuality is a sin or an abomination or any crap like that, tell me now and I'll walk right out that door and save us both a lot of problems."

My counselor stared at me for a minute. She was a very attractive brunette. "Well, the Original Documents say that a being can be whatever a being wants to be." The Original

Documents were copious volumes of scientific research allegedly originating from the leader of the church.

I scrutinized her carefully. She didn't look like she was lying. And the truth was most major religions had issues with homosexuality. Well, I thought, that sounds better than most religious organizations. "Okay," I told her. "I'm willing to explore this teaching further." We arranged to meet twice a week for the free mind-training sessions.

As my Spiritual Science studying continued, the script went out of control. Natasha was not a writer. For two years, she had struggled unsuccessfully to get a first draft on paper. For as unprofessional as she judged my writing to be, I had succeeded where she could not. I had written a complete first draft. As we labored to get a final draft complete, time rushed past, devouring my financial reserve in its wake. Natasha had a solution.

"Do you have a grandmother with any money?"

I did not like the question. "Well, yeah. My father's mother has some money saved that she's living on," I replied as we walked down Venice Beach one late August afternoon. The sun rested in an orange halo of smog on the horizon.

"Is she leaving you an inheritance?"

The knot in my stomach tightened. "Yeah. About two thousand dollars."

"Then ask your grandmother to give you the money now."

"I . . . I couldn't do that," I stammered, appalled by the idea.

"Look, you need the money now, not when she's dead." Natasha's voice was hard. "If you don't get the money, we'll never get this script done. And if the script doesn't get done, I can't get the funding."

My face blanched. My throat choked. My stomach contorted. My mind twisted rapidly trying to figure out how to please everybody in this scenario. "I suppose I could ask her if I could borrow the money," I said as I chewed on my lip. "I just couldn't ask her to give it to me. I just couldn't."

"Fine. Borrow it then," Natasha ordered. "Otherwise we're never going to get this film done. You've got to have a couple more months to work on that script. You can't be bothered with distractions like working in a market at three in the morning. And I can't do anything to get funding for this project until we have a professional script."

"Alright," I sighed. "I'll see what I can do."

* * *

"Why should I lend you the money? I may want to buy myself a Mark IV car." Her voice sounded like a teenage girl in the 1940s, play-acting to some B movie, trying to sound worldly and sophisticated by acting like a bitch. I could not believe that this person was my Born Again Christian mother who had always sworn how supportive she was of me and my career. She cared more about buying a fancy new car with lighted vanity mirrors on the sun visors than she did about me. I stared at her, stunned into silence.

"Mom," I said quietly, "I'm not asking you to lend me the money."

"Well, that's good," she replied. "I'd have to ask Sam and I really don't think he'd go for the idea. It's not my money, you know. It's Sam's."

That was a lie. Mom had been working in real estate when she married Sam, her high school sweetheart, and moved to Columbus, Ohio. She got her real estate license back there. A year or so later, she started working full time as an executive secretary for a real estate attorney. So it wasn't just Sam's money. She had a stake in the family fortune.

"I need to know if you could ask Grandma to lend me two thousand dollars," I proposed.

Mom's head rose to regal proportions.

"I know she has the money set aside for my part of the inheritance," I explained quickly. "I need the money now so I can finish this script. I would set it up like a business loan and pay Grandma back with interest. But I couldn't start making the payments until January. That would give me enough time to get another job if the film doesn't get funded immediately." I felt like I had the whole thing nailed down logically. Surely, my mother would support me on this. It was no risk to her.

Mom took a deep breath. "Just what is the subject matter of this film?"

The question hit me like a Mac truck on a moonless night. "What?" I asked.

"What is the subject matter of this film you're writing?" Her eyes looked like a cobra's, ready to consume in one gulp the rat it held in its tightly wound tail.

"Well, what difference does that make?" I squeaked, realizing that my grandmother was a devout Christian who did not know I was gay. "I mean, I'm asking for a loan that I will pay back with interest. It has nothing to do with the subject matter of the script."

"It's about homosexuality, isn't it?" Her cold eyes glistened with glee.

"Well, yeah," I stuttered. "But I still don't see—"

"I'll have to tell Grandma that she'd be investing two thousand dollars in a script about homosexuality," Mom pronounced haughtily, the word 'homosexuality' dripping from her lips like fresh venom. "I don't think she'd like that. She could give that money to missionaries, you know."

"Mom, you don't have to tell her the script is about homosexuality," I argued as panic seized my stomach.

"Oh, yes, I would have to be totally honest with

Grandma," Mom said humbly. "She trusts me implicitly. I'm like a daughter to her."

I felt like this was a battle for my immortal soul and I was not prepared to give into that.

Mom smiled and sipped her tea politely. Then she sighed. "Well, I just can't do it," she said finally.

"So now you're telling me you won't even ask Grandma?"

"No," she shook her head. "I just wouldn't feel good about promoting a script about homosexuality. If you want this loan, you'll have to ask her for it yourself. But I promise you, I will have to tell her that the script is about homosexuality."

"Fine," I said, my voice terse with anger. "I'll call her myself." Somewhere inside of me I knew that of anyone in my family, Grandma would support me. She loved me. She was my granny and she had always longed to be a writer too. "That is if you'll give me her phone number."

Mom's body made another movie-star pose movement as she put down her cup of tea. "Well, of course, I'll give you her phone number. After all, she is your grandmother."

I wanted to kill her, to lunge at her and choke the life out of her. At the same time, I felt like my own life was in terrible jeopardy. My mind raced to make sense out of this surreal conversation. But it had become a bizarre sort of mental chess match that I could only survive by detaching and becoming an emotionless observer, watching each cold, calculated manipulation as it was played by her.

"Yes, she is my grandmother," I responded tautly.

Mom's body moved again. She adjusted her bifocals and peered at me. "Now, tell me more about this Natasha person. I don't think I like her."

"She's a very nice woman," I remarked cautiously.

"How is she part of this script?" My mother's voice felt like a Nazi interrogator, couched in sweetness.

"She's the director."

"Has she directed anything else?" You would have thought my mother was knowledgeable of industry policies and procedures but she had never before been exposed to a film project. She was shooting in the dark.

"Yes," I took a deep breath and reached for a cigarette. "She's done some work with Jon Voight."

Mom's eyes widened. "Jon Voight?"

"You remember that movie we went to see together a couple years ago, called 'The Champ'?" I lit my Virginia Slim. "The one about the little boy and the boxer?"

"Oh, yeah," Mom's face lit up. For an instant, there she was, my real mother, Alice, grinning at me through those wonderful eyes. "Oh, I cried a lot at the end of that movie. That was a good movie," she giggled like a little girl of five or six.

"Yeah, that was a good movie, Mom," I smiled, relaxing as I saw her again. "Well, the guy who played the boxer—that was Jon Voight. Natasha knows him. She's going to ask him to help us fund the film."

"Oh," Mom nodded. She looked away for a moment and disappeared. The cobra was back in control again. "I'm worried about you," she said seriously. "I don't like this religious cult that Natasha has gotten you into."

The hair stood up on the back of my neck. Now it was all out war. "You just don't understand it, Mom," I said quietly. "If you study the technology a little bit, you'd feel more comfortable about it."

"No, I don't think so," she snapped. "I know you, young lady. I know what's right for you. And this girl isn't right for you. There's something wrong with her."

"There's nothing wrong with Natasha," I countered. But I could feel my resistance falling. It was as if some unseen magnetic force was sucking me into a black hole. I could barely breathe.

"No," Mom said emphatically. "There is something wrong with her and I know it's this religious cult."

"Mom—" I began.

"No!" Mom ordered. "I have been through too much with you, young lady and I am not going to stand by and let you drag yourself down into that psychotic hole again. Not when I'm the one who has to pick up all the pieces."

I felt myself grow stone cold. I stared at her, mustering what was left of my energy. "I am a spiritual being," I said firmly, marking her gaze with my own. A tiny smile crept at the edges of her mouth. Her eyes twinkled. "I have my own life," I said with slow deliberation.

My mother cocked her head slightly. "Well, dear," she said as she rose, "I have really enjoyed spending this time with you. I so rarely get to see what your life is like." She gathered up her brown, leather purse and her suede jacket.

I stood up. "When does your flight leave?"

"At eight-thirty tomorrow morning."

"Have a good trip back."

She gave me a hug and a kiss on the cheek. "I'll tell Grandma that you'll be calling her."

"Thank you."

With that, she was gone. It would take me another fifteen years to understand what really went on in that room that night.

I called my Grandmother two days later. Her words clasped me around my throat. "I could be giving this money to missionaries, you know. This is God's money."

"I know that, Grandma," I said sincerely. "I promise I'll pay you back with interest."

When she agreed to send me the money, I honestly thought that Mom must have changed her mind and not told Grandma about the subject matter of the script. She must have given me her stamp of approval.

"No," Mom told me later. "I told her the film was about homosexuality and that she could be giving the money to missionaries," Mom said flatly. "She prayed about it and made her own decision."

Well, score one for God, I thought. I don't know what I would have done if I hadn't gotten the loan. I was living on the brink of financial disaster. All of my hopes were pinned on this project. I knew Natasha would be proud of me for getting the loan. Now I could finish the script and she could get the funding.

* * *

"I don't want to have a relationship with you anymore." Her words whispered hoarsely through my body, numbing my mind and breaking my heart. I could not move. She sat curled in a fetal position in the overstuffed chair in the corner of her living room.

"Why?" I managed to mumble.

"I don't know," she snapped. "I just don't. It's not working. It was fun for a while. But now I feel suffocated."

I felt like a marble headstone on a frosty, winter night. My eyes stared blankly out of their sockets. Anger boiled deep below my belly but I could not feel it. I only grew colder.

"You're just . . . too sexual," she snapped.

The anger shot up into my eyes. "What?" I said.

Her body recoiled. Her eyes widened with fear.

"You think *I'm* too sexual?" I asked.

She nodded mutely, pressing her body more deeply into the chair.

I could not believe she would say that. She acted like a nymphomaniac with me, always wanting to make love, kissing me all the time, asking me to push her up against the door and kiss her when she was nervous. Natasha was loose and fast with her sexual energy. I was the slow one. The conservative one. The good one.

"Do you still want to finish the script?" I said as I opened the door to leave.

"Sure," she replied. "I don't see a problem with having a business relationship with you."

I turned back to her with one last question. "Have you started seeing Jane again?" My voice was soft and low. My heart weeping.

Her voice cracked slightly. She held her head defiantly. "Yes."

I walked out and closed the door.

The next two months were unbearably hard. Working with Natasha was miserable. But what choice did I have? My entire financial stability was riding on the success of this project. All she needed to get the funding was a finished script.

"The ending is all wrong," Natasha snapped as she lit a cigarette and paced across her living room. She ran her fingers dramatically through her hair as she exhaled. "Hillary wouldn't do that."

Exasperated, I lit up a cigarette of my own. "Natasha, this is the sixth ending we've gone through. What is it that you want?"

"I don't know," she moaned, falling onto the couch.

I took a deep breath, hoping that quiet rationality could prevail. "How did it happen in your experience? Between you and Judy? Did you ever have a confrontation with her?"

"God," Natasha moaned. "I have written and rewritten this story so many times over the last two years that I can't even remember what my actual experience was and what I've imagined."

I wanted to kill her. I could not believe that this was happening to me. She didn't want to finish the script. It would mean that she would have to get off her scrawny little butt and do something instead of just blowing a lot of hot air out of her ass.

"Well," I said calmly, "I think we should stick with the confrontation. It's just good dramatic structure."

"Oh, I don't know, I don't know." Natasha shook her head, rolling her eyes toward the ceiling. "I can't work anymore today. You're going to have to leave."

I stood up, collecting my notes.

"By the way," she added, "I took a scene from the script to an actor's workshop I go to and I had them act it out."

My heart soared. "How did it play?"

"It was fantastic!" Natasha jumped off the couch and bounced around the room.

"Great!" I grinned, feeling good that my work had been well received.

"Yeah," Natasha beamed. "I knew that scene I wrote would play well. I just needed to have it performed."

My heart sunk like an anchor to the ocean floor. "What do you mean?" I stammered.

"I always knew my words were good," Natasha pronounced haughtily. "Now I have proof."

"What do you mean, 'your words'?" I asked. "What do you think I've been doing for the last three months?"

Natasha stared at me defiantly. "Well," she smirked, "you wrote the first draft, of course. But that was the high school version. This version is my story. These are my words, my life. You just typed it."

Her words stabbed into my heart and twisted, burning with shame and deceit.

"That's what you think?" I said softly. "That I just typed it?"

Realizing she'd made a mistake, Natasha backpedaled. "Well, I mean, of course you wrote some of it. But this scene was mine."

I could not bear to look at her. I turned silently, gathered my notes and left. My head was reeling with pain and shame.

Kill her, a part of me whispered as I walked out the door. Kill her, destroy anything with her name on it, take the damn script, finish it yourself and sell it.

I wished sorely that I could somehow do that. But I did not have it in me to break away from her. Somehow she had invisibly wound herself so tightly into the fabric of my very beingness that to rip her away now would surely kill me too. We were locked in a death embrace, waiting for one or the other to collapse from the strain and release her grasp.

Shortly after that conversation, Natasha released her grip on me. She called one afternoon.

"This isn't working," she said sharply. "I don't want to work on this project anymore. It just doesn't feel like it's going anywhere."

"Okay," I replied coldly.

"So, you take your version of the story and do whatever you want and I'll take my version and go my way." Her manner was cold and deliberate. I did not want to argue with her. From the day she left my apartment promising to quit her job and to talk with Jon Voight, I knew in my guts that she was lost. But I was lost too and I had hoped against all hope that the feeling in me was wrong.

"What about Jon Voight?" I asked.

"What about him?" she snapped sarcastically. "I don't know him. I doubt if he'd even read the script."

My head spun. "What do you mean, you don't know him?" I asked. "You said you two took some classes together."

"Well, yeah, but that was a couple years ago before he got his break," she blabbered. "I doubt if he'd even remember me."

So that was an illusion too. I hung up the phone and stared out of the huge bay windows in my apartment. The September sun blazed orange in the smoggy air. I felt like a caged animal, trapped in a nightmare I could not awaken from. How could I have believed this maniac who lied to me? She had no intention of producing this film. She didn't know what the hell she was talking about. And now my life was slipping away like icing on a cake left out in the rain. I had quit my job at Ralph's. I owed my grandmother two thousand dollars and I had no way of paying it back.

My soul spiraled into a bottomless pit of numbness. I sat at my window, staring at nothing, chain smoking, my mind devoid of anything. Hours passed. The anxiety rose again. Very strong feelings of killing myself. Just like when my mother found out that I was having an affair with Joe, a man twice my age. I was seventeen; he was thirty-eight. My mother entered my bedroom, the rage seething in her eyes.

"You have never lied to me before, young lady," she began, her voice like sharp steel slashing my skin. "Don't lie to me now."

"What are you talking about, Mom?" I said, trying hard to control every nuance of my voice and body.

"Are you having an affair with Joe?" she asked with the harshness of a homicide interrogator.

I feigned innocence, crunching my face up in a 'you've got to be kidding' expression. "Oh, come on, Mom," I said lightly. "Why the guy's old enough to be my father."

It was a horrible scene. I lied my way out of it that afternoon. But that night, I lay in bed, my mind racing with thoughts of suicide. I could not stand the strain of keeping up this lie. But I knew my mother would have me incarcerated in a psychiatric ward if I told her the truth. I was still a minor in the eyes of the law. She was my legal guardian. In the eyes of the law, she could do anything with me that she wanted to and I was powerless to stop her. One thought kept me from killing myself that night. I had promised Niev and Emir that I would take them to the airport on Thursday. They were teenage Irish girls I had been taking care of all summer. They loved me. I could not bear the thought of them hearing that I had killed myself. So I told myself that I could not die right now. If I could just hold on for another month, I would be moving to Santa

Cruz to go to college. I would be safe there, far away from my mother's angry eyes.

On this soft September night as I sat in the darkness of my apartment, my mind raced again towards that infernal pit of despair. I searched for a thought to save me. My grandmother. I owed her two thousand dollars. She trusted me enough to give me that money. It was God's money. I did not want to disappoint her.

I reached for a phone and called Donatello, a gay artist friend I had known for several years. He would understand suicidal thoughts. He had attempted suicide when he was twelve.

My angel Donatello arrived within half an hour. I felt silly telling him my troubles but I knew if I didn't keep talking, I might do something really stupid. So I just kept talking.

Don was not the most sympathetic listener. But that did not even matter to me. Just seeing his warm body, his scruffy beard and that curly mop of blown dried brown hair, those sparkling blue eyes radiating out at me from behind his aviator glasses, that was enough to help me stay rooted in a safe reality.

"Well, the one word of advice I can give you," Don said sternly, "is this. Don't ever quit a job unless you have another one to go to."

"Oh," I nodded, hoping more for sympathy and understanding than a paternal lecture.

"You have to get another job to support yourself," he told me. "And just forget about this Natasha person. She sounds pretty screwed up."

I climbed into bed after he left and turned out the light. I slipped into the sanctity of my dreams, hoping that some Higher Power would give me an answer.

I awoke in a cold sweat the next morning. My head felt like lead. It took every ounce of strength in me to get my body out of bed and into the shower. I stood in the pelting rain of water, crying hysterically, an intense fear consuming me as I sunk to the bottom of the shower stall. I felt like I was acting in a movie, somehow there and yet detached. After awhile, I stopped crying and brushed my teeth.

I began searching for work. Every morning was a reenactment of the previous paralyzing fear. I owned one business suit that I would get dressed in to go on job interviews. I could barely eat; I was so scared. I did not feel capable or qualified to do anything other than menial labor.

Fortunately, I had a friend who had worked with me at the bookstore who was now working at Twentieth Century Fox Studios. I called Jim Murphy in early October in complete desperation.

"Jim, you've gotta help me," I beseeched him. "Do you know anybody at the studio that I could talk to about a job?"

"Oh, God," Jim moaned, "the only people I know work in the accounting office."

"That's okay," I chirped.

"No," Jim warned me. "You're a writer. You should be writing. You don't want to work in accounting. If you do that, you'll be stuck there for the rest of your life!"

"Jim," I argued, "I just need to get my foot in the door. Any door. I don't know how to sell my scripts. I need to get inside Hollywood to start making some connections."

There was a long pause. "Alright. I'll talk to George Adams and see what he can do."

"Thank you, Jim," I cried. I wanted to kiss his feet.

Within a week, I was sitting in the office of the Vice President of Accounting for Harry Glass Productions. George Adams was a handsome middle-aged man who graciously explained to me that while there were no job openings at Harry Glass Productions, he would gladly interview me as a favor to Jim Murphy.

Before I could respond, the phone rang.

"I'm sorry but I have to cut this interview short," George

said as he hung up the phone. "I've been called up to the Executive Bungalow. I'm going to have to turn you over to our Paymaster, Frank Ogden. He'll be able to finish the interview."

Frank Ogden was an attractive blonde in his early thirties who smoked copiously and drank tons of Coca Cola. Frank began the interview by explaining that he and George had different philosophies about hiring for the Payroll Department. In all his years of working, Frank had developed his own formula for evaluating prospective employees.

"It's like a Bell Curve," Frank explained authoritatively as he sucked on his cigarette and leaned back in his chair. Frank loved to pontificate. I listened with rapt attention as he talked at length about how certain types of people were skewed to the left while others were skewed to the right. He could see instantly that I was skewed in the direction that would benefit him and his department the most.

As I listened to him talking, I became keenly aware that a funnel of golden yellow light was descending onto the top of my head where it entered my crown chakrah. I remained expressionless, realizing that Frank could not see any of this. The energy brought a sense of total peace into every cell in my body, accompanied by a knowingness that this job was mine. And then the light disappeared. While I was becoming accustomed to these bizarre energy events, I still wondered if I was just going mad.

When I got up to leave, Frank told me that he could not promise me a job because George had the final say and George was definitely old school. Also there was no actual job opening but Frank wanted to get rid of one of the current girls in the payroll department.

There was not a scintilla of doubt in me. I almost said, "Look, I know I've got this job. Why don't you just hire me now?" But I knew he would think I was nuts.

"I'll call you next week," I told him.

"No, no," Frank instructed. "Don't call me. I'll call you if something opens up."

I just smiled and nodded.

On November 11, 1979, I began working in the payroll department of Harry Glass Productions located on the Twentieth Century Fox Studio Lot. Harry Glass was an independent television producer in Hollywood. I thought I was in heaven. The chubby, geeky little girl from the San Fernando Valley had finally made it to the Big Time. All I needed now was to sell a script. That wouldn't be hard, I told myself. After all, producers are always looking for raw talent and I knew I had that.

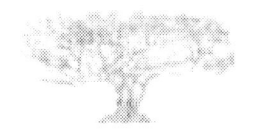

GLADYS

On November 11, 1979, I drove my 1977 brown Honda Civic Hatchback into the Pico entrance of the 20th Century Fox Studio Lot. Rounding the first curve, my eyes drank in Dolly Street as I drove to the Guard Shack. An old train station depot towered before me to the right of the gate. Green tarnished stairs lead up to an elevated platform where Dolly had said goodbye or greeted some well-known faces. I could practically hear Carol Channing belting out her song? Or was it Barbara Streisand? It didn't matter. In that brief moment, I fell in love with Hollywood.

Ernie, the guard at the gate, gave me a temporary pass that allowed me to park in the parking lot behind Old Park Row. I just had to follow the painted yellow stripe in the road and it would take me there. As I circled around the Executive Buildings and turned onto Avenue D, my mouth dropped open at the site of the gargantuan sound stages. Driving past production bungalows and around through Old New York Street, butterflies tickled the inside of my stomach. I wanted to scream with joy and to dance down the street. I worked in Hollywood! Inside a studio! The Back Lot sets looked so real. But they were all expertly constructed facades designed to seduce the senses into delusion. I had entered the world of master magicians and illusionists. Completely overwhelmed, I found Old Park Row and parked in the real lot behind it.

I spent my first day in Hollywood getting oriented. My boss Frank gave me a map of the lot. During the morning, Frank took me on a walking tour of the studio lot. The sound stages towered over us. I felt small and insignificant. Frank poured an encyclopedia of information into my mind as we walked from Old Park Row through the Western street facade that hid the Grip Department behind the Saloon. When we reached the Old Writer's Building, Frank explained that it doubled as a college set frequently used on "Charlie's Angels" and "Hart to Hart" and countless other shows. He pointed to the writer's bungalows sitting back on the grass. During production, grips would tent the buildings with blackout curtains so that any background could be superimposed. They frequently made the grass foreground into a cemetery filled with tombstones. We passed the Sound Effects building. I could hear gunshots being looped into some as yet unknown thriller or cop show. We wound around past Stages 1 and 2 where clouds of dust had billowed out when the cast and crew of some 1930's desert film tumbled out of the doors to get air during a camel-racing scene. The locked doors on Stages 3 and 4 had been frantically pounded on by Marilyn Monroe whenever she was late for her set call. (She was late a lot.) We past the editing bungalows where an infinity of film footage had been carved into seamless stories and had given birth to stellar careers and where countless careers had ended up on the cutting room floor. We made our way up Sixth Street to Avenue E where we turned left. We wandered past more office bungalows housing various production companies. Finally we came to the Commissary. Frank kindly and generously offered to take me to lunch my first day there. I had been so nervous about just getting to work on time that I had not even thought about what to do for lunch.

As we stood in line in the Commissary, I noticed a familiar face standing a few people in front of me.

"Mr. Alda," a pubescent young man asked forthrightly, "could I have your autograph?"

Alan Alda was one of the stars of a television war comedy called "M.A.S.H." It was the most popular show on television that year. In person, Alan looked just like he did on television. His co-star Mark Farrell stood next to him. They were dressed in their doctor's fatigues from the show. I caught my breath and watched, trying not to allow my excitement to show on my face.

"Gee," Alan said politely, "I'm really sorry but I make it a policy to not sign autographs."

The boy's face dropped. "Oh, okay," he mumbled as his face reddened and he darted quickly away.

That's terrible, I thought. Alan would not be where he is if it weren't for fans like that guy. I decided that Alan must be one of those prima donna type stars that I had heard so much about. I had no way of knowing if that were true or untrue. But that was the judgment I made based on witnessing his behavior for thirty seconds. And I felt completely justified in doing so. I was twenty-four.

In the meantime, the line continued moving. We were seated shortly after Alan and Mark. I looked over the menu and then around the room. I did not recognize most of the people in the room. Actually Alan and Mark were the only two celebrities present. Everyone else just looked like normal business people having lunch. Frank had a Cobb salad. I had the Fettuccini Alfredo. It was superb.

"Tomorrow, I'll take you onto a sound stage and show you what everybody does," Frank told me. "That way when you start learning payroll, you'll be able to connect the job title with the job. It will make more sense to you then."

"Great," I smiled and nodded. I did that a lot. Smiled and nodded and said 'Great' or 'Really?' I never realized how tense I was. I always thought I was relaxed and in control. But I was really terrified. I just didn't know it because most of the time, I was disconnected from my real feelings.

Yet even in all of my disconnectedness, by the end of that first day, I had fallen deeply and madly in love with Hollywood.

* * *

There weren't enough desks for me to have my own because the woman I was replacing was still there. In the meantime, I would have to sit in a side chair in Frank's office and do my work in my lap with a tiny hand-held calculator that I had brought with me from home.

My first experience in industry payroll was auditing musician's scoring-session contracts. It was basically checking figures that were almost always correct because the musicians usually worked standard hours and always made union scale rates. The simplicity of it helped to calm the ocean of terror filling my stomach. I felt like I was mentally retarded. And I hated myself for that. What the hell was I doing in payroll, for God's sake? I was a writer, I growled angrily. This was only a temporary measure, I told myself firmly. I once heard a professional writer say that Hollywood was surrounded by a huge brick wall. But the wall was filled with cracks. You had to just find whatever crack you could fit through and just go in. Well, this was my crack in the wall, I told myself firmly. I vowed to be a successful professional screenwriter within five years.

Working in Harry Glass Productions' payroll department was like working in a vacuum. I had left the freedom of the gay underground at Pickwick Booksellers only to feel like the outsider in "Mary Hartman, Mary Hartman." For all it's bright lights and supposed liberalism, the Hollywood I worked in was the most homophobic place I had ever experienced.

There were six of us in the payroll department. All women. All straight women. Straight women who loved talking about their boyfriends. I kept looking around the

20th Century Fox lot for all those homosexuals who were supposed to inhabit Hollywood. But I could find none. I felt like I had walked into the most Christian place on earth. I felt scared and all alone. My paranoia was not unfounded. There were no legal protections for homosexuals at that time. If someone found out that I was gay, I could be fired for that reason alone and there would be nothing I could do about it. Plenty of people hated homosexuals. It had only been seven years since the American Psychiatric Association had removed homosexuality from its list of mental diseases and had stopped performing lobotomies to 'cure' the 'disease.' Since Frank was a run-of-the-mill sexist chauvinistic pig, I did not think he would be especially supportive if he knew I was a lesbian. He might try to use it against me. I realized sadly that I would have to become invisible again in this place. I was skilled at not discussing my personal life. But I didn't like it.

Within a month of my being there, Frank called me into his office and told me that given my intelligence ratio and the fact that I was skewed to the left in his learning curve, if I didn't triple my salary in the first year, then there was something wrong with me. I proudly told my father that when he called me that evening.

"Now, don't be thinking you can take over the company," my father yelled at me. "You're just a cog in the wheel. They don't give a rat's ass about you. Why I remember when I got my first job at Benton Electronics. I thought I was God's gift to the company, hot out of the gate and I was going to show them how to run things . . ."Blah, blah, blah. He ranted on for ten minutes. Finally I began to cry. He stopped.

"I don't want to take over the company, Dad," I managed to choke out as I tried desperately to keep from openly sobbing. "I just wanted you to say you were proud of me. That's all. I was just happy that my boss thinks I'm a good worker and that I might be able to move up the ladder if I work hard."

"Oh," Dad mumbled. His voice was very soft as he spoke. "I'm sorry. I guess I went overboard. I just remembered what I was like when I first got a job."

"Yeah, well, I'm not like you," I retorted, sniffling and blowing my nose.

"No. I see that," Dad replied. "I'm sorry. Obviously you're doing a good job or you're boss wouldn't have said that to you."

I could feel his sincerity in my heart. "Thank you."

"Just don't let it go to your head." Dad could not control himself. "Well, I better go before I say something else wrong."

"Yeah," I agreed. "You better." I hung up the phone, feeling more lost and alone than ever. I was living alone in my Frank Lloyd Wright apartment that had been burglarized when I was with Natasha. They had stolen the tiny television my gay uncle had given to me so that I would not go crazy in the silence of solitude. Now I understood what he meant. I had been having nightmares about invisible spirits terrorizing me. I called Bree.

"I feel like I've lost all my friends," I told her earnestly. "All my friends were at the bookstore. Now I'm working with a bunch of straight homophobic women."

"That's tough," Bree said. "You know, I was thinking about moving."

"Yeah?"

"Yeah. Would you want to be roommates?"

I thought about it for a moment. There had been a time in the past when I really wanted to be Bree's lover. But she would have none of it. Now as I checked my feelings, I realized that that time had past. I could live with her without hoping to woo her. We could just be good friends. "Yes," I said. "Yes."

We found a nice two-bedroom apartment just down the street from my bachelor apartment. The other tenants were a bit standoffish at first. But then Bree found out that the previous tenants who had lived in our apartment had been drug dealers who physically harassed the other tenants. Once we convinced the neighbors that we were harmless lesbians, they could all sleep more easily.

Life with Bree was fun. We really didn't see much of one another. She had been promoted to a Regional Manager so she traveled quite a bit. When she was home, she liked to rearrange the living room furniture. She said she got bored with things always being the same. I never rearranged furniture. I never noticed it. Maybe that was because I didn't have any. My bed was a dense foam mattress lying on the floor. I had built a bookcase out of cinder blocks and plywood boards. My mother let me borrow her small used metal desk and a chair. And I had gotten a small two-drawer filing cabinet as a birthday present. I never paid much attention to material possessions. I told myself that was because I was more interested in spiritual enlightenment. But the deeper truth was that I was numb. I did not really know how I felt about anything because I lived in an intellectual box in my head.

"So I was talking with this Vice President in the home office in Minneapolis," Bree told me one night as we sat in the kitchen and drank beer and smoked cigarettes together. "And he said he had heard a rumor that some woman was able to single handedly do all the receiving in a multimillion dollar store. He said 'Frankly, I don't believe it. It's not possible for a woman to handle receiving that kind of load all by herself.'" Bree got a Cheshire cat grin on her face as she took a swig of beer. I started to laugh. "I told him 'It's the truth. I was there. I saw her do it,'" Bree stated as tersely as she had told the sexist pig.

I laughed really hard as pure lesbian feminist pride filled my body. "Thank God he told you that story! You saw me do it. I had a system. And it worked!"

"I know you had a system," Bree grinned as she sipped her beer. "I managed Topanga when you did just that all by yourself. Why it took two guys full time to do the same job that you did by yourself! I *loved* being able to tell that sexist pig V.P. that a *woman* could receive books better than two men!"

We both laughed heartily as we cracked open two more Buds. That was a great evening. I felt like I had my best friend back again.

A couple months later, one of the women in payroll was having a party at her house. I was invited and told to bring a friend. I asked Bree if she wanted to go. She said yes. I told her that she could not let anyone know that I was gay. My job security depended on it.

My first Hollywood party turned out to be just a regular party at a private home. No celebrities. Just lots of people. Lots of smoking. Lots of loud music, drinking, dancing and lots of sexual tension. As I was leaving, I noticed that Bree was standing in the corner with some strange guy. They were kissing passionately. I thought that was very odd.

On Monday morning, Peter approached me in the payroll department. Peter had started working in payroll two months after I did. At the time, he had directly asked me if I was gay. I was not going to lie. I told him 'yes' and I asked him to keep it to himself. He agreed. Now he looked pretty angry. "So what's the deal? You tell me you're gay but that you don't want anyone to know about it and then you run around at Lisa's party and tell everyone that you're gay?"

"What?!" I shrieked. Terror seized my stomach. "I don't know what you're talking about. I didn't tell anyone I was gay."

"Then how come a driver came up to me this morning and asked me if you were gay?" Peter demanded. "He said he had been talking to somebody at the party and that you walked right over and just said 'I'm gay' and then walked onto another group of people and said the same thing to them."

"That wasn't me, Peter," I told him as my mind raced to figure it out. Suddenly the image of Bree necking with that guy popped into my mind. "Oh, my God. It was Bree."

"The friend you brought?"

"Yeah. It had to be her."

"Is she gay?"

"Yes."

"Well, next time, tell her to keep her mouth shut," Peter admonished me. "I had to do some fast talking to convince that driver that you were straight."

That night, I confronted Bree. "How could you do that? After I specifically told you that I didn't want anyone to know I was gay?"

"I was drunk," Bree retorted. "People say all kinds of things when they're drunk."

"It was more than that, Bree," I told her. "You were walking around to everyone in the party, saying 'I'm gay.' Then you start kissing some guy in the corner. So people think you're straight and I'm gay. What the hell were you doing?"

"I was drunk," Bree insisted. "That's all there was to it."

As far as I was concerned, I could no longer trust her. My best friend had betrayed me. My mind could not make sense of it. Why would Bree want to sabotage my career? Was she jealous that I worked in the Industry? I felt lost and alone again.

A week later, Gladys Bird called me at my office. She had written a book that a producer was interested in turning into a screenplay. She needed a screenwriter willing to work on speculation. She was a member of the Church of Spiritual Science and had gotten my name from them. Would I be willing to meet with her and the producers at their Beverly Hills office to discuss a possible working relationship? I leapt at the opportunity.

On the agreed upon evening, I put on my one and only gray suit, packed all my notes into my briefcase and tried to look as professional as possible. I was terrified that they would think that I was not a professional writer. It did not matter that I had written two screenplays and a novel. In my mind, I could not call myself a professional writer until I was able to live off my writing income. That judgment existed in my own mind as solid as the Rock of Gibraltar.

I drove down Rodeo Drive in Beverly Hills and located the address Gladys gave me. I pulled my car into the driveway. Parked in front of me was an old station wagon. A little old lady slowly climbed out of the car. There was something very familiar about her. She reminded me of the Old Crone.

"Roxanne?" she asked.

"You must be Gladys," I smiled. I felt as if I had known Gladys forever; that we were old soul friends who had just picked up where we left off in some other lifetime. Like Humphrey Bogart and Claude Rains in "Casa Blanca." It did not matter to me that she looked like she was wearing clothes she had bought from a thrift store. We walked into the building.

Sophia Corleone was an incredibly sexy looking brunette, an ex-dancer with big brown bedroom eyes. But since she was the straight producer who would hire me, I shut off any speck of sexual energy. Sophia guided us into a conference room filled with a ten-foot long highly polished oval oak table. The sheer size of it intimidated me. I acted like I had been in many conference rooms as I walked around the table and sat on the side opposite the door. I was glad to have my briefcase. It gave me something to do to look professional.

Sophia sat at the head of the table. Her twenty-three year old son, Roy, sat across from me. Gladys sat next to him. They teased one another with the carefree abandon of close personal friends. They had all met through the

Church of Spiritual Science. I realized that I had to impress all of them. I gave them the very best pitch I could based on the limited information Gladys had given me over the phone. Sophia liked my ideas. Roy suggested that we rent some movies in the same genre and screen them in the conference room. He pointed to a spot on the ceiling

"That's a movie screen," Roy boasted. "It comes down from the ceiling. We could screen the movies right here."

I stared at him and nodded. A deep fuzzy energy rose up inside me. I wonder why these people are trying to fool me, I thought. I felt like I was being conned by a "Mission Impossible" team. I could not believe that a real producer would value my work. The feeling disappeared.

"You'd be working on speculation," Sophia explained. "However, I am nearly certain that my boss would produce the script if it is good enough."

Well, it's the closest thing I've ever come to working directly with an actual producer, I thought. "I would love to do it," I told her.

"We'll let you know what we decide by Friday," Sophia told me.

Gladys called me on Friday. "I am happy to be the one to tell you that you have the job, my friend!"

"Great!" I exclaimed.

"I'll get you a copy of the book and we can begin meeting with Roy next week," she told me. "He wanted to hire another writer, a man, but I fought for you."

"Thank you," I said. "I can't wait to read the book."

I read Gladys' book over the weekend. While I found it to be a fascinating account of how drug trafficking had actually increased with the formation of the Drug Enforcement Agency, I was not at all impressed with Gladys' writing abilities. She quoted liberally from other source materials throughout the book. She told me later that she deliberately quoted the source material extensively because she was terrified that she would be sued.

Gladys, Roy and I spent several months working out the story line for the script. When we reached the point where I was ready to write the first draft, Roy told me that he didn't want me to write a full script. He just wanted to sell the treatment. I thought that was ridiculous. I knew I could write a wonderful script and I deserved to get paid for that. Without telling him, I locked myself up on a three-day weekend and turned out a first draft. I gave the draft to Sophia. Sophia loved the script. But Roy was upset that I went around him. Sophia never took the script to her boss. The project died.

But Gladys was not going to be deterred from somehow getting her hands on the big bucks. She called me at work one afternoon and asked me if we could be writing partners. After my experience with Natasha, I was not sure if I ever wanted to write with another partner again. I took a few hours to think about the offer. Returning from the Executive Building, I walked through New York Street and pondered my future. Should I take Gladys as my writing partner or not? I had absolutely no feeling one-way or the other. She did not know how to write scripts but she was willing to learn. She said she had access to several other books that could be turned into wonderful screenplays. Secretly I had always been afraid that I would not be able to come up with good ideas to write about. Why not try partnering with Gladys. Maybe it would help. There was nothing better around.

Gladys was elated. She began inundating me with project ideas. In the face of all my silent self-doubt, she became my cheerleading section. She wanted to be my best friend. She maneuvered me into going on weekly hikes with her in Griffith Park. I would get up at five o'clock in the morning and meet her at the Observatory at six o'clock. It was cool then even in the heat of summer. We would hike up a wide, marked trail that wound around the mountain. We would talk about life and Spiritual Science and the nature of reality as we walked. Gladys loved that I was a deep thinker. We would stop at Dante's Peak and look out over Santa Monica and the ocean. Then we would continue climbing around to Captain's Roost where there were chairs and tables. We would eat a light breakfast of deviled eggs, brown bread and raw nuts and look out at the view of Burbank before we hiked down. I enjoyed those hikes. At that time, Gladys was the only person capable of getting me to hike up a mountain. She was sixty-nine years old and energetic enough to get her butt out of bed at five in the morning and go for a hike. The least I could do at twenty-five was demonstrate that I too was in good physical condition. Gladys talked to me a lot about food and healthy eating. She claimed that if she had known at my age what she knew now, she would not be suffering from her chronic ailments. She convinced me to drink herb tea instead of coffee and to drink water instead of diet sodas. Water! A hideous idea to me at the time. But when I returned home and took that can of diet cola out of the refrigerator and read all the chemicals it listed, I gagged and never drank another soda.

* * *

True to his word, Frank kept promoting me as the months went by and as my knowledge of payroll expanded. I devoured information, hungry to learn as much as possible about production in case I ever became a producer. I was soon paying my own show. Ironically, it was the ever-popular "Fantasy Cruise." I loved having to go down to the set to get crewmembers to sign their timecards. It gave me an opportunity to get out of the office, meet crewmembers and watch the actual process of making a television show.

At the end of my first year at HGP, there was a cast and crew party for "Fantasy Cruise." My first Hollywood wrap party was held on Stage 15 where most of the show had been shot. There was an actual small swimming pool on this stage. A live band played jazz all night. There was enough expensive, catered food there to feed a small city in China. Lobster, prime rib, chicken, pasta, salads, breads, deserts and above all alcohol. Hard liquor, wine and beer flowed like water from a Parisian spring. We all got solid brass belt buckles with the "Fantasy Cruise" emblem on them as wrap presents. By the time the party was over, I was totally bombed. It was well past midnight and there was no way I could drive home.

"You can sleep in one of the make-up trailers," Eddie told me as I staggered toward the stage door. Eddie was one of the show's Teamsters. "They're just around the corner. They're all unlocked. Just sleep it off in there."

"Thanks, Eddie," I slurred. Eddie was starting to look kind of cute for a homely older man. Then Peter walked over to us. "Hi, Peetie," I said loudly as I winked at him. "I'm drunk."

"I see that," Peter grinned. "You can't possibly drive home tonight."

"I told her to sleep it off in one of the make-up trailers," Eddie interjected.

"That's a good idea," Peter agreed. "Let's get you out there." Peter told his fiancée that he would meet her back at their apartment. He had to tend to his drunken lesbian friend. I knew his fiancée. I liked her. I didn't really like Peter though. I didn't like Peter because I had to do all of Peter's work because Peter was too busy looking through the trade papers to bother to do his payroll and my supervisor Claire was too wimpy to reprimand him. Claire was a beautiful blonde, very intelligent and incredibly good at accounting but lousy at reprimanding her employees. So I kept picking up Peter's slack. And I didn't appreciate it. But there was something about Peter. On the day I met him, I wanted to kiss him. An odd thing for a lesbian.

Unsettling really. Made me question my sanity. He wasn't particularly cute. There wasn't even anything sexy about him, at least not to me. There had just been that feeling of wanting to kiss him, just to see what it was like. I had had the feeling, judged myself insane and promptly forgot about it.

But on this late drunken evening, as Eddie and Peter walked me out to the make-up trailer, an energy began to swirl up inside of me. The two men managed to get the door open and get me inside. Then Peter and I just stared at one another. It was one of those long, lingering stares. One of those stares you see in the movies. Not an 'Oh, God I love you kind of stare.' Not at all. No, this was lust. Pure and simple.

Eddie looked at Peter. Then he looked at me. Then he looked back at Peter. "Oh," Eddie said. "I guess I'll be going then."

"Right," Peter and I grunted in unison.

Eddie walked out and closed the door.

Instantly, Peter and I were locked in lust. Erica Jong's *Fear of Flying* was a popular book title at the time. In it, she talked about the zipless fuck. That fantasy fuck that straight women (well, maybe all women) wanted. The hunky guy (or gorgeous woman) walks into a train car. They make eye contact. He closes the door and instantly they are locked in a passionate embrace as all their clothes fly off, completely unencumbered by buttons, zippers, bra snaps, etc. Well, that was kind of how this played out. Or at least what little I remember of it.

While we were doing that, I became distinctly aware of the part of me internally that was watching and the other part of me that was acting. That was what I learned in this experience. When I had sex with men, I always felt like I was acting. I thought that that was what sex was supposed to feel like—a performance. But when I made love with a woman, I didn't have to perform. I just melted.

"I don't know why you think you're a lesbian," Peter smirked as he zipped up his pants.

I stared at him in shock. That is exactly why I am a lesbian, I thought to myself. Because of arrogant pigs like you.

"I have to get going," he continued. "I've got to get home before Tammy wakes up. I wouldn't want her to suspect anything."

Oh, that's right. You're fiancée. You are such a pig, Peter, I thought. But I did not have the energy to reply. My head felt like a piece of lead. "What time is it?" I managed to mutter.

"Three-thirty," Peter said. "See you on Monday. Bye."

I groaned and fell back asleep. When I awoke, it was five-thirty. The trailer smelled stale and cheap. I felt like a whore.

"Oh, God, Roxanne," I moaned aloud. "What have you done? Jesus, girl, what kind of lesbian are you to be sleeping with men? Especially one as dorky as Peter? And my God, he's engaged to a woman you really like. Oh, you are such a cad, Peter. And you, Roxanne are such a slut." I looked at my watch. "Oh, God, and I'm late for my hike with Gladys! Jesus, I can't believe you!"

I chastised myself for the entire drive through Beverly Glen to my Sherman Oaks apartment. Once inside, I called Gladys and apologized for missing our hike. "I'm horribly hung over. But if you still want to write today, I can come over around noon."

"That would be great, partner!" Gladys chimed. "It's not a problem."

"I'm really sorry," I apologized again. "I'll explain it all to you when I get there."

I arrived at Gladys' jam-packed apartment at noon. She hugged me hard when I walked in the door.

"Ooh, you are such a sight for these sore old eyes," Gladys crooned. "I don't know what I did to deserve a partner as wonderful as you."

"Yeah, well, I wouldn't be too sure about how wonderful I am," I grumbled as I slouched into the overstuffed side chair that I usually claimed while we were writing.

"Come, come, my good friend," Gladys continued. "Whatever you did cannot be that bad."

"Oh, I wouldn't be too sure about that," I sighed.

"Tell me what it is," Gladys challenged me. "I can tell you that at my age, I've seen and done just about everything."

I grinned. I had to make a decision. Did I trust this woman enough to tell her that I was gay? I could just tell her about the sex and let that be the end of it. If she hated homosexuals, she could cause problems for me within the Church.

"You know I went to that wrap party last night?" I reminded her. She nodded eagerly. "It was really great fun," I began. "Lots of food, celebrities, presents, and, of course, liquor."

"Oh," Gladys nodded vehemently. "Liquor."

"I got completely drunk," I continued, grimacing. "Of course, I couldn't drive home in that condition."

"Of course not," Gladys agreed.

"And there were these make-up trailers outside the stage that were all unlocked," I mumbled. "So when Peter took me out to the trailer—"

"Peter?"

"Yes... Peter..." I sighed loudly.

Gladys grinned. "Who's Peter?"

"This dorky guy I work with," I moaned. "God, Gladys, I just wanted to kiss him, just to see what that was like. Honestly, that was the extent of it. But suddenly our clothes were all off and we were doing it."

Gladys laughed merrily.

"I am such a slut," I confessed.

"No, no," Gladys shook her head. "You're just human."

"No, Gladys, you don't understand," I began. "There's something about me that you don't know. I make a practice of not sharing this part of my life with someone until I know that they know me."

"Whatever it is, it won't change my opinion of you," Gladys insisted. "I can guarantee you that, my friend. You are the kindest, most generous, warm-hearted person I know."

"Thank you." I took a breath. "And I'm also gay."

"Huh?"

"I'm gay, Gladys. I'm a lesbian."

"But you just had sex with a man," Gladys stated.

"I know," I nodded. "But that was an accident. Honestly, I was just curious about kissing him and the next thing I knew we were having sex." I studied Gladys' face carefully, trying to access the emotions playing beneath her visage. This could be the end of a very short partnership, I thought. "I am quite capable of having sex with men. Believe me, I had plenty of sex with men before I came out. But it was not the same. Sure the body parts all fit together and move but when your heart's not in it, then it's not much fun. My heart opens for women, Gladys. I fall in love with women."

Gladys stared at me quietly for a long time. I knew she could easily tell me that this was more than she bargained for and that she could ask me to leave. She was, after all, sixty-nine years old. In her generation, homosexuals were classified as mentally ill perverts who at the very least deserved lobotomies and who were automatically condemned to the fiery pits of hell. I waited patiently for Gladys to digest this information. Finally, Gladys spoke.

"Well, I want to be honest with you," she began. "I never would have thought that you were gay. And I'm glad that you didn't tell me that right off because I think my judgments about it would have kept me from getting to know what a beautiful being you are. And you, my friend, are an exceptionally beautiful being. I've never met anyone who can compare with your brilliance. Which is why it's very interesting that you would be gay."

"Why is that?"

"Because my sister's first husband hurt her horribly. And he was a homosexual." Gladys stared at me. "I always thought he was a horrible person because he was a homosexual. Now I'm beginning to wonder if he was just a horrible person period."

"That's more the truth," I interjected. "There are just as many neurotic gay people as there are straight people. And just as many nice gay people as straight people."

"Well, he was an asshole," Gladys continued. "He and Harriet were married for five years, five miserable years for Harriet, before he finally told her that he was homosexual. He never should have married her to begin with."

"You're right," I nodded. "I'm sure he was an asshole and I don't want to play the devil's advocate. But society puts so much pressure on all of us to conform to a heterosexual model that sometimes we don't even know we're gay until later on in life."

"How old were you?"

"Nineteen."

"How did you know?"

"I fell in love with a woman named Whitney Dawn. She was the manager of the bookstore I was working in. She was beautiful. She had blue eyes and curly brown hair and a face that looked like Vanessa Redgrave. She was gay. She wasn't interested in me. But she's the woman who brought me out. And we never even kissed." I stared at Gladys. "Coming out is not some instantaneous event. It's a process that can take a long time. You have to accept a part of yourself that the entire world judges and condemns. But you have no choice. You have to eventually accept that this is who you are. If you don't, you'll live your entire life in a lie. It's difficult because it's not necessarily safe to come out."

We talked all afternoon about sexuality and society's struggle to transcend its own judgments and shame about sex in any form. By the end of the afternoon, we had not accomplished much writing but we had taken our friendship to a deeper level of intimacy. It was good to know that Gladys was willing to accept me for who I was. Indeed, Gladys became my staunchest ally. As a friend, she loved me with a fierceness that I was not accustomed to. I was used to being alone. Gladys insisted on communicating with me on a daily basis. Our lives became more and more entwined.

My relationship with Bree, on the other hand, had become very uncomfortable for me. I didn't like not being able to trust her. I decided to try to mend the fence between us. I asked Bree to read the thriller script. One Sunday morning I found her sitting dejectedly on the kitchen counter.

"I'm depressed," Bree told me. "I really liked your script," she said. "I love how you write. I got totally involved with these people." Then she crinkled her nose. "But then you kill off both of the main characters at the end. It's pretty depressing."

"Hmn," I mumbled. "I was going for a 'French Connection 2' kind of thing," I tried to explain. "You see, logically the French Connection guy should have died at the end of that film. But Hollywood wouldn't allow it. I was trying to make my ending more honest."

"It may be more honest," Bree replied. "But it's very depressing. Couldn't you let at least one of them live?"

"Hmn," I grunted. No artist likes to be criticized. "I'll think about it."

I showed the script to a director/writer friend of Gladys'.

"You write these wonderful characters that just leap off the page," Tooke told me. "And then you kill both of them. No audience is going to sit still for that. They'll lynch you."

I had not thought about the audience's reaction. I had been trying to be true to the story. I revised the ending, allowing the female lead to escape and to ultimately bring the evil villains to justice. That version got much better responses. I was determined to find a way to get the script to Jane Fonda. She would be perfect for it.

I wrote several scripts based on unpublished books that Gladys brought to me from different friends of hers. I also drafted several television movie-of-the-week treatments based on the life stories of some very interesting people that Gladys knew.

At the beginning of 1981, the film "9 To 5," starring Jane Fonda, began shooting on Stages 14 and 15 directly down the street from my office in Old Park Row. I knew this was providence. Now I would be able to actually talk with Jane.

Hollywood consisted of many closed doors. You went up to a door and you knocked. Someone opened the door. You explained who you were and what you wanted. They said 'No.' Then they closed the door in your face. That was pretty much my experience in Hollywood.

The first time I actually got within shouting range of Jane Fonda, I courageously knocked on the door to her mobile trailer. The door opened. I explained who I was. As I was standing outside the door, I glanced inside. I could see a dressing table with a lit vanity mirror. A woman was sitting at it being made up. All I could see was a gigantic eyeball turn to me and stare. A polite voice said 'No.' And the door closed.

I did not understand at that time that that experience was actually showing me how little self-esteem I had. At the time, I thought it just meant I was scared.

I was able to find out more about what the proper procedures were to submit a script to Ms. Fonda. I learned that she had a production company on the lot. I called her offices.

"She's not accepting any new material right now," her assistant told me.

"When will she be?" I asked.

"She's booked up for three years."

"Three years!" I screeched. The information would not process in my mind. I could not believe she would not even read a script for three years. "Well, when will she be willing to read a script?"

"Two and a half years."

I hung up the phone in disgust. I felt like Jane Fonda's character in "They Shoot Horses Don't They." It seemed to me that Central Casting had the whole thing sewn up before you even arrived.

I finally met Jane at a Campaign for Economic Democracy meeting in May. It was a fund raising event held at a producer's home in the Palisades. For ten dollars, you could get your picture taken with Jane. It was worth ten bucks to get the opportunity to talk with her personally. I waited patiently in line. When my turn came, the camera ran out of film and someone had to run off to get more. I was thrilled. It meant that I had more time to talk with Jane.

"Did you get a rose in your car this week?" I asked quietly.

Jane stared at me. Her eyes widened with surprise as sheer joy sprang up through her body. "Was that *you*!" she squealed.

I grinned and nodded.

And then a miraculous thing happened. Jane Fonda hugged me very tightly and with sincere gratitude. "That was so sweet!" she said in my ear.

I was in heaven. I knew she had been overseas for a few weeks and she returned to harsh criticism in the media for her political stances. I noticed that the window on her VW Rabbit was open one day. At lunch, I went out and picked up a rose and left it in her front seat with a note that simply said 'Welcome back, Jane.' I had no idea at the time that I would be meeting her. She had been my idol for years. She was such a strong woman, beautiful and outspoken. One of the first women in my experience to openly challenge the patriarchal system.

We sat down on a tree stump to wait for the film to arrive. We talked about her latest film shoot—a movie called "Rollover." She said that she had done a series of films for political reasons. But she did this one for the love of acting. She told me that she loved working with Sydney Pollack because he directed with a sensuous eye. I asked her if she would be willing to read a script of mine. She said 'yes.' I was elated. Of course, the thriller script was sitting with another actress. So I could not give that to Jane. Instead, I delivered a copy of a western epic I had written to her on that Monday.

Not to be outdone, Gladys hooked us up with a public relations expert who was in the Church of Spiritual Science. Bernie Baxter was a heavy set, loud-mouthed man who claimed he could greatly improve our careers. He convinced me to change the title of the thriller I had written to "Bodies In The Night" and to allow him to deliver it to Jane Fonda's office. He wrapped it in a box with a pair of false teeth attached to the script with a note that said "Sink your teeth into this." The teeth chattered when you removed them from the script. I was horrified when he showed us what he was going to do. But Bernie overpowered me with his bravado, assuring me that doing something outlandish would make the script memorable to Jane. I personally thought this approach was totally amateurish. But I went along with it, telling myself that my conservative approach had not worked so why not take a chance and be outlandish. The tactic did not work.

The script was quickly returned. I don't know if we got the teeth back.

By the middle of June, I was ready for a break. I ran into Bree in the kitchen one morning.

"I'll be taking my vacation on July 3rd," I told her. "I'm flying back to Boston to visit Mark and then I'll be going to Columbus to pick up my mom." Mark had worked with Bree and me at the bookstore.

"I'm going to New York on July 3rd," Bree told me. "Then I'm going to Boston to meet Rachel. We're going to tour Victorian houses in New England." Rachel had worked with Mark and Bree and me at the bookstore.

Bree and I stared at one another. Then we both grinned widely.

"I think we should merge our vacations," Bree suggested.

"Yeah," I nodded. "That sounds right."

"I'm flying into Newark, New Jersey on July 3rd. Why don't you come with me," Bree said. "I'll be meeting up with my friend Barbara. We'll spend a couple days in New York then go on into Boston."

"I'll let Mark know that you'll be coming too," I told her. "It will be like an East coast reunion of West coast book personnel."

It would be my first real vacation. My first time on the East Coast. I had reached the point in my bachelorettehood when I was yearning for a real relationship. Something wildly romantic that would last for the rest of my life. I had no idea what an unrealistic notion that was. I was twenty-six. There was a deep loneliness inside of me that I thought only another person could fill. That's what all the storybooks said. And up to that point in my life, storybooks were the only roadmap I had to go on.

Gladys and I took our usual six a.m. hike on Saturday June 27th. When we got to Dante's Peak, I looked out over the city. I felt deep inside my heart to see if I could locate my soul mate in the suburban sprawl down below. I could not feel anything. My soul mate was not in Los Angeles. I sighed deeply. Maybe she was on the East coast.

CARLY

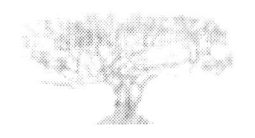

I met her in the New Jersey airport on July 3, 1981.

Bree's friend Barbara met us at the gate.

"We have to wait for about half an hour," Barbara explained to us as we struggled with our baggage.

"Why?" Bree asked.

"Carly is coming in for the Fourth of July," Barbara stated. Bree made a disgruntled face. Barbara shrugged goofily. "She insisted on coming down from Boston."

I had no idea who this Carly person was but I surmised that she was Barbara's lover and that she lived in Boston. Personally I really didn't care. I just wanted to get some sleep.

Barbara was chattering away about her life and her love affairs. I did not like what I was hearing. I began to wonder who this Barbara person was and why she was two-timing her lover. Then she turned to me.

"I hate to do this to you," she said. "But I'm going to have to ask you not to mention any of this to Carly. She doesn't know I've been seeing someone else."

I stared coldly at Barbara. Now she was asking me to participate in a cover-up. My father had cheated on my mother when I was in my teens. I did not like unfaithfulness. But my muddled mind was not prepared to fight for moral integrity. It was too early in the morning and the airport coffee tasted horrid.

I shrugged my shoulders. "Fine." I just wanted to see New York City, go to a Broadway play and see the fireworks. The sordid affairs of strange lesbians were not my concern. But my curiosity was peaking, wondering now who Carly was and why she was involved with such a chauvinistic woman.

Finally Carly disembarked from her plane. I watched her come down the ramp. Carly was a cute little Jewish dykette. Well, at least Barbara has good taste, I thought.

We drove to Barbara's parents' house in New Jersey. The East Coast was a visual color feast for my eyes. I had never seen so many vibrant shades of green before. The house was in the suburbs but unlike Los Angeles where property lines were boldly marked with fences, the green grass here rolled freely amongst the houses, unfettered by any manmade territorial markers.

The humidity was quite high and the mosquitoes plentiful. I didn't care. I was in love with the environment. We all sat and talked in an enclosed patio area where the view was spectacular.

Bree and Barbara talked boisterously about the old days they spent together. They finally got up, excused themselves and went back inside the main house where they could talk privately. I felt badly for Carly. Knowing what I knew about Barbara's disregard for their relationship, I was rapidly seeing Carly as the innocent victim.

"How do you like the East Coast?" she asked quietly.

"Oh, I love it!" I exclaimed. "I can't believe how green everything is."

She grinned. "Yes. It's green here."

We both chuckled at my enthusiasm.

"So what do you do in California?"

"I work in the film industry. I'm in the payroll department at Harry Glass Productions. But I'm really a writer."

Her eyes gazed up at me. A soft smile played at her lips. And then it happened. A twinkling white light shot out of her eyes at me. Literally. Like a soft, sweet star from her soul saying 'hello' to mine. My heart melted. I wanted to protect her.

Over the course of the next two days, that feeling grew very strong, primarily because Barbara was such an asshole. When we went into New York, Barbara attached herself to Bree like a barnacle to a reef. Anyone else would have thought Barbara and Bree were lovers and that Carly and I just happened to be casual friends trailing behind them. Personally, I thought it was rude.

We went to the Empire State Building. It was raining. I thought about that marvelous Cary Grant and Deborah Kerr movie, "An Affair To Remember." They meet romantically and fall in love on a boat trip or something. Each have their own separate lives to tend to before they can consummate their love. They agree to meet at the top of the Empire State Building at Christmas or New Years or something. Anyway, when Carey gets there, he waits forever. He hears the sound of a car accident but doesn't pay any attention. Unbeknownst to him, Deborah has been struck by a car and is paralyzed from the waist down. Or was he the one who got hit by the car? Oh, who cares?

We all arrived at the top of the Empire State Building. It was somewhat foggy because of the rain. But we could see the tops of the Trade Towers from the windows. Barbara and Bree disappeared. Carly and I stood quietly at the rail next to the glass. I had just gotten a 35mm camera and I wanted to take a picture but I wasn't sure how to focus it. I was quite aware that Carly was an amateur photographer.

"Do you know how to focus these things?" I asked shyly.

Her eyes gazed into mine. She had a softness about her, a childlike innocence. I felt a warm cocoon of energy surround me and begin pulsating between us as she stepped closer to my body and clasped my camera in her hands.

"These are the F-stops," she said, pointing to some part of the camera that I could no longer really even see in my delirium. "You have to adjust them to correlate to the shutter speed which you set here."

"Oh," I mumbled, not understanding or caring what she said but simply basking in that wondrous energy known as falling in love.

She took a couple of shots for me and then handed the camera back to me. We stared longingly at one another. Carey Grant. Deborah Kerr. The only question now was who was going to get hit by the car? We both sighed.

Then we glanced around guiltily, wondering if Barbara or Bree were watching us. They had vanished. We took the elevator down to ground level. Barbara and Bree were waiting impatiently below.

"What have you guys been doing?" Bree demanded.

I thought Bree was acting a bit queer. "I wanted a picture of the Trade Towers."

"Well, let's get going," she barked.

Why do I always get barking women around me when I'm falling in love?

We left the building. The rain had stopped. Millions of people pulsed along the sidewalks, talking in their own private conversations, swelling together in an ocean of noise, like a hive of bees humming together. It was like a dream. Carly and I talked quietly as we followed Barbara and Bree, heading for a nearby Thai restaurant.

Throughout dinner, the tension between Barbara and Carly escalated. My protective instincts for Carly intensified. We left the restaurant and proceeded to Christopher Street, to a bar called The Duchess in the heart of Greenwich Village. We stopped in front of the bar. They all looked at me.

"What do you want to do?" Barbara asked me. "We can either go dancing or we can go back to Hoboken to see the fireworks. It's your first time in New York. So it's up to you."

I stood awestruck by the magnitude of the decision. I hated making decisions. But this one held particular significance to me. If we go back to Hoboken, we could see the fireworks, I reasoned. I've never seen fireworks on the East Coast. But if we go dancing, we'll probably have a few drinks and something might happen between Carly and me. Suddenly I felt quite wicked.

"Of course, we might not be able to see any fireworks because of the rain," Bree complained.

"Let's go dancing," I replied innocently. "I can always see fireworks in L.A. I've never been to a women's bar in the Village before."

"Dancing it is then," Barbara said.

We entered The Duchess. It looked like any other bar, dark and dingy from too much cigarette smoke, with loud music and a small dance floor and, of course, the proverbial pool table in the back. We clustered around a tiny table near the dance floor and ordered drinks. Carly and I sat on one side of the table, facing Barbara and Bree. Barbara and Bree chattered away to one another as they slurped down their drinks. Carly and I sat quietly sipping our beers. "Bette Davis Eyes" began to play on the jukebox.

"You wanna dance?" Barbara asked Bree.

"Sure," Bree responded.

They vacated their seats and took to the dance floor. Carly and I sat in silence for a few minutes.

"Why do you stay with her?" I asked quietly. "She treats you like dirt."

"It wasn't always like this," she replied. "I'm not sure if we even have a relationship anymore. That's kind of why I insisted on coming down this weekend. To find out."

"What do you mean?"

"We've been having a long distance relationship for quite awhile now. I wanted it that way. I didn't want Barbara to move to Boston when I started at Boston U. I felt like our relationship was becoming suffocating."

"And how do you feel about it now?"

"I don't feel like we have a relationship."

I sipped my beer quietly. Who was this woman sitting next to me, stirring feelings in my soul that I had thought were dead and gone. I could see myself so clearly in her. She seemed so shy, so good. She reminded me of the me I had been when I was involved with Karole. I wanted to rescue her from that pain.

"You're a giver, aren't you?" I said.

She stared at me, amazed. "How did you know that?"

I smiled and shrugged. "You remind me of someone I knew once."

"Barbara used to be really overweight," Carly confessed. "She had never been with a woman before she met me. She had no self-esteem, no real identity. She was a teacher then. I helped her wake up to her own identity."

"And what happened to your identity in the process?" I asked.

We gazed at one another. Barbara and Bree returned to the table. They were quite boisterous.

"Do you want to dance, Roxanne?" Bree asked.

"Sure," I said. We took to the floor. I surreptitiously watched Carly as I discoed across the floor with Bree. If Bree and Barbara can dance, I reasoned, then certainly I wouldn't be out of line to ask Carly to dance. Returning to the table, I looked at Carly.

"Would you like to dance?" I asked.

"I'd love to," she said gleefully.

We stepped onto the dance floor. The previously fast paced music turned radically slow. Guilt seized my soul. I took hold of Carly like a schoolmarm holding an elderly man, keeping a healthy distance between any real body contact. After a long minute, Carly finally spoke.

"Do you always dance like this?" She sounded annoyed.

I was terrified. "Am I dancing too close?"

"You're not dancing close enough," she said firmly. "I

feel like I'm dancing with my father." With that, she pulled my body tightly against hers, pressing her ample breasts into my chest. I thought I was going to die. My pulse rate escalated to near orgasmic proportions. I was certain Barbara would murder me on the floor if she saw what was happening between Carly and me. Carly seemed completely carefree. I could barely speak intelligently.

"Do you think Barbara will mind?" I mumbled.

"No," Carly replied, rubbing her body against mine. "I just asked her if she cared if we dated other people. She said 'no.'"

"Oh," I said softly, feeling the weight of responsibility sliding off my shoulders and dissolving somewhere miles beneath the dance floor.

"As far as I'm concerned, I'm a free woman," Carly stated.

The rest of the evening became a blur of romance. We danced and drank and talked for hours. At some point, Carly left the table to go to the bathroom. Barbara and Bree chattered away to one another. Realizing that this moment was propitious, I seized the opportunity to leave.

"I have to go to the bathroom too," I stated to them as if I needed to justify my exit. They barely noticed.

I hurried downstairs to the women's room. It was large with six stalls. I was reeling slightly from the alcohol. I leaned against the wall, waiting for a stall to open. One did. Carly stepped out. Seeing me, she grabbed my arm and pulled me back into the stall.

My body felt like a wild beast threatening to break out of its cage. I pushed her up against the wall as we kissed passionately. I couldn't believe how much I wanted her. I felt like Conan the Barbarian consumed with insatiable lust. She must have felt the same way judging from her response. Finally, we broke apart, panting. The responsible part of my brain was informing me that we were taking up space in a bathroom stall that another woman could use for its primary purpose. My bladder was screaming at me that I had to pee.

"I really have to pee," I confessed.

Carly grinned. "I'll go back to the table so they don't get suspicious."

"Okay," I said, kissing her again before she left.

She opened the door. Another woman started to move towards the stall.

"She'll just be a moment," Carly informed her.

"Oh," the woman nodded with a knowing grin.

* * *

The Duchess was closing. As we all trundled out onto the street, we formed a line of women that snaked around the corner and into a doorway. We followed the line up a dark stairwell to a dimly lit second floor apartment where the party continued. Amidst the smoke and the swaying feminine forms, Carly and I grabbed a couple of beers and stood in a corner to talk.

"I don't see why you stay with her," I repeated. "You don't need her."

"No, I'm beginning to see that I don't," she said huskily as she pulled me into her body. I instinctively glanced around. Barbara and Bree were nowhere to be seen. "They're too immersed in one another to notice us," Carly whispered in my ear as she kissed my neck until her lips finally reached my mouth. My whole being felt warm and fuzzy. We broke apart and stared at one another.

"Hey, Carly!" Barbara's voice wafted up from the alley like a rusty grating gate. "Come on! We're going!"

Carly and I glared at one another in horror then turned perfectly innocent faces to the window and waved.

"We'll be right down," Carly called back.

"Oh, my god," I muttered as we rapidly wended our

way through the surging mass of swaying forms. "Do you think she saw us?"

"I don't know," Carly replied in a monotone. "I don't think so. I think she would have been really pissed off if she had seen us kissing. And she wasn't, so, I don't think so."

"Great," I mumbled. The *New York Times* flashed up in my mind, its headline bold and blazing: **YOUNG LESBIAN BRUTALLY MURDERED ON HER VERY FIRST REAL VACATION. WHAT A SHAME. SHE SEEMED LIKE SUCH A NICE GIRL.**

* * *

But I wasn't murdered. I left New Jersey on schedule and flew up to Boston to meet Mark and his girlfriend Melanie. Mark was like a brother to me. He and I had lived together for a few months when I had broken up with Karole and his old girlfriend Claire had left him. We spent many evenings eating matzo with butter and drinking beer while Ella Fitzgerald moaned in the background. Mark was also an aspiring writer and a hopeless romantic to boot.

"You have to call her," Mark intoned in his best rabbinical voice. "Things like this don't happen every day. When you're in love with someone, magic things happen!" Mark's eyes beamed at me. "Magic!" he repeated excitedly. "Let it happen. If you don't, you'll regret it. You'll always wonder what you let pass by."

The room glowed with a golden light. My heart raced with anticipation. I could taste the magic in the air.

"You're right, Mark," I gasped, turning to him, my body trembling. "Just before I left Los Angeles, I went for a hike with my writing partner Gladys. As I stood on top of Griffith Park, in my mind, I called out to the universe for help. I wanted so much to find my soul mate. And as I stood there, I could feel deep inside of me that she was not in Los Angeles."

Mark grinned. "Call her."

I jumped to the phone, picked it up and froze. "I don't know what her last name is."

Mark grabbed me firmly by the shoulders. "Think, woman, think. Her last name must have been mentioned at some point."

"No. No, it wasn't." My mind went numb. Terror gripped me. Oh, my God, leave it to me to meet my soul mate and forget to get her last name. The rest of my life will be ruined. I could barely breathe.

"Okay, okay," Mark whispered, rubbing my shoulders reassuringly. "There will be a way for this to happen. I guarantee it."

When I looked into Mark's eyes, I could see such sweet innocent sincerity. I believed him. My body relaxed. I took a deep breath.

"Plant Heaven."

"Plant Heaven?" Mark asked. "Where gardenia's go when they die?"

"It's where Carly works," I replied, a grin as wide as the Mississippi spreading across my face.

"Alright!" Mark gave me a high five as we both jumped up and down with joy.

I walked confidently to the phone, dialed information, and got the number. Suddenly fear seized me. I slammed the phone down and glared at Mark. "What if she laughs at me? She may not feel the same way that I feel about her."

Mark grinned. "Just call her and ask her if she wants to go out to dinner with us tonight. You won't be sorry."

Taking a deep breath, I nodded and dialed the number. The phone rang a few times before a woman's voice answered.

"Good afternoon, Plant Heaven."

"Hi, ah, could I speak to Carly, please?"

"Which one?"

"Huh?"

"Which one? There are two Carly's who work here."

"Oh... She's the bookkeeper."
"Hold on, please."
"They're putting me through," I whispered to Mark, my eyes bugging out. I took another deep breath.
"This is Carly." Her sensuous voice filled my ear and sent shivers down my spine.
"This is Roxanne," I responded softly.
She gasped. "Well, hi."
"I bet you didn't expect me to track you down."
"Well, no," Carly giggled slightly. "Actually, I hoped you would."
"Really?" My heart soared.
"Yes."
"Mmn," I sighed. "I'm in Boston now."
"You're in Boston?"
"I know this is short notice but are you free for dinner tonight?"
The air was still and silent for a moment.
"No."
The word weighed a ton on my chest.
"Oh."
"I'm sorry. I've got other plans tonight."
"How about lunch tomorrow?"
Another long pause.
"I don't know if that's such a good idea," she said quietly.
"What do you mean?" I implored her. "Look, I don't know if there's any possibility of anything happening between us but we can't just let this chance go by without at least exploring it a little more."
"I don't know," she countered. "I mean, realistically, you live in Los Angeles. I live in Boston. I just don't see where it can go. You'll be leaving when?"
"Thursday morning," I winced.
"Yeah. And I'll get all my hopes up and then you'll be gone. I just don't think it would be such a good idea." She sounded exasperated but she didn't hang up the phone.

"Carly," my heart opened completely, "please. I just want to see you one more time."

The wall of steel protecting her heart collapsed. "Take the Green Line," she began softly, "all the way to the end."

* * *

Boston's public transportation system consisted of a series of electric train lines labeled by color. The Green Line was not full when I got on. I found an empty seat by a window. As we raced along, I realized how different Los Angeles would be if it had similar public transportation. In L.A., survival necessitated owning a car. How odd to think of all those individual people suddenly converging on a railway system. What would they say to one another? Would they even speak to each other?

We journeyed far out into the industrial section of Boston. When Carly told me she worked at a nursery, I had images of flowers and plants and all kinds of green things. Something beautiful. When I got off the Green Line, I stood in a desolate area of red brick factory buildings, iron rail lines and smoke stacks. Hardly the setting for an erotic affair. I walked across the street from the rail terminal and entered the brick building with the large white sign that read "Plant Heaven."

I approached the receptionist. "Hi. I'm here to see Carly Goldman."

"Oh," the receptionist grinned. "You must be Roxanne."

I couldn't help but grin back. "Yes. I am."

"I'll let her know you're here." The receptionist jumped up and ran off into the back room to deliver the news. Carly quickly came out to meet me.

"Hi," she said, her eyes dancing with light.

"Hi." I couldn't believe I was standing in front of her again.

"I'm going to lunch," Carly told the receptionist. "Tell Sid I don't know how long I'm going to be."

"Sure," the receptionist grinned again and gave me the once over.

We walked outside. The air looked hazy. The humidity was high in the summer heat. But somehow none of that mattered. I was in love. We walked to her battered yellow VW Bug and climbed inside.

"I really want a hamburger," Carly said hungrily.

"Sounds good to me," I grinned.

She started the engine and we trundled off to Henry's All American Restaurant Home of the Red, White and Blue. Paul Revere had ridden by this place on his fateful ride through the city streets. Carly and I both ordered cheeseburgers, French fries and cokes.

"I'm starving," I sighed, looking around the cafe. Old men sat at a few of the tables. They looked like old fishermen, yawning through another recounting of a tale that should long ago have been retired.

Our order came up quickly. We took a table at the back of the room in the corner. I had hoped for something a bit more romantic, dimly lit, Italian. This place looked like it was lit by a high school gym teacher for a playoff basketball game.

I bit into my cheeseburger. My mouth exploded into ecstasy. "Oh, my God," I muttered. "This is the best cheeseburger I've ever eaten in my life."

Carly stared at me in disbelief as she swallowed her first bite. "This is the best cheeseburger *I've* ever eaten and I've eaten here lots of times!"

We both grinned.

"I guess it must be us," I said.

She looked at me then shyly away then back at me again as her body relaxed. "Yeah, I guess it is."

We both took another bite of our lunch. The energy between us was very soft and vulnerable and very safe.

"Does Bree know you're here?" Carly asked.

"Oh, God, no," I choked. "She and Raquel are leaving this afternoon to go on their tour of Victorian houses. I'll be so glad when she's gone."

"I couldn't believe how she and Barbara were acting together," Carly complained. "You'd have thought they were lovers."

"I know. So explain their relationship. I just don't get it."

Carly poked a French fry into a blob of catsup. "Bree and Barbara worked together in the bookstore when Bree was in New Jersey. Barbara was the first lesbian that Bree ever really knew."

"Oh, yeah," I gasped. "Now I remember. Barbara came to my apartment for a surprise birthday party for Bree five years ago. She was in L.A. visiting Bree so she came over with Bree. But Bree was still straight at the time."

"Yeah," Carly nodded. "I remember when Barbara went to L.A. So when did Bree come out?" Her eyes twinkled wickedly. "That's the story I'd like to hear."

"It was a few years ago," I explained. "It might have even been the year after Barbara was there. Bree had been working at the bookstore in Northridge for about a year. I was in charge of the Receiving Department at the time. She was dating a guy named Arnold who looked like he was mute and who carried a guitar around. I never did see what she saw in the guy. She threw him out when she caught him reading her diary."

"That sounds like Bree," Carly nodded.

"Well, it just so happened that our regional manager was a woman named Whitney Dawn. Gorgeous woman. A brunette with a face like Vanessa Redgrave and striking blue eyes."

"Was she gay?"

"As a goose. But very private about it. Hell, I fell in love with Whitney when I first started working there. That's when I realized I was gay. So why wouldn't she have the same effect on Bree." I sighed and shook my head. "But Whitney really liked Bree. So she started taking her out after work. For business purposes, of course."

"Of course."

"Well, Bree came into work one morning, looking particularly unapproachable so I left her alone. I was sipping my coffee and opening some special order books. She was sitting at this tiny little table top behind a partition that was laughably called her office. Suddenly I heard her voice wafting up over the wall.

"'I saw Lily Tomlin last night,'" she said.

"'Lily? Oh, god, she's great,'" I said.

"'I love her,'" she said.

"'Oh, I love her too,'" I said.

"I heard the creak of her chair as she pulled herself up to her full height and towered over the top of the partition. I turned around to look at her. She looked like a maniac.

"She shook her head and said slowly, enunciating each word, '"No, you don't understand. I *love* Lily Tomlin. I want to have her baby.'"

Carly started laughing. I grinned.

"Well, that's when I realized that Bree was telling me that she was gay."

"Oh, my God!" Carly squealed. "What a great story."

"She had been having all sorts of feelings coming up about Whitney and she wanted to talk to me about it, so we went to lunch and talked about Whitney."

"Did they ever get together?"

"Oh, yes. A passionate, torrid affair that lasted about a year, I think. Then Whitney went back to her old lover, Kay. Bree subsequently got involved with a very sexy butch woman who was extremely manipulating."

"Did you and Bree ever—?"

The question brought me back to the reality sitting across this Formica-topped table in front of me. My eyes softened as I gazed at her.

"No." The energy between us softened even more. "We kind of brushed up against the idea once or twice. Bree didn't want sex to ruin our friendship. She also told me I wasn't the right type for her."

"What type is that?"

"Weird."

We both burst into laughter.

"Well, no wonder she likes Barbara," Carly laughed. "Barbara is pretty weird."

Our hamburgers had long since been devoured. The watery dregs of coke lingered in the tall red cups, not wanting to be consumed too quickly, for once gone, it would signal the end of this visit.

I wanted to talk to her about us, to convince her to give us a chance to grow but I did not know what to say. The truth was she lived in Boston and I lived in Los Angeles and my mind could not logically build a bridge large enough to span those distances. So it just pretended we were neighbors.

Carly glanced at her watch.

"Oh, my God. I've been gone for three hours," she moaned. "I really have to go back."

"Okay," I nodded. We stared at one another for one more moment. Then I rose from the table. "I have to go to the bathroom."

"Me, too," she said.

We walked toward the restroom together. As we got to the door, Carly turned to me.

"The bathroom is just one big room with a toilet in it. Do you want to come in with me?"

"Sure."

We walked into the bathroom and locked the door. Instantly we were in each other's arms, our souls yearning to merge with the panting passion of young lovers propelled by some unseen magnetic force far beyond their own control. The heat of our desire could have ignited the entire building in a burst of lesbian love.

When we finally left the restroom and walked toward the entrance, the judgmental eyes of every old fisherman in the place grilled into us with a burning wrath. I almost felt like saying 'Geez, you guys, we didn't actually have sex. We just kissed a lot. That was the only private place we could find.'

Carly pulled the VW into her parking space at Plant Heaven.

"I'll walk you over to the Green Line," she said softly.

"Thanks," I said, feeling a heaviness filling my stomach.

The old car doors groaned open. We climbed out. The doors slammed shut. We walked in silence across the cracked asphalt of the parking lot, across the worn cobblestone street and into the transit terminal. We reached the turnstile and stopped.

"Well, I guess this is it, then," I said quietly.

"I guess so," she mumbled. Impulse seized her as she grabbed me and kissed me. "I wrote you this the other night and swore to myself that I'd give it to you no matter what." She stuffed an envelope into my hand. "You better go. You'll miss your train."

With that, she disappeared, leaving me alone and empty. I boarded the car and sat numbly in my seat as the Green Line sped out of the station, threatening to seal shut the crack of hope and love that had just opened up in my heart only days before.

I opened the letter and read it. My heart burst open. She was confused! She wasn't saying 'no.' She was saying 'I'm confused.' Of course I could convince her to follow her heart and move to Los Angeles where we could build a wondrous life together—with me as a famous Hollywood screenwriter and her as a happy accountant. By the time I reached Mark's apartment, I was ready to burst.

"You have to come to dinner with us tonight," I nearly shouted into the phone when Carly got on the line. "It's my last night in Boston and Mark and Melanie want us to go to the top of the Hyatt for dinner and drinks."

"Did you read my letter?" Carly asked after a beat.

"Of course I did. That's why I'm calling. Darling, together we can make anything happen. If we just trust the Love that's brought us together, it will show us what to do." I spoke with the certainty of an evangelical apostle who had witnessed the burning bush on Mt. Sinai. It would take me ten years and tremendous pain and hardship to understand what love even was.

* * *

"Move here and live with me."

Her sensuous voice filled my ears and stark terror flooded my stomach.

"What?" I whispered.

"Oh, my God, I can't believe I am saying this!" she shrieked as she grabbed my knee beneath the linen covered table.

"Yeah, Roxanne, move here!" Mark yelped in agreement, holding up his gin and tonic in a mock toast.

"Huh?" I grunted, quickly retreating into semi-consciousness to avoid making a decision.

"Move here, my love!" Carly repeated. "You could move in with me and my sister until you and I could find another place."

"But, my life," I stuttered. "My career—"

"Forget Hollywood," Mark argued. "It's filled with schmucks and imbeciles. True literary genius is cultivated in Boston, the hub of the universe."

"You could work on a paper," Carly suggested.

"Uh, uh," I stammered, taking a sip of my white Russian for spiritual fortitude.

"Now, come on, you two," Melanie's soothing voice saved me. "Let her have some time to think about this. You're asking her to give up a lot to move here."

"That's right," I rebounded. "I've got a budding screenwriting career. I'm making great money in the film industry. What kind of work could I find here?"

Carly looked at Mark and frowned. Mark pursed his lips.

"There is another way to approach this," I said softly. "You could move to California."

"What?!" Carly shrieked. "No way!"

"Oh, come on," I cajoled. "Don't just toss it out the window without thinking about it. You're an accountant. It would be easier for you to find work out there than for me to find work here. There's no film industry in Boston."

"I hate to say it but she has a point," Mark conceded with a grimace.

Now I felt in control and Carly looked terrified.

"You don't have to decide right now," I assured her. "But think about maybe taking your next vacation in California."

"Well, I don't know," Carly grunted.

"Come on," I cajoled again. "I took my vacation and here I am. Why can't you consider taking just a week to come visit and see what it's like?"

"Well . . . maybe. I'll have to think about it."

By the time we reached Carly's apartment, I was so tired, I could barely stay awake. But this was our first and last night together. So I mustered all my energies to make love. Grover Washington played 'Santa Cruzin' in the background as Carly and I ebbed and flowed on top of her sheets. The heat in the apartment was stifling, the humidity suffocating. Cockroaches scuttled across the kitchen sink, looking for drops of water to soothe their parched throats. Carly's bedroom was tiny, barely containing a bed and a bookcase with her stereo on top. We opened the window, hoping to catch any hint of a breeze but the air was still and lifeless.

I felt like I was performing in some kind of play. Like part of me was in and part of me was gone, watching from some box seat, waiting for the climactic moment to applaud. But there was no climactic moment. I couldn't have an orgasm. I was just too tired. I was falling asleep for seconds at a time and jolting back into my body as she made love to me. She didn't have an orgasm either but she didn't mind. She was like a little kid on Christmas Eve, too excited to sleep, not caring what presents she got but more excited about the adventure of the unknown.

When we awoke at six-thirty that morning, the skies were gray and dreary. The air was thick.

"I'll fix us some coffee," Carly said as she kissed me softly and stood naked before me. She had a beautiful body, athletic and buxom.

"I need to take a shower," I said.

"We don't have one."

"Oh."

"You'll have to take a bath," Carly suggested as she padded into the kitchen and called back to me. "But you really don't have time for that."

I jumped out of bed. I did not want to miss my plane flight. I scooted into the kitchen, kissed her on the back of the neck and continued towards the bathroom.

"I'll just take a cat bath," I called as I climbed into the bathtub and grabbed a clean washcloth from the towel rack over the toilet. There were no shower curtains so I felt a bit obscene kneeling naked before the spigot, trying to wash my crotch out by cupping water in my hands. No, I could not live in a place like this. Not when I was used to making five hundred dollars a week and living in roach-free apartments.

We downed our coffee quickly and Carly whisked me off to the airport. The bleakness of the skies reflected the bleakness of my soul. If I moved here, I would die, I thought. So I ran from this place, hoping with all my heart that she would love me enough to come to me instead.

ALICE

The flight to Columbus from Boston was fairly short. I literally passed out in my seat before takeoff. The next thing I heard was a woman's soft voice whispering in my ear.

"We've landed now," she said sweetly. "In California."

A big grin spread across my face. "Ohio," I mumbled in response as I pulled my eyelids open and chuckled at the stewardess standing next to me.

She grinned broadly. "We thought you were gone."

"I was. I didn't get much sleep last night."

"We could tell," she replied with a wink.

Basking in the afterglow of Carly, I disembarked from the plane and walked across the steaming hot asphalt towards the terminal. Peering at me from the terminal windows, my mother waved wildly. I waved wildly back.

"Mazels!" I mouthed at her as I raced toward the terminal.

This was my nice Mom, the one I could play with. Sam had died in April and I had come to collect my mother and drive her crosscountry, back to her rightful home in California where both of her daughters lived. The last time I saw Mom, she and I spent the morning racing all around Columbus, looking for a cheap putter to put in Sam's coffin.

"He'd kill me if I broke up his set of golf clubs," Mom explained as we went from one variety store to the next.

"I'm giving his set to Ben. But I just couldn't let Sam go to his grave without a putter. He just loved golf so much. Do you think I'm crazy?"

"No," I grimaced. "I think it's very sweet. Sam's probably laughing his ass off watching us."

We both laughed. On April 11, at 4:11 p.m., Sam Spenser dropped dead while playing a round of golf. He had finished the eleventh hole, turned around to pick up a towel he had dropped and just keeled over dead. He was fifty-four years old and in perfect health. It was just his time to go.

"Sam always said he wanted to die like his brother Timothy," Mom told me as we drove to the mortuary, putter in tow.

"How was that?"

"Timothy died on the eleventh hole of that same golf course while he was playing golf," Mom said. "Eleven years ago to the day."

Goose bumps covered my skin. I grinned. "Well, I guess Sam got what he wanted."

An awkward silence filled the car. I looked out the window to the red brick buildings and weather-worn, white slat houses that were Ohio, spanning out flat with only the river running through it to give it life.

"Something kind of creepy happened," Mom said quietly, in a little girl voice.

"What?" My voice was soft with concern.

"Well, when they took Sam to the hospital, I was at the Church. They pulled me out of class to go to the phone."

"Yeah?" I was still amazed that my mother had joined the Church of Spiritual Science after she had so vehemently condemned it when I first became involved.

"Sam and I had had an argument that morning about the Church. He didn't like my being involved in it. I wanted him to take a class on how to communicate. I thought it might help our marriage."

I nodded. "I took that class. It was excellent."

Mom shook her head as she maneuvered the car around a corner. "He just yelled at me and walked out to play golf." She pulled the car into the mortuary parking lot. She turned off the engine and looked at me. "Roxanne, when Sam died, I was doing an exercise to free myself from an obstacle in my life." She took a breath. "Sam was that obstacle."

I gasped audibly then instantly masked the look of fear and surprise on my face. I had heard that some of the Church's teachings were dangerously powerful. But I could not fathom that my mother would be responsible for Sam's death.

"I wonder if I killed him." Her voice was very small and sad.

I put my hand on hers and squeezed her. "No, Mom, you didn't kill him," I assured her. My mind scrambled back through all of my metaphysical and religious studies. In all of them, the soul had free will. "It was Sam's choice to leave when he did."

Mom heaved a huge sigh of relief. "Yeah, I think it was his choice. He was very stuck in his ways. And I think it threatened him that I was becoming more independent." She peered over her glasses at me and grinned. "Guess I'm not a murderer then, huh?"

"Well, I don't know about that," I teased her. "I hear you're murder to live with sometimes."

"Roxanne!" She playfully hit my arm. "That's no way to talk to your mother. And I am your mother this time around."

"How could I ever forget that?" I retorted grinning.

Inside the funeral home, we approached the open casket. I glanced around to see if anyone was watching. Well, it really didn't matter if anyone was watching. A golf putter was a pretty hard thing to hide. Mom placed it along side Sam's body in the coffin.

"Here you go, baby," Mom said quietly. "Now you can play golf in heaven."

I placed three white golf balls and a yellow tee inside the coffin. I wondered what an anthropologist in the future would make of this if they discovered a skeleton buried with a golf club and golf balls. The idea amused me. Then I noticed Sam's hair and make-up. I nudged Mom.

"Mom," I whispered. "Don't you think Sam looks kind of odd?"

She nodded solemnly.

"I mean, his hair looks really weird. He looks kind of like . . . Dracula."

Mom's body began to shake. To the untrained eye of people in the pews, it appeared like the widow was sobbing. The greater truth was, she was laughing.

"Stop, stop," she giggled. "You'll make me pee my pants."

I tried to keep from busting up myself. Sam would have been horrified at the make-up job the mortician did. Too much rouge. The hair was air dried and blown back. I half expected Sam to sit up and start talking to me.

"The mortician didn't have a picture of Sam to work from," Mom explained to me later that night at her condominium. "There must have been a high wind on the golf course when he died," she started to say as the laughter barreled out of her body again. "This is terrible," she said, scrunching her legs together to keep from peeing her pants. "He was so vain, though. He'd die if he saw how he looked in that coffin." She ran into the bathroom. Then returned and climbed into bed.

"It's been very odd sleeping in this bed alone for the last three months," she said.

I stared at her and the bed. Suddenly I realized that this was my mother. She had been married for three years to her high school sweetheart and he had just died. She was fifty-one years old now and a widow. "That must have been hard, Mom," I said softly.

"No, not really," she said, blowing her nose. "Actually, I'm glad he's gone."

"Really?"

"Yeah. He was becoming a real asshole." She wiped her eyes. "He was always picking on me and making fun of my weight. I didn't like it. We hadn't made love in six months. He always thought he was such a stud. I think that's why I didn't wait for him in high school."

"Did you want to marry him then?"

"Yeah," she sighed. "He was so stubborn. He wouldn't ask me. So when your father came along and proposed, I said 'yes.' Sam got so mad, he threw my picture out his window."

So there you are. Thirty years later, the two high school sweethearts met again at their class reunion. Sam was divorced and had one son, Ben. Mom was unhappy in her second marriage. When she returned to California, she filed the divorce papers.

Now Mom and I were loading up her Chrysler with her last belongings, saying goodbye to her past and heading once more for California.

"I feel really weird," Mom said as I piloted this boat of a car across Route 5. "Like I'm moving down a long dark tunnel and there's a light at the other end."

Sounds like a near death experience, I thought. I glanced at her and smiled. "Well, you're starting a new chapter," I offered.

"Yeah. Sort of like being reborn, I guess," she laughed. "I don't know who I am. Feels sort of scary."

She sounded like a little girl, so innocent and fragile. I felt very strong sitting next to her, carrying her home. I had complete confidence that I had found Carly my true love, that she too would come home with me, and that my writing career would soar with all this love and support.

* * *

It was in Kansas when Mom unleashed another side of her soul. The landscape was flat and barren. I could tell by the air currents waving off the asphalt that only hot winds blew outside the cool interior of our air-conditioned car.

"I just want you to know that I don't approve of this homosexual thing," Mom said rising up in her seat from what had been a sound sleep.

The statement rocked me and amused me at the same time. With the feeling of Carly still satiating my soul, I could smile at this old woman trying to control me. Sooner or later, she would accept me.

"That's okay, Mom," I grinned. "I don't need your approval."

My response stymied her. "Well, you've never discussed it with me," she grumbled.

"I was just waiting for you to bring it up," I replied. "I wasn't trying to hide anything from you."

Actually, I thought I had always been pretty forthright with Mom when it came to my personal life. Seven years before, when my sexuality was rising up inside of me with a clarity I could no longer deny, I knew that she would be upset. But I also knew that if I tried to keep this part of my life from her, we would drift slowly apart and she would never know why. So one evening at her Canoga Park home, I maneuvered an after-dinner conversation with her husband Arnold into the subject matter of homosexuality. My mother could hear strains of the conversation from her seat on the couch in the living room where she talked with my sister.

"Is there something Roxanne wants to tell me?" Mom asked Susan.

Susan squirmed.

"HOMOSEXUAL!" The word shot out of the kitchen like a cannon ball.

Mom gave Susan the evil cobra gaze. Susan succumbed.

"Well, she has been thinking about having an affair with a woman," Susan stammered. Mom's eyebrow arched menacingly. "But she hasn't actually done anything yet."

The following Sunday, Mom and Arnold came to my house for Mother's Day dinner. Susan and I shared a house with her friend Carrie. We had just gotten a sweet little puppy dog from the pound who peed on the floor every time a new person arrived at the front door. Mom avoided talking to me for most of the afternoon. When she was preparing to leave, she approached me as I sat at the kitchen table. I could feel the anger emanating from every cell in her body. I stared at her.

"I just want to say that I heard that conversation you had with Arnold the other night," she began, her body quaking with rage. "I don't want to discuss it right now," she snapped.

"That's fine, Mom," I said calmly. "We don't have to discuss it."

"I'm just going to tell you," she continued, her voice blustering like a bazooka ready to explode, "that no daughter of mine is a homosexual!"

The words cut into the very heart of my beingness like hot steel searing me with incredible pain.

Tears formed in my mother's eyes. "When I was a little girl, my mother told me that homosexuals only did it with cows and with dogs. Lesbians kept them specifically for that purpose. No daughter of mine will ever be a homosexual!" she commanded. "That's all I have to say." She turned on her heel and marched out the front door.

My eyes followed her movement as she vanished and the door slammed shut. My body felt like lead. My mind was numb. My eyes fell upon our little puppy playing with a toy on the living room floor. Great time to get a dog, I thought. What kind of pervert would tell their daughter those kinds of lies? I felt sick to my stomach.

* * *

"The idea makes my stomach feel sick," Mom explained, her voice sounding once again like a little girl as we drove through the barren heat of Kansas.

"That's okay, Mom," I said softly. "It just means you're scared about it, that's all."

I did not really understand why my mother would be scared of me being gay. It was not as if I had changed overnight into some hideous monster because another word was added to the expression of my soul. Yet that is how her judgments felt to me. I felt very sad that she could not simply be happy for me. I wondered if she had ever really known me all these years of raising me. Hadn't I always been the good child, the 'A' student, the responsible adult? Hadn't I always been there when she needed me? Why would she be so scared of me now?

We did not discuss the subject any further. I took refuge in fantasies of Carly moving to Los Angeles and the future we would build together. It was easier to fantasize than to deal with my mother's homophobia.

When we arrived back in L.A., Gladys had pulled in another writing project for us to do. The woman who owned the story rights insisted that she could get financing for a movie-of-the-week if we wrote a script. We decided to form a production company and open offices in Venice. Sensing the moneymaking potential of this venture, Mom insisted on opening her own talent agency and representing me. I was very uncomfortable with that idea but I did not know how to say 'no' to my mother. I agreed in order to placate her.

I told Carly about everything as it was unfolding. I was very excited. I was certain that this would prove to everyone that we were real producers. Carly called the day after we opened the offices.

"I was going to send you flowers for your opening,"

she apologized. "But I forgot. But it's the thought that counts, isn't it?"

I felt sick to my stomach when she said that. I choose to ignore it. "Yeah," I said. "That's what they say."

Carly said she would be coming out in September to spend a week with me. She would not commit to moving yet. First she had to see how she felt about Los Angeles.

I was certain that once we had some time alone together, she would realize that we were indeed soul mates, that Destiny had brought us together, that together we could change the world.

CARLY: PART TWO

"I never have orgasms," she said.

I pulled my head out from between her legs. "Huh?"

"I don't know why. I just don't," Carly explained calmly. "It's okay though 'cause I just love how everything feels."

I stopped what I was doing and crawled up to lay next to her. We both reached for a cigarette. I lit hers first, then mine. We both laid back and exhaled as we considered what she had just said.

"I thought all lesbians had orgasms," I said, breaking the silence. "I mean, I never had orgasms with men but I thought that was just because they didn't know what they were doing or that they were just too self-absorbed to care about my pleasure. But two women can just keep going until they both have orgasms. At least that's what I thought."

"Yeah, well, I can keep going forever and I still don't come." She shrugged. "Go figure." She pulled the glass ashtray off the nightstand and placed it between us on the bed. "I talked with Sarah about it before I left Boston. She recommended a book on learning how to masturbate."

"How was that?"

"I really didn't have time to do what it said before I came out here." She flicked the ashes off the end of her cigarette. "I mean, you have to take long baths in candle lit rooms and basically get to know your body very gently."

"Well, that sounds nice."

"Yeah," Carly grimaced. "Maybe I can get around to it when I get back home. It's not easy to get privacy when you live with your sister."

"Oh," I nodded and took a drag off my cigarette.

"So I hope this isn't a problem for you."

"For me?" I repeated innocently. "No." My mind flashed back to my affair with Paul. He was almost old enough to be my father. I was seventeen. I couldn't have orgasms with him. No matter what he did. It bothered him. He felt like he had let me down, had failed somehow as a man. I said I really didn't care. But I did. And secretly I blamed him. I wondered if Carly would begin to resent me as the years rolled by and she still could not climax. It did not occur to me that I might begin to resent her for withholding herself from me that way. Well, I could not possibly tell her those feelings. So I moved to some other ones that I'd had on my drive across country.

"I want to give you the world," I told her, "to provide you with anything your heart desires, to spend the rest of my life with you." I did not, however, want to marry her. Marriage was an institution that literally made me nauseous. The idea of a public ceremony declaring my love for another woman made me physically ill. I never told anyone that. I was terrified that it meant that being gay really was bad. So whenever that feeling arose in me, I turned away from it.

As luck would have it, Carly came to visit me during Labor Day week. My sister was getting married that weekend. Carly came to the wedding and spent the day with my family.

I was one of six bridesmaids all dressed in peach. Carrie, my sister's best friend, was the Matron of Honor. Everyone was excited for Susan. This was the one day in her life that she had always dreamed of. She really had. Throughout her adolescence, Susan would say "I want to get married, have children and live in a house with a white picket fence."

Throughout my adolescence, I didn't. I resented the idea that a woman's biggest goal in life was to marry a man. I wanted to have a career, to make my own mark on the world.

So as I stood near the altar in this Catholic Church in Orange County, the Republican Christian capital of the world, I felt like an outsider. I looked back at Carly sitting in the pews. My family had never acknowledged that the five years I lived with Karole constituted a marriage. Now as I stared at Carly, I knew in my heart that they would refuse to recognize my marriage to her as well. In their eyes and in the eyes of society, I would never really be married unless it was to a man. What kind of hideous institution would deny love in all of its diversities? By the end of the evening, I was glad to get out of my bridesmaid's uniform. There was no real place for me in the heterosexual world and yet I was condemned to live in it.

* * *

"I can work with homosexuals," Bernie Baxter bellowed. "I don't care how many babies they murdered in their past lives." Bernie was teaching my mother how to be a talent agent. He sat on the chocolate-colored, crushed-velvet, modular couch in my gay uncle's living room. Bernie did not know that I was one of the alleged past life baby killers.

"What?" I exclaimed. "I thought the Church said a being can be whatever it wants to be."

"Oh, sure," Bernie waved his hand dramatically. "Of course. But it also says that homosexuals are the most dangerous people on the planet. It's in the Original Documents. Chapter Twenty-Two."

My stomach clenched. Oh, great, I thought. Here we go again. Cast as the villains, the devil incarnate. I was getting pretty tired of being cast out of everywhere I went.

I quickly told myself that this was not a reason to cast aside Spiritual Science. After all, most major religions had taboos about homosexuality. I had no idea why but it made me nervous that they all did. I wondered why my first Spiritual Science counselor had not told me this when I asked her directly. Now I knew I would have to watch my words whenever I dealt with Spiritual Scientists. Damn I hated living in a closet. But I did not think I had any choice in the matter. If I were open about who I was, I would be expelled from the Church. If I were open about who I was at work, they could fire me. No, I would just keep my sexuality invisible the way I always had, hidden in some dark chamber of my mind. I had already invested too much of myself, my time, my energy and my money into this religious practice to throw it out because of a disagreement. I decided that I would be the one to prove to all of them that gay people were just as normal, just as spiritual and just as able to reach enlightenment as anybody else.

"Could you get me a cigarette?" I asked Carly as we drove through the darkness of the Ventura Freeway back towards my apartment in Sherman Oaks. She lit a cigarette for me and handed it to me. "Thank you," I said.

"If one more person says 'Thank you' to me, I'll scream," Carly responded tersely.

A burning sensation shot through my stomach. "Huh?"

"Oh, come on, don't tell me you didn't notice it?" Carly snapped sarcastically. "I've never heard so many 'thank you's in my life. I mean politeness is one thing but to say 'thank you' after every god damn sentence is ridiculous."

I honestly did not know what she was talking about. Certainly anyone who has studied Spiritual Science knows that one of the foundations of communication is acknowledging the other person's transmission. Obviously, Carly needed to study Spiritual Science. Then she would understand and it would not bother her.

"Well," I began diplomatically, "Spiritual Science

contains some very precise training in the art of good communications. 'Thank you' is simply an acknowledgement that the person has duplicated your communication."

"That's ridiculous," she fumed. "I mean, sure, everybody wants to be understood. I just think saying 'Thank you' all the time over does it."

"Well," I replied, "you're right. Sometimes Spiritual Scientists get so used to talking to one another that they forget how it sounds to someone on the outside."

This seemed to satisfy her. Her shackles went down. Okay, I told myself, better omit 'thank you' from your vocabulary whenever you talk with Carly. She's probably just scared by all the bad press that the Church has gotten. She doesn't have to join the Church to be my partner. But I just know that once she sees how much it improves my life, she'll want to study it too. But I'm certainly not going to push it on her.

As I held her tight one last time before she boarded the plane to Boston, I whispered softly in her ear. "Think about it. We really can do this together."

Carly's sad brown eyes stared at me. She impulsively kissed me on the lips. "I'll call you when I get home."

I watched her disappear down the boarding ramp. When I got to my car in the parking lot, I stood on top of the hood. Carly's plane taxied down the runway and pulled itself magically into the air. I waved my arms high above my head, hoping she could see me. My heart and soul were on that plane.

"I need some time to think about all this," Carly said softly over the phone that night.

I stretched out on my foam mattress on the floor in my room and stared at my brick and plywood board bookcase. "Of course," I replied, sad that she was so reluctant.

"I'm not sure about this Spiritual Science thing," she confessed.

"Well, you don't have to join," I assured her.

"I know," she sighed. "I just don't know how I feel about living in L.A. It's so hot there."

What the hell does that matter?, I thought. I'm here. Doesn't that count for anything?

"We do have air-conditioning," I countered.

"Right," she snorted. We both clung to the silence. "I miss you. I'll call you in a couple of weeks when I've had a chance to sort this stuff out."

"Okay."

I hung up the phone and lit a cigarette. According to all of my spiritual studies, I created my own reality. Well, if that was true, then I steeled my heart with the conviction that Carly would move to L.A. I would not allow the least hint of doubt to corrupt that truth.

PRISCILLA

"I'm not moving."

The words rumbled through the phone line like Sherman tanks through a thick forest, crushing every cell of hope in my body, destroying my dreams of a happy, secure future.

"Why?" I whispered.

"I've talked with my therapist about this and I am just not emotionally mature enough to handle leaving my life here in Boston behind and moving three thousand miles to be with you." Her voice was crystal clear and calm as a quiet pond.

"I don't understand," I said.

"Look," Carly explained, "if I were to move out there and live with you right now, I'd just cling onto you. I don't know how to be independent yet. I haven't developed those skills and I know I would just latch onto you and expect you to save me. And pretty soon, I'd become a whiney bitch and you'd hate me for it. And I'd probably hate you too."

I didn't like what she was saying to me but I knew she was right.

"So what do we do now?" I asked quietly.

"I don't know," she sighed. "Barbara and I had a long distance relationship for quite awhile. But I don't know that I want to deal with that."

How could she be so damn logical when she was discussing our future together? Where was the passion?

The intensity? The desire for consummating our mutual love? Didn't she know I was her soul mate? How could she let our future together just slip away so easily?

"You sound very mature," I told her graciously. "I'm glad you're taking care of yourself. It just makes me love you that much more."

"And your understanding makes me love you more too," she giggled.

Carly delivered this well thought out revelation in October. By December, frustration had consumed me. Love letters go so far to satisfy the passions of the soul but the body yearns to be touched and held, kissed and caressed.

"I made love with a woman last weekend."

My body went numb. My mind went blank.

"It was so nice to feel my body again." Her voice sounded so innocent and sincere. "I feel like my sexuality has opened up again. After being with Barbara for so long, I felt pretty dead."

What did she want me to say? Why was she telling me this? Didn't she know this was tearing my heart out?

"I wish it had been me who did that for you," I said quietly.

"Well, that would be sort of hard since you're three thousand miles away," she chuckled.

"So I guess this really won't work," I said.

"I don't think so."

"How long do you think you need to get mature enough before you can move out here?" I asked, my voice sharpening.

"I don't know," Carly replied, surprised by my question. "It might be a couple of years. I don't know what I want to do with my life right now."

"Well, I don't know how to do whatever it is we're doing right now, so I guess I'll just have to start dating again." I clenched my teeth.

"Are you angry?" Carly asked, her voice getting cold.

"No," I snapped. "I'm just really frustrated, that's all. I wanted you to move here, to build a real life with you and you don't want to do that for a couple of years, so I guess I'll just have to start dating and see what happens in my life."

"Are you upset that I slept with Mary?"

"No. No," I lied. "It's probably the best thing that could have happened. I mean, I don't own you, for Christ's sake. I can't expect you to be celibate. I just wish it had been me, that's all."

"Can we still be friends?"

"Of course," I snapped. "We're both mature adults. Of course we can be friends."

When I hung up the phone, I threw my notebook across the room. I was furious.

"Well," I said out loud, "so much for that one!" I stomped across the room and got a cigarette. "Jesus Christ, Carly, can't you see what you're throwing away? Don't you have a clue how hard it is to find your soul mate? You don't just fucking toss her down the toilet because you're too scared to make a commitment! God! Why the fuck do these things happen to me?!"

As if in response to my ire, another woman entered my life. T.J. was an attractive blonde director whom I had first met at the Dummy Up several years before. I met her again at Bree's New Year's Eve party. She was interested in discussing film with me.

"California women just seem to jump into your bed, make love and then leave," T.J. complained as she fixed me broiled chicken and mashed potatoes at her apartment the following weekend.

"Do they really?" I asked. "I hadn't noticed."

"On the East Coast, women bond for life," she explained. "I'm from New York. Ever since I moved here, I've had a hard time understanding the lesbian population. They just seem so . . . flighty."

She could have been talking about the differential housings on a Boeing 747 for all I cared. I just wanted sex. I had always despised men who just wanted sex. Now I was one of them. How could I live with myself in the morning? I really did not care how I felt in the morning. I just wanted sex. And I wanted it now.

We talked well into the early hours of the morning. I was waiting for a sign from within myself. I did not want to use this woman. I knew too well how it felt to be used and thrown out. But I also wanted to make love with her without commitment. The debate ran on inside my head until finally at two o'clock in the morning, I gathered up all my courage and I leaned quietly over and softly kissed her lips. She moved into my arms.

"I could not have done that," she whispered as she kissed me again.

"I didn't know if you wanted to," I said, kissing the nap of her neck.

"Oh, yes," she moaned softly, "I wanted to but I just couldn't make the first move."

Our breathing merged as we gently explored one another's bodies. She was so soft and vulnerable. She made me feel very safe in her arms. We flowed together as easily as two dolphins surfing in the sea.

When I left in the morning, I was scared. By the time I reached my apartment, I was angry with myself.

How could you use that woman that way, I admonished myself. You know you love Carly. What are you going to do? Get involved with T.J. and then dump her when Carly moves out here? Why couldn't you just wait?

Wait? For what? Two years? And what if she didn't come in two years? What if she and Mary had some incredible romance and decided to move to Manhattan together for Christ's sake? How am I supposed to know what's going to happen? What am I supposed to be? A monk?

I never did understand how people could date casually, make love and then date someone else. I was the type that bonded instantly like crazy glue and then tried to make it work with the other person regardless of who that other person was.

The same seemed to be true with T.J. We saw one another a few more times before I began to feel suffocated and terrified. T.J. sensed my withdrawal.

"I know you don't like that I smoke pot," she said over drinks one night. "I'll stop." Her energy was eager to please.

"No!" I insisted, horrified. "Please, don't change for me. You're fine just how you are. You're you. Don't start changing yourself to please me. That's not healthy."

I did not realize at the time that T.J. was mirroring back to me the part of myself that instantly changes to please my partner. It was too terrifying to behold. So I broke up with T.J. Well, I didn't exactly break up. I sort of snuck off. I felt like a real weasel but I just could not confront telling her directly that I did not want to see her again. So I stopped answering the phone and I did not respond to her postcard.

I plunged into my work at the studios. We were in the midst of a massive computer conversion. I was helping to create the first fully computerized residual system in the motion picture industry, complete with a payroll interface capable of tracking pension ceilings automatically. To do this, I needed the services of two brilliant computer programmers—a Chinese fellow named John and another man who would influence my life in infinite ways. I first met him over the phone.

"This is Trevor," a chipper male voice said politely.

"Hello, Trevor, this is Roxanne," I said in my most commanding voice. "I'm Residual Paymaster at Harry Glass Productions."

"Oh, yes," Trevor replied. "I'm happy to meet you."

"Yes," I said. "What is the status of the Residual system?"

"Well," Trevor began sweetly, "I was just assigned to this the other day. I have a few screens I'm working up. Actually, John and I were planning on meeting with you around Thursday."

The hair stood up on the back of my neck. I had dealt with computer programmers before. They were notorious for promising me everything and giving me shit. I was not going to diddle around until Thursday naively assuming that all would be well and that I could trust these people.

"No," I said curtly. "That will not do. I was told that this system would be ready and waiting for me to start my conversion when I arrived yesterday. QPC will cease making any residual payments at the end of this week. That gives me one month to get a fully operating residual system up and running and capable of cutting a month's worth of checks. If we don't make that deadline, the guilds will charge us with penalties."

I am quite sure I sounded like the female version of a pre-menstrual Patton. There was dead silence on the other end of the phone. I waited for several long moments.

Trevor drew a breath. His voice sounded quite soothing as he said, "I'll be over at four o'clock this afternoon with some input screens for you to start using."

"Thank you," I replied, my voice softening.

At four o'clock, Trevor appeared in the Payroll Office doorway. He cut quite a dashing figure. Standing five-foot-eight inches tall, he had jet-black hair with a neatly trimmed mustache and beard. He had the body of a dancer and a walk like Charlie Chaplin's. His blue eyes sparkled confidently at me as he crossed the room. I knew in that moment that I loved this man, an old soul mate come to greet me again. He made my heart smile. I was very impressed with his efficiency and his manner. He reminded me of a softhearted English gentleman without the accent.

Within twenty-four hours, we had ascertained that both of us were gay and that both of us were artists in our own rights. He was a composer. Show tunes. He had been raised in Las Vegas. So it should not have shocked me that we would share a mutual friend. But it did.

One night at two o'clock in the morning, Trevor was pecking away at his keyboard with the fury of an inspired maestro. I dutifully entered player work histories on my terminal. It was a boring job but comprised the bulk of the system. The room was silent save the tap, tap, tapping of our fingers on computer keys. Without missing a beat in his rhythm, Trevor's voice rose as if from some unopened grave.

"Do you happen to know a lesbian named Whitney Dawn?"

Chills ran up my spine as an involuntary shriek leapt from my throat. "Whitney Dawn?!"

We both stopped typing and stared at one another.

Trevor grinned. "Yes. I guess you do know Whitney."

My eyes bugged out of my head. I'm quite sure my hair was standing on end. I nodded. "You know her?" I squeaked.

He lit a cigarette. "I went to high school with her."

"Oh, my god," I gasped, grabbing a cigarette of my own. "This is too weird. What made you bring up her name now?"

"I don't know," Trevor puffed. "It just popped into my head. I really didn't think you'd know her. I mean, it's been ten years since I graduated and I had only heard a rumor that she had moved to L.A. So I really didn't think that you'd actually know her."

"I worked with her," I replied. "She's the woman who brought me out."

"Oh, you poor thing," Trevor shook his head.

"Was she as crazy in high school?"

His face blanched. He nodded.

"Was she mean to you too?"

He nodded again. "Awful. I didn't know I was gay when I was in high school. And she made a point of calling me a fag in front of people. She and Basil were always doing weird things."

"Basil!" I screamed. "She'd talk about Basil with me. She said they hopped a train car together and ended up in L.A."

"Yeah," Trevor nodded. "They wanted me to go along but I was too scared. She was just too out there for me. She'd just collapse in the middle of the crosswalk and wait for someone to come pick her up."

"Weird," I shook my head. "But very attractive."

"Yes, that's true," Trevor grinned. "Is she the type you look for in a woman?"

"Why do I feel like you're fishing here?" I asked suspiciously.

He grinned. "Because I am. Are you single, honey? Are you dating anyone?"

"Ugh," I grunted. "I've given up on love. I was passionately in love with a woman in Boston and she just dumped me. I'm not interested in getting involved with anyone right now."

"Oh, I'm not talking about involvement," he said innocently. "Just a casual meeting."

"What's her name?"

"Priscilla."

"Is she gay?"

"Well, she's not really sure," Trevor said cautiously.

I glared at him. "Has she ever been with a woman?"

"Yes, yes, she has," he replied gleefully. "She's just not sure if that's what she really wants or not. She just wants to talk, that's all."

"She wants to talk," I repeated. "Okay. I'll talk to her."

"Great!"

We all went out for pizza one night. Priscilla looked quite sexy in a solid red silk teddy and black slacks. She was not the type of woman that I was normally attracted to. Her lips were very tight. She seemed very chipper. We all went back to Trevor's apartment and drank beer, ate pretzels and talked.

Trevor passed out on the couch around midnight. Priscilla and I sat on the floor, leaning against the backside of the couch. She looked at me coyly. After six beers, I was not feeling much of anything. I knew she expected me to kiss her and for some reason, my body began moving towards her. Suddenly I heard a loud, baritone voice reverberating inside of me.

"Do you *really* want to do that?" the voice said sarcastically.

But it was too late. I felt like I was caught in some strong magnetic current that was pulling me toward her lips. Our faces connected. My life disintegrated. I instantly felt bound to this stranger, that I had to take care of her, that if I left her, she would kill herself.

Within a few weeks, I was moving into her cottage in Santa Monica. As I packed up my belongings, I sobbed hysterically. My mind had short-circuited. I felt completely out of control, trapped and committed to something I did not want to do. I could not see any way out. I wanted someone to come and save me from my fate. An outsider would have assumed someone in my family had died. The truth was that I was the one who had died. And I was going to hell. In another instant, those feelings stopped. It was as if someone had turned off a switch inside of me, as if that pain had never even existed. I packed up my car and drove to Priscilla's cottage.

As I drove over the 405 freeway towards the 10, I told myself that I would give this relationship a year to bloom. That's fair, I thought.

Priscilla lived in a tiny two-bedroom dollhouse on 23rd Street in Santa Monica. It was very dark inside. Every inch of wall space was covered with some article of furniture, nick knacks or pictures. A huge red tapestry rug covered the wood floor in the living room. White shutters covered the front windows. An antique red love seat acted as a couch. It looked like a French bordello. There was nowhere to breathe. The white kitchen was tiny. The stove was covered with grease. Pricilla constantly fried bean burritos or tacos on the stove. Priscilla was a vegetarian who hated vegetables. She refused to eat meat or fish or chicken. She wore plastic shoes and considered it politically incorrect to sit on a leather saddle while horseback riding. She was always more concerned about political correctness than about anything inside of her own soul.

Priscilla had a natural talent for theatrical performing. When she was five years old, a talent scout saw her tap dancing in a school play and immediately approached her mother. Priscilla's mother had failed at acting. She would not allow Priscilla to go to Hollywood. Priscilla spent the rest of her life pursuing an acting career with undeniable fervor. She acted in countless Community Theater productions and had won numerous awards and accolades from the critics. She had a tremendous talent inside of her. It would take me a few months to realize that along with her talent, Priscilla also harbored a massive amount of inner pain.

From the beginning of the relationship, I told her about my feelings for Carly. Priscilla did not seem concerned. Looking back, I believe Priscilla knew from the outset that this was a temporary arrangement and she was going to get the most for her time.

I, on the other hand, thought I was trying desperately hard to make the relationship work. But the truth was, I did not love Priscilla. No matter how many times I compulsively said those words to her. I collapsed into this relationship because I thought if I couldn't have Carly, then I had to make it work with anybody. I could not just be me alone.

Priscilla told me she had been diagnosed manic/depressive by her psychiatrist. I wasn't sure what that even meant. The words just bounced off of me like rubber balls in a padded cell. I didn't know who I was or why I was in this relationship. I only knew I had to wait for a year before I could leave, otherwise, I would be an evil person.

Priscilla smoked her cigarettes like Bette Davis, taking deep draws, sucking the smoke into her mouth tightly, until her lips looked like a lizard. Her hands were not large and secure like many lesbians. Hers were short-fingered and small like a monkey paw. She loved to act out dialogue from the "I Love Lucy" shows. The worst part was that she expected me to join in. I felt like an outsider to her theatrical group of friends. They would all start singing show tunes at the drop of a hat.

I, on the other hand, was crusading for Spiritual Science. Spiritual Science could cure any ill, right any wrong, even raise the dead. At least that's what I thought at the time. But it could not get me Carly back. And it could not make Hollywood buy my scripts.

Sexually, we were diving into a blackened pit. Priscilla needed to get stoned to make love. I resented that. But I also wanted to have sex. I hoped that if Priscilla could relax and feel the softness of a woman, she would love herself more. Our lovemaking went from something seemingly normal to strange requests. Please don't touch my breasts. Please don't kiss me down there. Please don't lie on top of me. Please don't breathe on me. We stopped having sex. Then her pain came forward in full dramatization.

At two o'clock one morning, I awoke to a very odd sound. A sound unlike any I had ever heard before. A very hollow sound, yet somehow simultaneously metallic. I opened my eyes. Priscilla was not in bed. I could see a light coming from the living room. And then the sound again. I sat up, my mind trying to decipher the sound. Suddenly, my stomach filled with dread. I knew what she was doing.

I rose quickly from the bed. In an instant, I was in the living room. Priscilla jumped nervously from the couch over to the display case harboring her collection of "Gone With The Wind" memorabilia.

"Priscilla," I said firmly, "what are you doing?"

"Nothing," she said, her voice sounding like a two-year-old.

"Come back to bed then," I said gently.

She scampered back into the bedroom. I walked across the wooden floor to the lamp by the loveseat. Then I saw the heavy duty hammer lying on top of the small wooden coffee table. My heart ached. Priscilla had been smashing the metal head of the hammer against the top of her knee. That was why the sound had been hollow and metallic at once.

I took several deep breaths to calm my own anxiety. She did not need my judgments at this time. She needed my gentleness and my love. What the hell had happened to her in her life that would make her want to do this?

The next morning, Priscilla came to me when I was getting something from the bedroom closet.

"I did something bad last night," she said in a tiny little girl voice.

"I know," I said quietly.

She pointed to her knees. They were black and blue.

"What happened, Priscilla?" I asked gently.

She scrunched up her shoulders and shook her head. "The heebee jeebees."

I took her in my arms and held her. I was frightened for her and I was frightened for myself. I had no real understanding of how to deal with someone with so much pain. I had thought that the Church had all the answers I needed. Just get her some counseling and she would be fine. She refused to go. She could not afford the prices.

By September, I was nearly dead. My skin tone had turned to gray. Priscilla was slowly draining my life force from me, like a vampire quietly sucking blood. She had written her first screenplay while I was there. I encouraged her to pursue her creativity. She in turn tore me apart for pursuing mine.

At the beginning of the relationship, I tried over and over to talk with her about our relationship. She was always too busy, deliberately filling up every ounce of time with social engagements and activities. Dodging me with excuses about working on her film with Tom, her childhood sweetheart. The two of them were like Lucy and Ricky together. At his birthday party in June, I overheard her whispering to him that they would go to Europe together the following year. She never mentioned going to Europe with me.

I told Priscilla that I needed time alone to think about things. She still refused to see that we were having problems in the relationship. I spent a three-day weekend in Carmel alone.

When I returned home Monday night, she had the living room filled with candles. She stood by the loveseat, dressed in a tight red dance skin and black fishnet stockings complete with black garter belts. The most hideous part of this disguise was the wig. A big brunette bundle of hair. I knew that she was trying to look sexy but to me, she just looked like a whore. My stomach turned. I didn't want to tell her how I really felt because I knew she would launch into a tirade attacking me and I could not take anymore of her acerbic tongue-lashings. The neurotic nature of this existence was literally killing me.

We had planned a trip to New York in November.

"Priscilla, we need to talk about us before we go to New York," I told her one October morning as she combed her short butch haircut. (As our relationship passed through time, Priscilla had undergone a bizarre transformation. When we first met, she had shoulder length brown hair and a petite body frame. As time moved past, her hair got progressively shorter and shorter until finally she looked like a Marine recruit. Her hips grew proportionately wider to the shortening of her hair. She looked like a large, unattractive pear.)

"Sure, sweetheart," she chirped merrily from the bathroom. "I'm so excited about getting to the Big City. Broadway. The Theatre District. I've made arrangements with Scott to take us to a Broadway play."

"Great," I muttered. "Priscilla, I need to talk with you."

"We'll have plenty of time to talk in New York," she insisted, rubbing rouge heavily on her cheeks and covering her lips with blood red lipstick.

"I want to talk before we go to New York," I insisted wearily.

"Well, I really don't think that's going to be possible," she countered, true chess champion that she was. "I just don't have any time right now."

With that, she trundled out the front door and plopped her wide butt into her red Carmengia, hung a cigarette between her blood red lips and gunned the car out of the driveway.

I collapsed into the overstuffed living room chair.

"Fine, Priscilla," I muttered out loud. "Have it your way. We'll break up in New York. Frankly, my dear, I don't give a damn anymore. You are just such a self-centered bitch, I can't even believe it."

So there we were, stuck in an ancient ninety-story hotel in New York's theatre district. The room was scorchingly hot. There was no thermostat control in the room itself. The temperature was controlled by some unseen being deep in the bowels of the basement. Consequently, the thermostat read a solid ninety degrees. I opened a window, hoping for a brisk breeze from the thirty-degree wind outside. Our window looked out into an enclosed courtyard. The buildings around us towered upwards into the sky, blocking any hope of a breeze. The air was stagnant and smelled like the decaying garbage that lay in heaps at the bottom of the buildings.

I wanted to vomit. I pulled my head back into the room and looked at the only other available view—Priscilla. She looked manic. A smile plastered across her face so tightly her skin could crack at any second. Everything in me froze. I felt like I had to be extremely careful about every word that came out of my mouth, that I could not even breath without fear of setting off this human time bomb.

"Let's call Scott and see if he wants to go to dinner," Priscilla chirped.

"Sure," I intoned with all the enthusiasm of a corpse.

Scott was a fellow thespian who had gotten a part in a Broadway play. He had made his break into the big time. He was truly a charming fellow. But frankly, I was so dead by this time that the whole experience of meeting him was like moving through a dense cloud, garbled and foggy.

We returned to the hotel late that night. I got into bed quickly, hoping to fall asleep before anything remotely sexual could develop. Priscilla turned the light out and crawled in next to me. She wiggled her body up against me in her most sexual manner. I felt nauseated.

"I feel like all of my skin has been stripped off of me," she cooed into my ear. "Do you still love me?"

I felt like an invisible claw had wrapped itself around my neck and was beginning to pull the most secret parts of me out of my intestines. I could not stop myself from speaking the truth.

"No," I heard myself say quietly.

An icy cloud filled the room. Priscilla's body recoiled to the other side of the bed. For a long time, there was silence. Then her voice split my ears.

"How could you say that to me?!" she screeched. "I just told you that I have the heebee jeebees and you take a knife out and stab me to death!"

"Oh, god," I gasped. "You have the heebee jeebees? I didn't know, Priscilla, honestly, I didn't know."

"How could you not know?" she railed. "I just told you my skin was stripped off. When my skin is stripped off and all my nerves are exposed, I have the heebee jeebees!"

"I'm sorry, Priscilla," I said sincerely. "I didn't understand what you were saying." That was true. I was so terrified, my mind had not connected her words with the reality she was trying to describe to me.

"I can't believe this is happening to me! How could you bring me three thousand miles away from my support system to dump me like some piece of shit! Thanks a lot! You could have waited until we got home. Then at least I would be able to talk with Trish or with Tom and not just run out and slash my wrists, for Christ's sake. Who is it? Carly? Is that it? Have you decided to go back to her now? Is that what this little trip is all about? So you can get back in the sack with the great love of your life? Is that it? Huh? Say something, will you? Or did you just want me to bleed to death quietly once you plunged that dagger deep into my heart?"

"No," I said. But my mind was frozen. I was terrified. I felt like I was trapped in an insane asylum with a lunatic capable of killing me or herself or both of us. I knew I had to speak very carefully. "Priscilla, I didn't plan on telling you this here."

"Oh, when then?" she chirped merrily, happy to be the bitch in control.

"I wanted to talk to you before we came," I began.

"Oh, right!" she moaned. "Like you couldn't talk to me."

"I couldn't, Priscilla. You wouldn't let me."

"Right!" she snapped. "We live in the same house for Christ's sake. All you had to do was yell 'I want to break up' and you'd have had my undivided attention. But no, you decide to dump that news on me after you drag me off to some foreign land where I have no friends. Well, you're just going to have to take care of me until we get home."

I felt so guilty and so scared and so angry all at once. But I could not for the life of me express any of my feelings.

They just rumbled around inside of me while I listened to Priscilla rant and rave and whip me with her words and accusations until she finally collapsed into tears and let me rock her in my arms.

After a few hours of sleep, Priscilla got up and took a shower. I felt like I'd been run over with a steamroller. What else could possibly go wrong? Suddenly a bloodcurdling scream came out of the bathroom. I ran in to find Priscilla shaking in horror. She pointed to the bathroom counter. Hundreds of baby cockroaches covered her make-up bag. In the night, a pregnant roach had given birth inside Priscilla's make-up kit.

When we got back to Los Angeles, Priscilla milked the melodrama for as much attention as she could get. I wearily played the part of the bad lover. I moved into the spare bedroom and began looking for apartments. I just knew I had to get the hell out of this house by January or I'd be dead before my next birthday.

Priscilla became very loving when I told her I was moving out. She even started taking some Spiritual Science workshops, saying she really wanted to understand my world, that she wanted to fight for my love, that she was not going to let the best thing that ever happened to her slip away without a fight.

I would have been slightly flattered if I did not know Priscilla so well. You see, she didn't really care about me. She just enjoyed a good dramatic role. She needed something juicy outside of herself to sink her teeth into so she could avoid dealing with the horrific pain inside of her own soul.

I moved into a one-room apartment in Brentwood. A friend of Priscilla's was going overseas for nine months and needed someone to sublet the place. That would give me enough time to get reoriented. I called Carly once I moved in. When I had seen her in Boston, she told me she would move to California and live with me when I left Priscilla.

"I can't," Carly said quietly.

Oh, great, I thought. Here we go again. "Why not?"

"I had an anxiety attack when I was visiting my sister in New York," she explained.

"My god, Carly, what happened?"

"Honestly, Roxanne, I don't know. We had been walking down the street and this guy snatched this woman's purse and ran off. There was a cop standing across the street and he didn't do anything."

"Did he see what happened?"

"Oh, he saw it but he just turned and walked the other way."

"That's awful," I said as I lit a cigarette.

"Yeah. I knew I was upset by it, but I didn't realize how much until we got back to Sandra's apartment. I decided to take a bath." Carly's voice cracked.

I waited for her to continue, taking a drag off my cigarette, wondering where all this was leading to. What the hell had happened to her?

"I got into the tub," she said quietly, "but I couldn't get out."

"What do you mean?"

"I stayed in that bathtub for six hours."

I sat up in my chair and took a deep breath. "Oh, my God. What happened?"

"I don't know," she said. "I couldn't move. I couldn't breath. I was terrified. All of a sudden the world wasn't safe anymore. The only safe place was being huddled in the bathtub."

"Oh, honey, I'm sorry. I wish I could be there right now to hold you."

"I wish you could too."

"Have you talked to your therapist about this?"

"Yeah. She doesn't really have any ideas about why the anxiety would be so severe."

"Oh." I could feel the pain in her heart. How I longed

to hold her. My voice was soft and low. "How did you finally get out of the tub?"

"I crawled out on my hands and knees."

"Oh, my God."

"Yeah, it was pretty scary. Sandra brought me a bathrobe and I crawled out of the bathroom and down the hall to the bedroom. I was such a wreck."

"When did the symptoms finally pass?"

"They haven't really."

"What do you mean?"

"I can't leave my apartment without checking to see if I locked the door."

"What's wrong with that?" I asked.

"I have to check it twenty times before I feel safe enough to walk away."

"Oh, my God," I muttered. "This just doesn't sound like you."

"You're telling me," she sighed. "I don't know what happened. It's like all of a sudden I have no faith in myself, no sense of security. It's like the whole world suddenly got terrifying."

"How bizarre."

"So you see, my darling, I can't possibly move out there right now," she apologized. "I know you must think I'm a real basket case. I'm sorry."

"No," I sighed, "you're not a basket case, believe me, I just finished living with one."

She laughed. "It must have been awful for you."

"Only the worst year of my life," I replied. "But that's over with now. Now we have to get you feeling better so you can move out here."

"Yeah. I just hope therapy can help me through this."

"Me too. I love you."

"I love you too."

I hung up the phone, my stomach sinking with the

feeling that she was never going to come. If she had only come in 1981, everything would have worked out fine. My writing would have taken off and we would have made a real home for ourselves by now.

But the truth was that the older I got, the harder life was becoming. Within six weeks, I gave up all hope of ever having a relationship with Carly. She called to say she just didn't know if she would ever be able to move. Priscilla appeared on my doorstep on Valentine's Day, sporting cupcakes and a new figure.

"I'm taking the Spiritual Science class you recommended," she said proudly as she walked into the apartment.

"God, that's great, Priscilla," I said in shock. Maybe there's hope yet, I thought. Of course, I thought the Church could make the dead walk again if they could just afford to get a little counseling.

The problem with Priscilla was not that she was crazy. It was that she had crazy spells. In between the spells, a very attractive and sometimes even supportive person would come out to be with me.

We made love that night. In the deep loneliness of my soul, I wanted so much to be held, it really did not matter much by whom. Priscilla and I began dating.

I began having nightmares again. They always had the same flavor to them. The characters changed and the sets rotated but always the same dynamic of evil spirits trying to get me.

I would wake up with a start at two, three or four in the morning, my body wet with sweat, my heart racing wildly in my chest. It would take me a moment to get my bearings. The dreams were always more real than my own life. Then I would get up, check the apartment for signs of poltergeist activities, smoke a cigarette and try to go back to sleep. I was never afraid of burglars. I always knew I could club a burglar to death if I had to. But these unseen spirits, they were my biggest fears. There was no escape from them. I could not control them. They had no form, no substance to wound. They appeared randomly in my dreams, turning normality into choking terror. The worst part was being afraid to go back to sleep for fear that they would be waiting to attack me again.

Priscilla played her final trump card on Easter Sunday. She came over to my apartment for breakfast. After we ate our eggs benedict and sipped our homemade mimosas, she lit a cigarette and rose dramatically from the couch.

"I don't know how to say this," she announced, her voice laced with false humility. "But this just isn't working for me."

"I overcooked the eggs?" I kidded. She stared at me solemnly. "What are you talking about, Priscilla?"

"Our relationship," she said sternly. "It just isn't working for me."

"What do you mean?" I asked. I was totally thrown off-guard by this pronouncement. I felt like she had plunged a gutting knife into my heart and twisted it several times for good measure.

"I mean, I'm leaving you," she said pointedly.

"I don't understand. I thought things were going along fine."

"No," she stated, walking slowly around the room. "Not for me. I just can't deal with your religious views. You're obsessed by them. And I don't want to invest any more energy into the relationship. I never should have come back to you in the first place." She quickly gathered up her sweater and her purse and scampered to the door. "But I honestly thought we could work things out." She opened the door. "I was wrong." She walked out and closed the door.

I collapsed on the couch and burst into tears. How could she do this to me? I thought we were getting along so well? I cried for a few minutes when suddenly a very deep thought arose from within me. Why are you getting so upset? You didn't want this relationship. You still have Carly.

I sat bolt upright. "Jeez, that's right," I said out loud. "What the hell do I need Priscilla for? I can call Carly."

So I did. Carly was smart enough to realize that this would probably be the last time I would ask her to live with me.

"Yes," she said. "Yes, yes, yes. I'll come out in six weeks. I just need time to wrap stuff up back here."

"I'll come back and get you," I offered, knowing too well that a lot could happen in six weeks. "I'll make a plane reservation tonight. In the meantime, I'll find us a house to live in."

"A house?" she giggled.

"Yeah," I said, feeling strong and powerful and finally in control again. "What kind of house do you want?"

"One with a big tree in the backyard," she said gleefully.

"You got it," I promised. "One big tree for Carly."

Finally, all of my dreams could become a reality.

CARLY: PART THREE

True to my word, I found a two-bedroom house for rent in Brentwood, one of the more elite areas of town. There was a monstrously large rubber tree growing in the backyard. The house itself was on Darlington, just off Barrington before San Vicente Boulevard. Hamburger Hamlet's restaurant across the street offered live jazz every Saturday night and there was a plethora of shops and restaurants to walk to along San Vicente. Just the sort of neighborhood that Carly would love.

The house had a small kitchen, a dining area that adjoined a decent-sized living room, one bathroom, an extra bedroom and a large sunken master bedroom that was actually a converted garage. It took me about a month to get moved in and unpacked. Then I flew to Boston to get Carly.

I envisioned a wildly romantic road trip adventure with my soul mate, culminating in building a wonderful life together in Hollywood. The reality was starkly different. It was a horribly hot August. Carly's yellow VW Bug did not have air-conditioning. It was packed to the brim with her life's belongings. I had no idea what it even meant that she was giving up her entire life in Boston to move to Los Angeles with a virtual stranger.

The trip was long, hard and hot. By the time we reached

the mountains leading to Brice Canyon in Utah, Carly short-circuited. She pulled the VW into a turnout.

"I can't do this!" she exclaimed.

I stared at her, scared by her outburst.

"The car's too loaded down. We'll never make it up this grade. And I can't possibly drive through that tunnel." She glared at me, then at the mountain before us.

My mind scrambled for a logical solution. "Why don't I drive for a while?" I suggested.

"We have to turn back and find another way," she insisted. "We can't possibly make it up this hill."

I stared at the Winnebago lumbering past the turnout and heading up the incline to the tunnel. If a Winnebago can get up this hill, then surely we can, I thought. We can't possibly turn around and find another route. I have to be back at work on Monday and a change in plans would cost us another day.

"We'll just take it slow," I said calmly.

"No!" she shouted. "I can't go through that tunnel."

"Honey, I'll drive us through the tunnel," I said firmly.

"You don't understand," she shook her head. "I'm having an anxiety attack. I can't go through the tunnel. There's no air in there."

"No air," I sighed, nodding, trying to appear compassionate while wanting to choke her. I felt like I was dealing with a two-year-old.

I got out of the car and walked to the wall at the edge of the lookout point. What's the big deal about driving through a damn tunnel, I asked myself silently. I peered over the wall of the lookout point. An extremely sheer cliff dropped into a cavernous canyon. My head began to spin. I looked up at the mountain and the tunnel. The tunnel stretched across eternity. My stomach dropped. I staggered back to the car.

"Who the hell built that fucking thing?" I demanded as I fell into the driver's seat. "It's fucking huge."

Carly grinned, happy to see my anxiety. "It's twenty-three miles long," she announced as she closed the AAA travel book.

"Look, I can drive us through that thing," I told her, my pupils dilating. "But we have to go now before I lose my nerve."

"We can go," Carly replied calmly.

"Huh?" I could not believe this radical reversal. "What changed your mind?"

"There are air holes in the tunnel," Carly explained victoriously. "It said so in the travel log."

"Air holes," I muttered, starting the engine. "Great." I could give a shit about air holes. I was terrified that the sheer weight of the mountain would collapse on top of us before we could get through the damn thing. But I couldn't tell Carly that. She was finally relaxed about the air holes.

We headed up the hill. About a hundred yards into the tunnel, I broke out into a cold sweat. My clammy hands clutched the steering wheel. It was pitch black inside the tunnel.

"Why aren't there any lights in here?" I muttered.

"There's an air hole coming up!" Carly squealed excitedly.

My neck and shoulders relaxed slightly as I saw light pouring through the side of the mountain. The air holes were also light holes. This I could live with. We inched our way from hole to hole until we finally reached the other side of the mountain.

Brice Canyon stretched out like an artist's canvas in its surreal perfection. Thousands of blue and pink misty haloed spires of rock had been chiseled by wind and rain. I stood motionless in the midst of heaven. It was too beautiful. The kind of awesome splendor that forces the mind to make less of it lest the ego should become infinitesimally small and vanish entirely.

"I had the same reaction when I first saw it," Carly

whispered, breaking my reverie. "Would you like to hike down and take some pictures?"

I hated hiking. I hated hiking in heat. But I didn't want to be a dead head on our first trip together so I put on my best happy face. "Sure."

Carly hopped down the hillside like a mountain goat, giggling, happy, carefree. I lumbered down awkwardly, uncomfortable with my body's ability to maintain its balance. Dignity at all costs was my silent motto. I was just happy that Carly was having fun. We had come through the worst mountains of our journey. It would all be downhill from here.

* * *

"I can't fucking believe I'm doing this!" Carly shouted angrily as our car plodded along the steamy desert blacktop. "This is fucking ridiculous!"

My stomach spasmed. I stared at her, unsure of how to respond. What had happened to that sweet woman I fell in love with two years ago? I knew she should have moved in '81. She's turned into a bitch. Oh, god, I hope she's not like Priscilla. I can't take another one like that again. Carly's nothing like that, another part of me insisted. She's just too hot. It is hot. You're driving through a desert during the day. Of course it's hot.

"Maybe we should find a motel and get some rest right now," I suggested as I put a wet, red bandana from the ice chest on the back of her neck. "We could drive the desert leg at night."

Carly held the bandana on the back of her neck, then wiped her face with it and returned it to her neck again. "Fine," she grumbled.

We pulled off at the first town we saw. We waited until ten o'clock to start driving again. We drove like nomads through the darkness, searching restlessly for home.

* * *

Carly loved the huge rubber tree in the backyard. It was the rest of L.A. that she hated. The ugly urban sprawl. The heat. The traffic. The people. The smog. And most of all, she hated the food.

"There are no good bakeries here," Carly complained on a regular basis. "I don't get it. L.A.'s big. Why don't they have good bakeries?"

A hungry New Jersey Jew. That's all I needed. I had no idea what I was getting into when I fell in love with this woman. Why did I do that? Fall in love with strangers and think we should just magically get along? Wasn't that what love was all about? Weren't you supposed to fall in love because you could get along and have fun together?

Carly and I had been living together for three months. I originally told myself that she would need a period of adjustment to get used to L.A. and to find a job. I just assumed that she would love my friends. She didn't. I felt like I couldn't do anything right to please her.

"I don't know, honey," I shrugged. "I was raised on Van de Kamps. I always thought that was good stuff."

"Van de Kamps?" Carly grimaced. "Ugh. No, if you have to go with store bought bakery items, then Entenmann's is the only way to go."

"Maybe we should get a pizza," I suggested hopefully. "Numero Uno's is good."

Carly made a face. She would have none of it. "I'm calling Maria. Maybe she can bring me some blueberry muffins when she comes out next week."

Please let her have the muffins, I prayed silently to God. It would give me some peace.

Maria arrived the following week, sporting blueberry muffins and fresh bagels.

"Oh, my God!" Carly squealed with delight. "You

brought both!" She stared at the bakery boxes like they were gold. She heaved a huge sigh.

"And now for the piece de resistance," Maria said in her best Bostonian French accent. She dug into her suitcase. Carly's eyes grew as big as saucers. "I hope this didn't get squished," she muttered as she pulled a white pizza carton from the small suitcase.

"OH MY GOD!" Carly squealed like a pig. "Oh, my God! I can't believe you! How did you do this?"

Maria solemnly placed the Lucy's pizza carton on the table in front of Carly.

"You won't believe what it took to get this here," she began with Italian bravado. "I told them to only cook it half way so we could finish baking it here. Then I carried the suitcase like it was the pizza carton and put it under the seat."

There really is a God, I thought. It was the happiest I had seen Carly in three months. She was like a little girl with food, savoring each bite with intensity. She was the same way at Christmas opening presents. She would sit and stare at the present for a long time, ingesting every detail of the wrapping paper. Then she would slowly undo the ribbon and gradually ease the scotch tape off of the paper. Once the present was unwrapped, she would stare at the box for a long time before opening it.

I wanted to buy her a briefcase as one of her Christmas presents but she was so particular about getting the exact shade of maroon that I finally gave up trying to surprise her with it. Instead, I bought her the most expensive piece of darkroom equipment I could find. She had always wanted a darkroom of her own to work in. She was awed by the Hasellblad when she unwrapped it.

"Oh, Snuggies," she gasped. "I can't believe you got me this!"

"You like it?" I asked timidly. "I did good?"

She kissed me. "You did very good. I just hope I did

okay with your present," she said, biting her lip as she pulled a large box out from under the Christmas tree. "I know you said you wanted a VCR with four heads and that freeze frame thing."

I could tell from her voice that that wasn't what she got me. I froze any speck of disappointment inside of me, hoping she would not see it on my face. This is your first Christmas together, Roxanne. She moved to L.A. for Christ's sake. Don't give her any grief about not getting you what you wanted. "I'll love whatever it is," I said supportively.

She shoved the box in front of me. "You've spent so much money on me," she said guiltily.

"Don't worry about it," I said firmly. "I make good money and I wanted to spend it on you." I carefully unwrapped her present to me. It was something I had never heard of before. "A Laser Disc Player," I cautiously pronounced the words on the box. I had no idea what that meant. "What is it?"

"Oh, Snugs!" Carly squealed, jumping up and down excitedly. "It's the latest thing on the market. The salesman told me that it'll be bigger than VCRs because the picture and sound quality is incomparable to tape players." She was so excited, you'd have thought I had given her the present.

I stared at her blankly.

Her face fell. "You hate it," she said sadly.

"No," I shook my head lamely.

"We'll take it back and get you a VCR."

"No, no," I protested. "No, I just don't know what it is. Why don't we set it up first and try it out and see what it looks like." I desperately wanted to make this the best Christmas Carly had ever had to make up for how miserable she was living in Los Angeles. I wasn't going to ruin it by not liking her gift even if it wasn't what I really wanted.

I spent the rest of the afternoon reading the instruction manual and setting up the laser disc player. Carly had gotten me a laser disc of Alfred Hitchcock's 'Rear Window' to watch on it. I wondered how much money I would be investing in future laser discs since all my movies were on tape.

"Is the popcorn ready?" I yelled to Carly.

"Hot and buttered," she called back from the kitchen.

"Well, bring it on in here. The movie's about to begin."

Carly brought a huge bowl of popcorn and two Budweisers into the living room. We cuddled up on the couch. I pressed the remote control for the laser disc and the movie began. The first few bars of the theme song swelled through the television speakers.

"Jesus Christ," I gasped. "I've never heard such clarity."

"It's because it's all done digitally," Carly explained excitedly.

The first picture frame flashed out of the dark screen. Crystal clear.

"Look at that picture quality," I gasped, leaning forward with my mouth gaping open.

"It's digital. You can't get that on tape. The laser reads it," Carly squealed. "You like it, Snuggies?"

"I love it," I replied, kissing her gently and then settling in for the movie. I really was impressed with the picture and sound quality. I'll just have to buy myself a VCR with freeze frame capacity, I told myself.

* * *

While my relationship seemed to be under control at the beginning of 1984, my writing career was another matter. After twenty-one months in operation, our production company collapsed in the middle of 1983. The funding for our original project had evaporated. We were forced to give up the production offices. My mother insisted that I keep my desk.

"Possession is nine-tenths of the law," she informed me

somberly. The business partnership had dissolved into a dispute over the original contract agreement with one of the partners.

Gladys was in a tizzy. "I can't believe I ever signed that contract," she wailed one day.

My mind flashed back to two years before. Gladys lay in a heap on her bed. "I'm so ill," she whispered. "I need that five hundred dollars to go to the doctor's. If we don't get this contract, I'll die."

"Gladys," I said quietly now as she railed about her stupidity, "I only agreed to do this project because you said you needed the money to go to the doctor's." And I gave you my half of that five hundred dollars so that you could do just that, I added silently.

Gladys whirled on me like a pit bull attacking. "Don't *ever* do that to me again!" she shouted. "I don't care how sick I am!"

I was shocked and hurt by her ingratitude. It was the first time I began to see how manipulating she was. That was in May of 1983.

The Gladys who appeared before me in January of 1984 beamed like a full moon in summer. "This is it!" she exclaimed, thrusting her index finger into the air. "This is the big one!" She had pulled in yet another screenwriting opportunity.

"Great," I replied, weary of hearing her claim to fame and fortune before anything real had transpired.

We were at the Los Angeles Sports Arena at an Automotive Expo. We were meeting Joe Kenly, the inventor of the Quest Car. The Quest was a fully electric automobile capable of racecar acceleration. It could get two hundred miles per gallon of fuel and it could be driven from coast to coast without ever stopping to recharge the batteries. Joe Kenly came from old money. He understood the politics of breaking into the automotive industry. He fancied himself another Henry Ford or Tucker. Joe began building the Quest after the first Arab oil embargo. He was appalled to see America brought to its knees by a foreign country.

"I want to prove that one man can still make a difference," Joe told me as we discussed the project. "You can still make a car in your garage without being put in jail. But you sure can't get it to market without stirring up a lot of trouble."

"Joe's had death threats," Gladys nodded knowingly.

"Is that what you want the film to be about?" I asked, immediately seeing the dramatic possibilities.

"No," Joe said firmly. "That's another story. Which I just may ask you ladies to write once we've gotten the car manufacturing up and running."

"Oh, goodie," Gladys cooed.

"No," Joe continued, "I want this to be a family film about college kids who build the car as a school project. Then they enter the car in a race that runs from San Diego to San Francisco. That way we can show off all the bells and whistles that will be on the new version of the Quest."

"Isn't that wonderful?" Gladys squealed. "I think it will be a very suspenseful film."

"Mmn," I nodded, annoyed because Gladys did not know suspense from a hole in the ground. I was the one who would have to figure out how to make this subject matter interesting and family oriented. I was not too happy with the idea of writing another script on spec for a guy who had no producing experience. But as Joe explained how he would raise the funding, I began to see that this really was a possibility.

"He's got lots of backers," I exclaimed excitedly as I told Carly about the meeting when I got home that evening.

"Who are they?" she asked suspiciously, her voice coiling around my throat like a cobra.

"I—I don't remember their names," I stammered. "There were too many of them. Roy helped build the Quest. He's a retired navy officer. Larry is a stock broker—"

"That doesn't sound like they have money," Carly interrupted.

Her words stabbed into me like a hot knife. "Joe's floating stock in a limited partnership to raise funds," I replied, trying to remember all the details to defend my enthusiasm but my mind was quickly turning to mush.

"What's stock got to do with anything?" she snapped.

My body began to vibrate with rage. I stood up from the couch. "Why are you being so unsupportive?" I asked, my entire body trembling.

"I'm just being realistic," she snapped back.

The rage filled my body with heat. I stormed out of the living room and into the master bedroom. A deep unbearable primal pain swelled up inside of me, threatening to explode. My eyes locked onto a small but heavy trampoline by the bed. My body picked it up as I screamed at the top of my lungs.

"AAAAAAAAAAAHHHHHHHHHGGGGGGGGG!!!!"

I hurled the trampoline across the room where it crashed against the wall.

I stood shocked at my barbarism. Out of the corner of my eye, I saw Carly's body bounce up off the couch, hop around the living room like a pogo stick and disappear into the kitchen. The back door opened and closed. The VW engine fired up and gunned out of the driveway. I collapsed into a sobbing heap on the floor in the darkness of the bedroom.

Formless images raced through my mind as I sobbed for half an hour. Wordless pain pulsated through my body, quivering in fear and humiliation. Why couldn't she just believe in me? I cried until I was exhausted. Then I laid down on the bed and shut my eyes.

Carly returned after awhile. She quietly entered the bedroom.

"I'm sorry, Roxanne," she whispered sincerely. "I shouldn't be so critical."

"I'm sorry too, Carly," I said quietly. "I don't know what came over me. I've never thrown a trampoline across a room before."

Carly looked around. "Is that what that was?" She grinned. "It scared the shit out of me."

"Me too," I grinned sheepishly. "You looked like a pogo stick bouncing out the door."

Carly giggled and curled up beside me. "Yeah, I guess I did. I never heard a scream that sounded like that before. It just sort of lifted my body up and out the door. I drove around and got an ice cream cone."

I laughed and put my arm around her. "That's probably what I should have done. I can't explain it, Carly. It was like some deep primal pain in me. I just couldn't bear you not believing in me."

"I'm sorry, Shnuggie," she kissed my cheek. "I'll try to be more supportive."

We curled up together and fell asleep.

The Quest project evolved over the next year. Joe wanted to contract us for two hundred thousand dollars a piece to write the script. However, he did not want us to start working until he had all the funding in place. Gladys was ecstatic.

"This is it!" Gladys proclaimed when we hung up the phone after I had negotiated the deal. "Whooeee! We're gonna be rich!"

I grinned. I wished I had as much enthusiasm as she did. But I felt a heaviness inside me, a lingering doubt. This was too good to be true. Four hundred thousand dollars was twice the going rate for a feature film script at the time. I was worried that Joe did not know what he was doing. He budgeted the film at sixty million dollars. He would be wiser to make it for twenty million. How was he ever going to raise sixty million dollars?

"You don't seem very excited," Gladys poked at me. "I don't want to hear any doubts on this."

In Spiritual Science, doubt was considered the ultimate sin when creating your reality. A being was supposed to maintain pure intention to manifest the desired result. My problem was my gut kept giving me one message, while my Spiritual Science intellect demanded the opposite.

"Gladys," I said wearily. "I've been through this so many time, I just can't get excited until I deposit the check in the bank."

"Well, I have enough excitement for both of us!" Gladys exclaimed. "You just wait, my friend. We'll have the money in the bank real soon."

"Okay, sweetie," I grinned, giving her a hug. "That sounds good to me."

At the end of January, I decided to stop by Gary Stein's office on the studio lot. Gary was a producer on "Fantasy Cruise," a popular weekly network series. He had dropped into my office on Saint Patrick's Day in 1983 when the Accounting Department gave a party and invited the production executives to drop by and see the new accounting facilities. The company had just moved from the Fox lot and had relocated at the old RKO Studio lot in West Hollywood. Gary was kind enough to stop by and talk to me about how he got started in the business.

"It was basically luck," he told me. His balding Jewish head glistened under the overhead florescent lighting. "I had just graduated from law school."

"You were a lawyer?" I asked shocked.

"I never got a chance to practice law," Gary explained. "I'd gone from working in a coal mine in my teens to studying law. I passed the bar and was considering my options when a friend of mine told me that CBS was looking for story editors. So I sent in a resume, more on a lark than anything else. Turned out the producer went to the same college that I did. So he called me. Here I am, thirty years later."

"Oh," I nodded. The old boy's network again. Well, that shoots my chances, I thought. To hell with that, I thought. "Gary, if I wanted to submit some ideas to you, would you let me?"

"You write?" Gary's eyes opened wide.

"Yes."

His mind churned wildly as his eyes glazed over. "Sure. If you've got an idea for a pilot for a series, that's what we're looking for now."

"When can my partner and I come to see you?"

Gary snapped back into the present. "Well, we're doing the cruise shows in two weeks. We won't get back from China until June. Bring me your ideas in July."

"Can I submit story lines for the 'Fantasy Cruise'?"

"Sure, sure," Gary nodded as he walked to the door. "Bring me a series pilot. That's what we really need right now."

"Okay," I said excitedly as I watched him walk down the hall. Then I ran back into my office, clenched my fist in victory and whispered "YES! I'll bring you a pilot, Gary. But I'm also going to drown you in 'Fantasy Cruise' ideas."

When Gary returned in June, I called him and set up a pitching session for the beginning of July. Gary was so sweet. He was willing to have the pitch session after I got off work one night. Gladys met me at my office and we walked across the lot to Gary's office. Three hours and twenty-two storylines later, Gary was laying on the floor glassy-eyed.

"Well, that's quite a lot of work you've done there," he mumbled. Dragging his body up off the floor, he staggered to a chair and looked over the one-line plot synopses that filled three pages. "I'll make sure that Jeff sees these and I'll get back to you."

"What did you think about that pilot concept?" Gladys

asked. They were the first words she had uttered in three hours. I always did all the talking in our pitch sessions. Gladys just sat and nervously twiddled her thumbs.

"Huh?" Gary looked dazed. "Oh, it's fine. We don't need a pilot right now. But I'll submit that to Jeff as well. You never know what the network is looking for."

"Thanks for spending so much time with us, Gary," I said as Gladys and I left. I knew the only reason he did that was out of friendship to me.

Months passed with no news. I had assumed that Jeff rejected all of the ideas and that Gary felt bad about telling me. In January, I had to drop off some paperwork to Gary. He was sitting at his desk in his office.

"Jeff's taking one of your ideas to New York," Gary said off-handedly.

"Oh," I nodded, my brain going numb.

"I'll let you know what happens."

"Thanks."

I left his office and returned to my building. As I sat in my chair and smoked a cigarette, a dull sense of excitement began to cut through my numbness.

"Jeff is taking one of our ideas to New York," I mumbled aloud. "I guess that means he liked it." A big grin spread across my face. I decided not to mention this to Gladys. She would go over the top and I didn't want that desperate energy clinging to our one shot at a prime time script.

A month later, I got a call from Chris Stein. Chris was a heavyset, Jewish story editor who dressed like a ragamuffin.

"So, Roxanne," Chris muttered into the phone, "Gary wanted me to call you and see if you and your partner would be able to come in for a story meeting on Friday. It seems that Jeff really liked one of your ideas and he wants me to help you elucidate it."

I felt like I was receiving a message from God. My eyes glassed over. My heart stopped. My ears hummed. "Uh, sure," I managed to say.

"How's about six o'clock," Chris suggested. "We don't want to interfere with your residual duties."

"That would be perfect."

"We'll see you then," Chris crooned as he hung up the phone.

Like a stunned fish in a circle of hungry dolphins, I sat with my mouth gaping open for five minutes.

"I think this means we're getting paid," I muttered aloud. "The Writer's Guild Basic Agreement states that if the producer has a story meeting with the writers, then he has to pay them the scale for story payments." Well, why the hell didn't he just say so? an annoyed voice in my head demanded. Maybe you don't fall under the Writer's Guild regulations. You aren't a guild member.

"What do you think it means?" Gladys asked nervously.

"I think it means they want to buy the story, but I'm not positive. We need to go in on Friday and talk with Chris about it."

"Oh, my God," Gladys whined. "I don't know how to write the story outline."

"It's okay, Gladys," I replied wearily, "I'll do all the talking."

"Well, I don't want to look like an idiot."

"You won't," I assured her. "You'll just look really cute."

Trying to look as professional as possible, we walked into Chris Goldman's office on Friday night.

"Good evening, ladies," Chris said genteelly. "Please have a seat on my couch." We sat down. He paced slowly around the small office. "You probably should know by now that we are buying your story. The Writer's Guild requires that we pay you for the story if we have a story meeting with you."

"I thought so," I replied professionally.

Gladys's eyes just bulged as she twiddled her thumbs frantically.

Chris continued, telling us about the format of the show.

He gave us a sample story outline. "Why don't you two go home and noodle over this together. Then bring back a fully developed story outline and we'll go from there."

"Sounds good," I said rising. "When do you need it?"

Chris shrugged. "A week."

I walked Gladys out to her car.

"What am I going to do?" she muttered. "I can't write this story. You're the screenwriter. I'm all thumbs when it comes to this stuff."

"Gladys," I smiled and patted her on the shoulder. "Just do the best you can and give it to me. I'll write the final draft. Don't worry, sweetie. It'll be fine."

"Oh, God," she sighed. "I don't know what I did to deserve you, my friend. But you are a lifesaver."

I hugged her frail little body and made sure she got out of the parking lot safely. Gladys could not see well at night. She had a fierce will that refused to be cowed by the continual ailments of her aching flesh. That was what I admired in her.

"Carly, we got the story assignment!" I yelled as I ran into the house that night. "I'm gonna get paid to write!"

"Snuggies, that is wonderful!" Carly squealed as she ran into the living room and hugged me. "So we should celebrate. How about Chang's for dinner?"

"Sounds wonderful," I grinned as I kissed her.

At last, my writing career could soar wild and free. I spent the weekend writing the outline. I knew that Gladys' outline would be useless to me and we did not have the luxury of time to train her on this one. I delivered the first draft of the story to Chris' office on the following Wednesday. He called me on Friday morning.

"Can you two come into my office tonight to discuss this outline?" He sounded annoyed.

"Sure, Chris." I was surprised. "Is something wrong?"

"Didn't you study the outline I gave you?" he asked like a schoolteacher reprimanding a student.

"Well, yeah."

"I don't see how you could have," he continued. "You're story doesn't match the format of the show."

"It doesn't?" I was totally confused. I thought my outline was perfect.

"No. So just get in here tonight and we'll go over it together."

"Sure, Chris. No problem." I hung up the phone, feeling like an idiot. My big chance at breaking into Prime Time television and I screwed it up somehow. I called Gladys. "We have to meet with Chris tonight."

"Tonight?!" Gladys shrieked. "I'm supposed to meet Michael tonight about an interview for Premiere Magazine. I don't know if I can cancel that."

"Gladys, we're going to make four thousand dollars apiece on this story," I said sternly. "You get paid seventy-five dollars an article at Premiere. You've got to make a choice here."

She was silent for a minute. "I'll call Michael and tell him I have to reschedule the meeting."

"Good. Be in my office by five forty-five."

We met Chris at six.

"You see, ladies," Chris explained as he pointed to a color-coded breakdown board of the show, "each episode weaves three different story lines through the whole hour. So each storyline has to be laid out in the same manner that the other ones are. The show takes place over two days and one night. Now your story takes place over three days and two nights. It's a very nice story. But it doesn't fit in the formula of the show."

I felt very uncomfortable with his criticism.

"Why the hell didn't he just explain that to us in the first meeting?" I grumbled to Gladys as we walked back to her car. "I mean, really, these people need better communication skills. It's no wonder shows cost so much to make. There's so much wasted time."

"Can you fix the story?" Gladys worried. "I really need the money to start that wheat grass cleansing program."

"Of course I can fix it," I snapped. I could feel the pressure of the world on my shoulders. I did not need to hear about the condition of her bowels. "I'll rewrite it this weekend."

"Do you want me to rewrite it too?" Gladys offered. "I know my writing isn't very good but maybe you can get something from it."

"Thank you, sweetie," I said sincerely. "But no. There's no time. I can write it faster by myself. Chris needs this by Monday morning. It's not a problem."

Gladys climbed into her car and gave me a grin. "If anybody can do it, my writing partner can!" she cheered. "You're the most talented writer on the planet.!"

"Thanks, sweetie," I smiled. I watched her car pull out of the lot. What the hell am I doing with a partner who can't write scripts? Why is she going to get half the money on this when I'm the one who has to do all the work? I shut this part of my mind off, knowing it would only distract me from the task at hand. I spent the next weekend rewriting the story.

Chris called me on Monday afternoon. "Gary loves it," Chris told me.

"Great!" I beamed. "Does that mean we get to do the teleplay?"

"Ah, no," Chris replied. "No, we'll call you if we want you to do the teleplay."

"Oh." My heart fell. "Okay."

A month passed with no word from Chris.

"Any news from Joe?" I asked Gladys. I was depressed about my failing writing career. I thought things were supposed to take off now. Instead, the energy was slower than molasses in winter.

"Yes," Gladys told me. "He's called a meeting of the group at the Hilton this weekend. We're all required to attend. It doesn't sound good."

"Great," I moaned.

"I'm being forced to abandon my original plan to build the Quest and make the film with entirely American funds," Joe announced that Saturday morning. "It is a dark day for America," he intoned angrily. "But the truth is, the Big 3 have a strangle hold on car manufacturing and the oil companies are in cahoots with them. So we'll just have to change the game plan and go around them."

"Go, Joe!" Gladys yelled from her seat next to me.

"Thank you, Gladys," Joe grinned. "I've devised another funding plan. I'm going to broker the licensing rights to foreign countries. That way, they can build their own Quest cars using their own people. We can raise enough money this way to finance the film and to begin manufacturing the first hundred thousand cars."

He had a good idea, I thought. Bazooka Films used the same procedure to raise funds for their films. They would pre-sell the foreign film rights to finance the making of the film. They became quite successful at it. Of course, Bazooka Films made low budget features, not sixty-million-dollar epics.

We left the meeting with high hopes that Joe would pull off this next major coup.

A week later, Chris called my office. "Don't ask me why the producers waited for a month to decide to tell you that we want you to write the teleplay and we need it immediately."

"Oh, my God," I gasped. "Really?" A mix of emotions swept through me.

"Yeah," Chris replied, his grin sounding in his voice. "Can you two ladies do that for us?"

"Of course!" I shouted. I hung up the phone.

Later that day, I ran into Gary. "When do you need the first draft?" I asked seriously. "I can get it to you in a week. Is that okay?"

Gary's eyes glazed over like a newly recovered alcoholic in a bar. "A week? . . . A week would be good."

"Great! You'll have it in a week."

I spent the weekend locked up in my office at home writing the first draft. Gladys wrote her first draft also in the hopes that I could use some of it. It was useless. The dialogue was horrid. She had no sense of character.

"Gary loves it," Chris told me when he called me on the following Wednesday. "He thinks your writing is terrific."

"Great!" I beamed. "What do we do now?"

"Nothing," Chris replied. "We'll take it from here. Thank you and your partner for your very good work."

"You're welcome," I replied. I hung up the phone. A sense of depression filled me. It had all happened so quickly and then vanished with a few kind words. What am I gonna do now? I thought. My residual office looked like a tomb again, trapping me in accounting. It took me seven years to build up a friendship with Gary. I don't know any other producers. I don't know how to sell this stuff. What the hell am I going to do now? I felt like an orphaned child with no hope for the future. Come on, a drill sergeant in my head ordered sternly. Snap out of it. You've got to stay focused on Joe's project. Keep that mind programmed. No doubts. You know you can do it.

I was able to send my grandmother an extra five hundred dollars in interest on my loan. I had paid off the loan in full some years before. Now I just wanted to give her something extra to say 'thank you for believing in me enough to support my talent.' I knew she would be pleased that I had written for "Fantasy Cruise."

"I wish he'd lower the budget on this thing," I remarked to Gladys one day in June. "Sixty million is awfully high even by today's standards."

"Don't talk to me about any doubt," Gladys commanded. "I won't hear of it. As far as I'm concerned, it's a done deal."

Well, forget sharing your fears with Gladys, I told myself

as I slipped into silence. The Church insisted that a being created his or her own reality. Why did I feel like I was fumbling around in the dark, bumping into walls that somebody else put in front of me? I was trying as hard as I could to hold my mental programs in place but these damn doubts kept creeping into my mind. The realities of all my experience in Hollywood told me that sixty million dollars was too high a budget for a first time producer to finance. But instead of honoring that voice inside of me, I was just like Gladys. I thought that by telling doubt to disappear, that that act of self-suicide would ensure the survival of my dream of being a financially successful writer.

It didn't.

Joe fought long and hard to get the funding for the project. He had the support of a hundred grass roots people. We rallied round this gargantuan ego and followed his lead. He and his partner purchased an international bank in the Marshall Islands. I had never known anyone capable of buying an international bank. But Joe moved in a world very different from my own. And the power mongers in that world were not pleased with his valiant effort to save America from foreign oil dependency. Joe got a call one night from a political ally.

"Don't be surprised if your bank license is not renewed," the caller informed him. "The king of the Marshall Islands wants to turn it into a deep sea fishing resort to attract high class tourism. To do that, they need a trade agreement with the U.S. government. I happen to know that before Congress will pass that agreement, the king will have to allow two American government officials to sit on the board of the international banks there. Those two officials intend to rewrite the banking regulations so they can exclude your bank and shut it down permanently."

That was exactly what happened. The Quest project collapsed after two years of valiant efforts and all of the deep dreams of its supporters. I was not alone in my sense of disillusionment.

As my film career was disintegrating before my eyes, my spiritual base was simultaneously collapsing. The Spiritual Science Church was under siege from within its own ranks. A group of high-ranking church officials dubbed themselves "The Treasury Guard" and began a series of very Gestapo type attacks on the small satellite organizations around the country. The Treasury Guard would sweep in unannounced and threaten to shut down the organization if they did not pay large sums of money to the main Church. This extortion effectively destroyed the satellite groups. Within the main church itself, the Treasury Guard expelled most of the highly trained Spiritual Scientists, claiming they were dangerous to the church. These highly trained Spiritual Scientists formed their own groups, determined to practice their religion in its original form.

"Phillip Crown has opened a center in San Luis Obispo," Gladys exclaimed to me one day over the phone.

Phillip Crown was renowned amongst Spiritual Scientists. He had worked personally with the Founder on developing some of the higher levels of counseling.

"Are you going to take courses there?" I asked.

"I don't know yet," she replied. "If I do and the Church finds out, I'd be expelled for life. It's pretty risky since I have a lot of PR contacts that are in the Church. But frankly," her voice became spunky, "I'm so damn mad at what the Treasury Guard has been doing that I don't know if I'd want to go back to the main church even if I had the money to get counseling. I've been in the Spiritual Science Church for twenty years and I have never seen such Nazi tactics and such absolute idiocy in all my life. I personally think the Founder is being held captive by that Clout pipsqueak, if the Founder is still even alive. I trust Phillip Crown. I've known him for years. He's such a gentle man. He has tremendous integrity. If anyone can keep the technology intact, Phillip can."

I wondered if anything could keep my marriage intact. It too was liquefying like a mountainside in a mudslide. This was not something I could discuss with Gladys or anyone else for that matter.

BONNIE

"There's nothing to do in L.A. I hate it here," Carly complained.

It had become her perpetual litany. I didn't try to fight it anymore. For the past year, I had felt personally responsible for her misery. After all, I had promised her the world and happiness if she would move to L.A. and be my wife. Now I hated her guts. We had become her parents—passive-aggressive children.

We were sitting at the dining room table. The house felt like it had shrunk to the size of a matchbox. I stood up.

"There are lots of things to do in L.A.," I countered calmly, placing the Calendar section from the Los Angeles Times Sunday paper in front of her.

"You never want to do anything," she replied.

I could feel anger arise in me. Yes, I did prefer to stay home. I could easily have become a couch potato. I did not know why. I worked hard all week and then worked at my writing career. I was tired on the weekends. But I was not going to let Carly place the blame on me. If she wanted to go out, fine, we'd go out. "I don't have a problem going out. We can go wherever you like. We could go to the museum."

"It's too far away."

"To the beach."

"I don't feel like swimming."

"To a movie."

"You always want to go to the movies. I'm sick of movies."

"To a play."

"No."

"A concert."

"There's nobody I want to hear performing here."

"Well, pick something and let me know what you decide and we'll do it," I said. Then I retreated to the bedroom and took a nap, content that I had won the debate.

By the following weekend, I wanted to go to a play at the Mark Taper Forum. Carly did not want to go. We were sitting at the dining room table.

"Look, Carly," I began calmly. "You're the one who's always complaining that we never do anything.

"I know," she said softly. "I just hate it here."

I stood up. "Well, you'd better do something about it or I'm going to start doing things by myself."

She stared at me with little girl eyes. I sighed and sat down.

"I'm just scared to go anywhere."

"Have you thought about going back into therapy? Or getting some counseling?"

"I know. I will, Shnugs."

A week later, Carly grabbed me when I walked in the door and hugged me. "I think I've found my answer," she said gleefully.

"Yeah?" I asked, happy to see that she was happy again.

"Yeah. It's called Terrap. It's a therapy group for agoraphobics."

"What's an agoraphobic?" I asked.

"It's what's wrong with me," Carly explained. "I heard about it on the radio while I was driving to work this week. They described all the symptoms that I have. It's a disease where you're afraid to go out of the house. It actually means 'fear of the market place' or 'fear of open spaces.' It started back in New York when I couldn't get out of the bathtub. So I called this group and talked with a really nice woman named Clarice. She was so understanding that I started crying. It was just so good to finally talk to someone who could relate to my symptoms."

I felt a tremendous relief. So what if she wasn't going to do Spiritual Science classes? At this point, I didn't care. If this technique could help Carly have a life again, then I was all for it.

She began attending classes the following week. It was late October in 1984. The classes were designed to educate the agoraphobic and her significant other to the nature of the disease and in methods of behavioral modification.

I attended the classes with Carly at Carly's request. Clarice was impressed with how supportive I was. I was determined to make this work. I wanted my relationship with Carly to be fun again. We attended classes from October through December. I learned that agoraphobics picked partners who were controlling. I didn't like that idea. I had always considered myself fair in discussing things. Now I was being told that for a little while, I would have to let Carly have it her way all the time.

"We realize this is going to be very difficult for you partners," Clarice told the group. "But it's only for a little while. She needs to feel that she is safe to express herself. Don't be surprised if she turns into a bitch. And please, remember to take care of yourself too. You may need to take some time to go out alone for a while. That's okay too."

Great, I thought. But I was willing to try anything at this point. I hoped that it would improve our sex life, which had dwindled down to nothing. I wanted passion in bed. Carly was more like a baby, sucking and cooing. I was hurt that she still couldn't have orgasms. I felt like there was something wrong with me.

By the end of the classes, Carly was able to get into

elevators again. She had learned some very good skills at managing her own anxiety levels. We still weren't having sex. I told myself it wasn't important.

Instead, I turned my attention back on my writing career. The pitching season had opened up again for "Fantasy Cruise." Gary had left the show along with the entire story editing staff. I called the new producers and set up an appointment to pitch to two story editors. It was February of 1985.

Gladys met me outside the Writers Building at Warner Hollywood Studios. We had a ten a.m. appointment with Bonnie Bergman and Clyde Hopper. Clyde invited us into their office. We sat on the couch.

"Bonnie will be here shortly," Clyde apologized. He was a gentle man in his mid-thirties, lanky and unassuming. He and Gladys struck up a conversation. I kept checking my watch, aware that I had snuck out of my office to make this meeting.

Bonnie finally arrived at ten-thirty. She was a lanky blonde with big blue eyes, and a dynamic energy that indicated she was very much the master of her fate.

"Sorry I'm late," Bonnie said casually as she leaned back in her chair and put her feet on her desk. "I had to sign my escrow papers."

I knew nothing about escrow procedures and I really didn't care. I thought she was rude. Very attractive. But rude. I could lose my job being in here and she's off signing escrow papers. She's known about this meeting for a week. Couldn't she schedule that at another time?

I squished all those thoughts into a tiny box and booted them out of my brain. She's obviously the one you have to win over. Clyde seems like he's asleep.

I began to pitch the first of ten ideas. Gladys nervously twirled her thumbs. Bonnie stopped me after the first idea.

"I hate to have to say this," she began as she removed

her feet from the desk and sat forward, "but are all your ideas in that same format?"

My stomach dropped. "Yes."

"Well, I know you guys put a lot of work into those but that's not the format that Jeff wants on the show anymore."

"Really?"

"We were brought in to pump up the show for the final season," Bonnie continued. "We're getting away from the bathing suit scenes and trying some innovative things like a choreographed dance numbers, a forties take-off. We'll be playing around a lot more, shaking off the formula."

"Shaking off the formula," I repeated, my head bobbing numbly. "Well, then these won't work," I conceded. "Could we come back and pitch something else?"

"Certainly," Bonnie nodded. "I'll give you a sample of some of the shows we've already lined up."

I stood up. Clyde stood up. We shook hands.

"Well, thank you so much for allowing us the time."

"Of course," Clyde said.

I turned to Bonnie. She did not get up. She extended her hand. As I took hold of it, time slowed, the universe expanded. Her hand seemed to be surrounded by a golden light. It was a strong hand with long, tapered fingers. A lesbian hand. My heart stopped. Then time boomeranged back to normal.

Bonnie stood up. Gladys got off the couch. We said our goodbyes. I walked Gladys back to her car.

"What are we gonna do?" Gladys complained.

"Write more ideas over this weekend," I told her. "There's still a chance for some spots in the first thirteen episodes. After that, we'll go after the back nine."

When I called Bonnie to arrange a second pitch session, I noticed how sultry her voice was on the phone.

"Call me back in two weeks," she told me. "We're swamped right now."

"Sure," I said, my voice dropping low. I hung up the phone. What the hell are you doing? I scolded myself. What about Carly? How can you be having sexual feelings for Bonnie when Carly is your soul mate? What kind of low life scum are you anyhow? You're just going to have to cut off those feelings. Oh, stop making such a big deal out of it, for God's sake. It's just a feeling. Maybe if Carly and I would start having sex again, maybe then I wouldn't be feeling this way about Bonnie. The feeling will just go away.

But it didn't go away. I called Bonnie two weeks later. I was able to schedule the next pitch session in the middle of March. In the meantime, the thought of Bonnie had gotten into my brain and was gnawing away at my libido. I struggled valiantly to divorce myself from these feelings but the harder I struggled, the more powerful they became. And the bitchier Carly got.

Gladys returned from San Luis Obispo with rave reviews about Phillip Crown's group

"It's so beautiful down there," Gladys cooed into the phone. "You just have to go."

Fear swept through me. Even though I had basically dropped out of the Church when Carly moved in, I had planned on returning when I saved enough money to continue my course work. The Church was not a forgiving parent when it came to going to outside groups. But as I listened to Gladys argue that the Church had no right to resort to Gestapo tactics or to throw out the most trained members, I could feel myself being swayed.

"I'll think about it, Gladys," I conceded. "But first, I have to focus on these 'Fantasy Cruise' ideas."

"Of course, my friend," Gladys replied cheerily. "You're the best partner anyone could ever want. How did I get to deserve you?!"

The pitch meeting was scheduled for March 15th. Beware the Ides of March, Shakespeare had said. What was he? Psychic? Gladys was unable to attend. It didn't matter. She never did anything in the sessions anyway.

I pitched six new storylines. Three of them were too close to scripts already underway. The other three were met with lukewarm enthusiasm by the two story editors. The worst thing about pitching to people who have no power to say yes or no is that you have no way of knowing if they have any understanding of what you're pitching or if they will duplicate that when they tell the next one up the chain. It's like that telephone game. By the time the message gets to the last person, it's completely distorted.

So there I sat, staring at two people who politely listened to me. The energy in the room was as flat as a piece of paper.

Well, this meeting is a bust, I thought. Do you want to pull out the trump card? I don't know. I could swear Bonnie is gay but there's no way of telling how she'll react. But it may give you an idea. She'll certainly know that you are. Oh, what the hell. I'm tired of all this heterosexual crap anyway. Let's liven up this place.

"I do have one other idea," I began quietly as I pulled a typewritten page out of the bottom of my stack. "I included it in your packages but I haven't completely flushed it out yet."

"Oh, that's okay," Bonnie nodded. "Let her rip."

"Okay," I smiled and relaxed. "In this story, the Captain is very lonely. He's questioning his life as a ship's captain. His daughter has grown up. He's wondering what will bring him a sense of fulfillment again. And then he meets a woman. She's close to his age. Attractive. Dynamic. And he falls madly in love. They begin seeing a lot of one another. They just have a lot of fun together. The crew is beginning to talk amongst themselves about it. Finally, the Captain musters the courage to pop the question. She, of course, is extremely flattered. But she can't marry him."

"Why not?" Bonnie asks, leaning back in her chair.
"Because she's a lesbian."

Bonnie nearly fell out of her chair as she tipped backwards and hit the wall behind her. Clyde choked and coughed a few times. Bonnie struggled to get her feet on the floor as she wrestled through her papers to find the storyline.

"Which one was this?" she muttered, looking wildly at Clyde.

"It's the one on the bottom," Clyde replied calmly, a grin pulling at his lips, threatening to destroy his poker face.

I sat back on the couch, completely relaxed, enjoying the commotion I had stirred.

Bonnie's eyes devoured the words on the page which she held covetously close to her breasts. After a few minutes, she put the paper down on her desk. She looked at Clyde.

"What do you think we can do with this?" She looked worried.

Clyde grinned. "Well, I'm sure Jeff will like it."

"Oh, well, Jeff, of course," Bonnie said with a laugh.

Jeff was the executive producer on the show. It was common knowledge that he was gay although he had been married and had a son. The social mores in highly monied circles dictated that the appearance of heterosexuality was paramount to a successful career. Homosexuality was accepted only if it remained gagged and bound in the closet.

It was 1985. To even pitch an idea with the word 'lesbian' in it was extremely radical. But I had nothing to lose. They weren't going to buy my ideas anyway.

"I don't think the Network will go for it," Bonnie muttered, her eyes again devouring the words.

"You never know," Clyde said quietly.

"Well, that's the lot," I said, rising from the couch. "Let me know if anything pops." Clyde stood up and shook my hand. "Thanks for listening," I said.

"Sure."

Bonnie rose from her chair. "I'll call you next week and let you know."

She called me in my office the following week. "I'm sorry to say they passed on all of your ideas."

My stomach dropped. "Oh," I said. Then trying to salvage any possibility of hope. "Is there any hope for pitching more ideas?"

"Well, right now, the first thirteen are completely locked down," Bonnie said. "We won't know about the back nine for another month."

"Oh." My life collapsed inside of me.

"You may still have a shot," Bonnie offered. "Call me in a month."

"Okay." I hung up the phone. I felt sick to my stomach. There's always the back nine, I told myself firmly. Don't let any doubt creep in. Make the decision that it's already done and let it go.

I decided to go to Phillip Crown's group on weekends. When I first arrived in San Luis Obispo, I was nervous. When I began doing the course work, my body began to visibly shake. I felt like there was something wrong with me, that there was something wrong with Spiritual Science. My whole sense of self-confidence evaporated. As I drove home that first Saturday night, a frantic sense of panic began to rise up inside of me, choking me.

"How was your class," Carly asked as I walked in the door.

"It was okay," I sighed. "The drive's pretty long though."

"Guess that's just the price you have to pay," Carly retorted.

Her words dug into the pain in my stomach, wrenching it even tighter than it already was. Why was she treating me like this? Couldn't she see the pain in my eyes?

"What's for dinner?" I asked, walking toward the kitchen.

"I already ate," she replied as she turned on the television in the living room. "I had no idea when you'd be home."

"Great," I muttered under my breath. I opened the refrigerator door. The contents stared back at me, lifeless. My body ached. I wanted to tell her how scared I was but I knew she would just use that to tell me how screwed up the Church was. "I'm going to bed," I announced.

"Great," Carly snapped. "I've been waiting all day just to see you and you're going to bed. I can see what the next two months are gonna be like."

My heart turned to stone. I walked silently back to the bedroom and shut the door.

That night, I had a dream about Bonnie. We were laughing and running along the beach. The sunlight played through her hair, turning it golden. Her blue eyes sparkled at me as she moved close to my body. Her lips met mine softly as she penetrated my mouth with her tongue. I moaned in ecstasy.

I jolted awake, terrified that Carly had heard me moaning. The room was pitch black. The digital clock on the nightstand read three a.m. Carly slept soundly on her side of the bed. I lay back down, my heart racing in my chest.

What kind of asshole are you, anyway? I admonished myself silently. Cheating on Carly in your dreams? You're just like your father.

I closed my eyes, hoping to drown out this voice in sleep.

The following weekend, I drove to San Luis Obispo again. I was more relaxed, happy to get away from Carly. But the same anxiety filled me as I began the course work. By the end of the day, I was a wreck. I spoke to one of the counselors about my feelings. She was very easy going about it, telling me to simply come back when I felt better. As I drove home, I realized that I would not finish that course. Something inside of me was telling me to let go of the Church. It had been a solid foundation for my spiritual beliefs to rest on. I had thought it would hold me forever. Now that foundation was disintegrating rapidly beneath my feet. There was no other support in sight. I felt lost and all alone yet strangely free. I talked with Gladys about my decision. She didn't understand what the anxiety was but she was very supportive about my decision to stop going for now. For all her moaning and complaining, Gladys always tried to be supportive when it came to my problems.

It came time to call Bonnie again about the back nine.

"God, I hate to be the bearer of bad news," Bonnie sighed. "Jeff wants to keep the back nine in-house. We're closed up for the rest of the season."

The blood drained from my face. "It's not your fault," I heard myself reply. "We'll just have to try again next year."

How could this have happened? My entire future collapsed inside of me. Nothing mattered anymore. The pitching season was over. Every series in town would already be booked. We wasted all that time preparing those ideas, my mind droned on. Well, how the hell was I supposed to know? They were good ideas. I worked really hard on them. How could they pass on all of them? Why is this happening to me? No matter how fucking hard I try, this crap keeps being shoved down my throat. How the hell do they expect me to make a living at this when I have to work forty hours a week doing fucking accounting for Christ's sake? My life faded to an infinitesimal speck of dust beneath a residual check.

My mind went numb. I stared at the wall for an hour. The phone rang. I answered it. It was Gladys.

"Have you heard any word from Bonnie?" Her voice strained to sound chipper.

"Jeff wants to keep the back nine in-house. They're closed up for the rest of the season."

"Oh, God!" Gladys screeched. "What am I going to do? I need that money to go to the doctors. I just don't know how I'm going to make it."

"I know," I muttered. I didn't care about anything. I felt completely dead but my body would not die. I was sick for a week with the news.

Life went on. But oddly enough, my feelings about Bonnie did not die with the loss of the 'Fantasy Cruise' scripts. I began running into her at the lunch truck. She was always very polite when she saw me. Hiding behind her sunglasses, she looked like an ivory tower ready to topple with the tension in her body. I wanted to crack through that wall and explore the woman inside.

"Are you gay?" I asked her bluntly one afternoon as we sat alone at a lunch table, waiting for our orders to come up. I studied her face intently. Nothing moved. She stayed safely contained behind her Foster Grants.

"I never discuss my private life," she replied after a moment. A soft smile crept at her mouth.

"Tuna melt," the order cook called out from the truck.

Bonnie rose and smiled at me. "Well, gotta go. We're doing lunch in the office today. Lots of work to do."

"Have a nice day," I replied. I watched her get her sandwich and walk past the buildings to the parking lot. "I don't discuss my private life," I repeated out loud. "Sounds like a 'yes' to me." My body filled with excitement at the possibilities.

"Veggie burrito," the cook yelled.

I rose, picked up my burrito and strolled out to the parking lot, passing Bonnie's office window on the way back to my office. I wondered if she was watching me through the screen.

* * *

Carly and I had not made love in over six months. I didn't know when we stopped. She still didn't have orgasms. I guessed she never got around to those candle lit baths. I began to feel like I was making love to a baby. The idea made me nauseous. I felt like it was incestuous. What was this sick feeling that would overwhelm me? I didn't know. It didn't make any sense. I was terrified that it meant that my mother was right, that homosexuality was evil and that I was really straight. Nonsense, I told myself. I just want to make love to a passionate woman, not some cooing, gurgling baby for Christ's sake. Well, what the hell am I going to do? I worried. I can't possibly tell Carly I don't like having sex with you because you act like a baby. How the hell is that going to make her feel?

Since I didn't know how to discuss this with her, I simply withdrew.

"Oh, Shnuggies," Carly would coo into my ear as she crept up behind me in the kitchen and pressed her body against my back. "I miss you."

"Mmn," I would reply as my stomach knotted and I felt like vomiting. "Me, too," I would agree as I continued doing the dishes. Then I would yawn. "Maybe we can do something romantic this weekend. I'm really tired right now."

The weekend would come and go with no romance. I was quite adept at the art of avoidance.

"What's wrong, Shnuggie," Carly would ask in a sad little girl's voice.

"Nothing, sweetheart," I would reply. "I'm just tired, that's all." And I was. I felt weighted down by all these feelings I could not express. I would fall asleep and dream about Bonnie. I hated myself for that. As the weeks went by, fantasies about Bonnie began filling my mind at work. No amount of self-control could stop it. Finally, my fear about having an affair drove me to overcome my fear about making love with Carly again.

"Why don't we get out of town for Memorial Day," I suggested. "Maybe we could go visit Jan and Sue."

"That would be great!" Carly squealed with delight. "I'd love to go to San Francisco."

I just wanted to get the hell out of town and to get as far away as possible from Bonnie.

Jan and Sue were ecstatic to see us. Carly and Sue had been roommates at Boston University. Sue wanted to give us a tour of the city. We all piled into her Mustang. Carly sat in the front with Sue. Sue was a saucy blonde who wrote music reviews for the local papers. Physically she reminded me of Natasha. I sat in the back with Jan. Jan was more reserved with shoulder length brown hair and a more conservative manner. I felt very comfortable with Jan. I rested my head on the backseat and listened to Carly and Sue reminisce about their college days. We drove past a park. I had no idea where we were in the city and I really didn't care. My body began to relax. My shoulders loosened. At last, I thought, safety.

"Oh, look, honey," Carly chimed as if on cue, "Bonnie's Bakery."

My body jolted with horror and anxiety. My eyes glazed over. My jaw dropped open. What?! "Is that some chain from Boston?" I croaked innocently.

"No," Carly sighed. "I was just reading signs."

"Oh," I muttered. Great, I thought. I drive four hundred miles to get away and just when I think I'm safe, my lover begins reading signs. Bonnie's Bakery. Can't I have a vacation from Bonnie? Jesus. Will this never end?

After awhile, I calmed down inside, assuring myself that it was all pure coincidence. There was no great plan to make me leave Carly and run to Bonnie even though I felt compelled to do just that. I was not my father. I was clear of my past.

That night, we went to the Red Dragon Restaurant in China Town. The food was terrific. We were all relaxed, drinking, laughing, enjoying a wonderful Memorial Day weekend together. After dinner, we walked along the street, window-shopping.

"Let's go in here," Sue suggested, entering a Chinese

five-and-dime type store. We all followed and began browsing around. Carly went down one aisle. I went down another. There were tons and tons of tchotchkes. It reminded me vaguely of when my mother was PTA president when I was in grammar school. She was responsible for getting all the prizes for the yearly school fair. Our garage would become filled with boxes of Chinese toys, finger puzzles and the lot. My sister and I would play with them but we couldn't keep any. That would be stealing. Carly walked up to me.

"Oh, look, Shnugs," Carly said, "little kitties." She picked up a small porcelain kitten and showed it to me.

"Cute," I nodded. I spotted some Chinese finger puzzles. I picked one up and put it on my right index finger. "Hey, I used to play this when I was a kid." I put my left index finger in the other end. "The harder you pull to get out, the tighter it gets on your fingers. The trick is to relax."

"Great," Carly nodded and smiled. She caught site of Sue heading for the door. "Looks like we're going," she said as she turned to leave.

I managed to get my fingers free of the puzzle and put it back on the shelf. Then something caught my eye on the bottom shelf. A blonde-haired doll. I stooped down and picked it up. What's this?, I thought. A Chinese Barbie doll? I looked at the title on the box. My eyes glazed over. My head began to spin. I threw the box down as I gasped for air and fled from the store.

It was a 'Bonnie Doll.' The name was clearly marked on the box. Now I knew I was in hell and there was no escape. I spotted Carly, Sue and Jan a few doors down the street. My mind went into overdrive. What the hell does it mean? Why am I seeing signs of Bonnie all over the universe? Am I supposed to leave Carly? What the hell does it mean?

By the time we got back to Sue and Jan's, I was numb

inside. Carly and I got ready for bed. We could hear Sue and Jan giggling in their room. I crawled into bed first. Carly turned off the light and climbed in next to me. She rubbed her body up next to mine and kissed my neck. We began making love. Carly had her first small orgasm. I wanted to feel overjoyed and ecstatic. Instead I felt empty and alone. It was too late. In my heart, I knew our relationship was over.

* * *

"Can you please not talk about Hollywood with my friends," Carly complained on the drive home. "That's all I hear about in L.A. with your friends."

"Carly, that's my life," I replied, shocked that she would expect me not to discuss it, hurt that she wasn't proud of my accomplishments.

"Well, I hate Hollywood," she snapped. "And I'd just appreciate it if you'd not discuss it with my friends."

"Fine," I fumed angrily. We drove the rest of the way in silence.

A month later, Sue and Jan came down to Topanga to spend the Fourth of July with us. I was relieved to see them. Sue would keep Carly occupied and I could relax and talk with Jan. By Sunday morning, the tension between Carly and I was palpable. We were all sitting on the floor around the coffee table, finishing off the remains of the cream cheese, lox and bagels and scrambled eggs that we had devoured for breakfast. Carly and Sue were engrossed in a conversation about college chums.

"More coffee, Jan?" I asked, rising to go to the kitchen.

"I'd love some," Jan replied, following me to the kitchen.

"I'm glad Carly is having fun," I sighed as I threw the used coffee filter into the trash.

"Yeah," Jan nodded. "I'm glad Sue's having fun too. We've been having a bit of a tough time recently."

"Really?" I was happy to hear that.

"It's nothing, really," she insisted. "Just an adjustment period. I'd rather not talk about it."

"Sure," I nodded as I watched the coffee dripping into the pot.

"You know, I studied film history in college," Jan continued. "I wanted to ask you what you thought about Hitchcock."

"Oh, I love Hitchcock," I replied, a grin as bright as the sun beaming from my face. Then fear gripped me. Carly had forbidden me to talk about the industry. But this wasn't about the industry. This was about a filmmaker. And besides, Jan brought it up. What the hell was I supposed to say? Oh, sorry, Jan, Carly said I can't discuss it?

"I was amazed at how the majority of his films dealt with innocent people caught up in bizarre, sinister circumstances," Jan said as she poured herself a cup of coffee. "What motivates an artist to create that way?"

"Well, a film professor I had had her own theory about that," I began as I made my own cup of coffee. "Apparently when Alfred was a young boy of five or six, his father sent him down to the police station with a sealed note for the Constable. The Constable read the note then immediately grabbed Alfred, threw him into a jail cell, locked the door and walked away without one word of explanation."

"Oh, my God!" Jan gasped.

"Yeah, pretty sick, isn't it?" I agreed. "Apparently, Alfred's father finally arrived a few hours later to get little Al out. He told him that he wanted to teach him what it was like to get thrown in jail so he would be sure to avoid breaking the law when he grew up."

"How cruel."

"Pretty cold, if you ask me. Can you imagine how scared and confused that little boy was being locked up and left with no explanations at all?"

Jan shook her head.

"Carly, do you want more coffee?" I asked from the kitchen.

"No, thanks." Carly barely broke stride in her conversation.

"Sue?"

"No."

"They seem thoroughly engrossed with one another," Jan sighed as she watched them debating the merits of living in a brown stone.

Jan and I walked back to the coffee table and sat down.

"Well, that would certainly explain his predilection for that theme," Jan continued.

"Absolutely," I replied.

"Did he have some sort of thing about blondes?"

"It sure looks that way."

"I don't think he liked them," Jan proposed.

"Actually, he didn't." I sipped my coffee then lit a cigarette. "A friend of mine knew him while she was growing up. She called him Uncle Al."

"You're kidding!" Jan's voice lifted with excitement.

"Her father was head of ABC for years. Hitch would go to their house for dinner."

Jan looked amazed. "What was he like?"

"Lily didn't like him," I replied. "She said he was mean to Tippi Hedren when she was doing 'The Birds.' I guess he'd—"

"Oh, God! Please!" Carly groaned loudly, interrupting our conversation. "Don't bore her to death with another Hollywood story!"

I glared at Carly. I could feel battle lines being drawn between us.

"Oh, she wasn't boring me," Jan replied innocently, tensing with the electricity filling the air.

"Believe me, it's always boring," Carly replied snottily. "Why don't you talk about something else."

Nine months of pent-up frustration rose up to my throat.

In the past, I would have cut it off because of the social circumstances but not so now. I stood up.

"No, Carly." I turned to Jan and Sue. "I'm very sorry for having to do this in front of you but I have to say this now." I turned to Carly. "I am sick and tired of you telling me how much you hate L.A., you hate my friends, you hate my career, you hate Hollywood. I am not going to sit here and let you dictate what I can and cannot talk about. Hollywood is my life. And you either better get used to it or move back to Boston alone."

Dead silence filled the room.

"Girls, girls," Sue chimed in, "come on. Let's talk about something we can all discuss."

"Yeah," Jan said. "Like bagels ... or nuclear proliferation."

My body stood as taut as steel. My gaze fixed on Carly. She gazed at me like a reprimanded two-year-old.

"I prefer talking about bagels," Sue said lightly. "Nuclear proliferation is so arduous. Where bagels are an amazing creation."

The discussion turned to lighter topics. But the battle lines had been drawn.

A few weeks later, I woke up one morning, rolled over and discovered a total stranger sleeping next to me. She was Carly, of course. But something fundamental had changed. A feeling of dread arose very deeply within me.

Oh, my God, I thought, I'm acting out my parents! The idea made me want to vomit. But there it was as clear as a newly polished windowpane. It was as if some huge projection screen had suddenly vanished, leaving only Carly sleeping peacefully in bed next to me. I was horrified. She was not the woman I wanted her to be.

Instantly, I knew I had to call my father.

"Hi, Dad," I said quietly from the phone in the upstairs bedroom.

"Hi, Babe," my father's boisterous voice boomed up

from his big belly. "Hey, you guys," he called to someone in the background, "it's Roxanne." He returned his attention to me. "You're sister's here with Dave and little Billy. We're just having a barbeque. What's going on with you?"

"Dad, how do you feel about God?"

Dead silence filled the phone line for a full minute. Then Dad cleared his throat.

"Ahh, hang on a minute," he mumbled, "let me take this on the back phone." He put the phone down. I heard his muffled voice calling to his wife. "Ruth, hang this up for me, will you? I'm taking it in the back."

I waited for a minute, wondering if my father thought I had gone absolutely insane. We never talked about serious subjects unless, of course, it was astronomy or mathematics. But not really important issues like God. I heard the other phone line pick up.

"Okay, Ruth!" Dad called out. The phone clicked as she hung up the outer extension. "So," Dad said, trying to sound relaxed and fatherly, "ah, what brings up this subject?"

I started to laugh. "I'm sorry, Dad," I said. "I didn't mean to just spring it on you like that but I really need to know how you felt about God and religion and spirituality when I was growing up. I remember Mom was always seeking spiritual stuff. She got us into Transcendental Meditation and the Science of Mind. For some reason, I always thought you agreed with her spiritual pursuits. But this morning, I realized that maybe you didn't. That maybe you were just going along with Mom to be nice or something and I just really need to know the truth about that right now."

The sheer earnestness of my voice diffused my father's usual comic bluster. His voice was very soft as he spoke. "Well, actually, I was just going along with your mother," he admitted.

I felt a great relief inside my soul. "So you didn't agree

with the Science of Mind either? You seemed like you like it."

"No, not really," he grumbled. "I felt like it was a panacea for the masses. Most of us are just going to be stuck in the middle class for our whole life. So we need something to keep us going, to give us hope for making that million dollars. And the positive thinking stuff makes people think they'll be able to do that. They won't, of course, but I guess it doesn't hurt them to have something to hang onto. Probably keeps them from killing themselves or grabbing a bazooka and killing everybody else. I just never really bought it, that's all."

"So, how do you feel about God?" I asked. "I remember you saying once to me that you felt like God created the universe and then went off to play golf. Is that how you really feel?"

"Yeah, that about captures it," he guffawed. "I just don't believe all this religious crap about some guy watching us and making detailed decisions about each one of our lives." His voice began to throttle in his throat as his anger rose up like a primordial beast from his past. "I had this crap shoved down my throat for twelve years when I was a boy. I didn't believe it then and I don't believe it now! There is no big guy in the sky who is going to save you. Life is chaos. There is no power controlling anything. Things just happen, that's all."

My ears reverberated with the sound of God's wrath echoing over the phone. No wonder he never talked to me about that Spiritual Science book I gave him a couple years before. I assumed he would love it because it blended science and religion. Now I realized he thought that was crap too. My mind immediately assumed an intellectual defense.

"So, are you an atheist?" I asked calmly.

His entire demeanor changed. "Well, no," he replied quietly. "I wouldn't say that. I don't know how the universe was created. I just know that the traditional Christian crap is just crap designed to bring money into the church and make people into sheep. I get really angry when I hear these preachers filling people full of bull!"

I grinned. "Well, I can tell that," I said. "Were you mad about Mom pushing us into the Science of Mind and TM?"

"No," he said. "I just kind of went along with it to make her happy, that's all. It was just easier that way, I guess."

We sat in silence for a moment, each taking in what the other had said.

"So what brings up all this?" he asked. "Something must have happened to make you call and ask about this. Is everything okay?"

I lit a cigarette and took a long drag. "No, not really. Carly and I are having some problems and I just realized that it might relate back to how you and Mom were."

"What do you mean?"

"Well, I always thought that the two of you shared the same spiritual beliefs," I began, fingering the ashtray I had placed next to me on the couch and staring out the window at the canyon hills stretching into the distance. "But every partner I get involved with seems to play the devil's advocate to my spiritual searching and this morning I realized that I needed to know how you and Mom related to spirituality."

"Oh," Dad mumbled. "Well, I guess you could say we never really did share the same views about it. Your mother was always searching for something that way. I wasn't. I was more science oriented."

"How do you and Ruth get along on this subject?" I asked. "I mean, she's Jewish. Does she have strong convictions about this?"

"No," Dad replied. "She doesn't really care about religion either. Actually, we both get along quite well because of that. When I was with your mother, I always felt like I was being dragged into things that she wanted to explore."

"So you guys just don't care about God," I repeated. "I'm just amazed because that's all Susan and Mom and I ever talk about when we get together."

"I know," Dad groaned. "That always drove me crazy."

"God, it must have," I laughed, as the pieces of my dilemma fell more into place for me. "Well, I guess that answers my questions."

"You know, I did have an experience once," my father said suddenly. "I don't know if this qualifies as a God experience or not. But when I was living in that horrible little apartment on Lankershim when Faye threw me out, I came home one night and I had such a horrible pain inside of me, I thought I was going to die or go crazy if it didn't stop hurting. It was so bad that I actually got down on my knees and I prayed. I asked God to please take the pain away, that I just couldn't handle it. When I woke up the next morning, the pain was gone. It never came back."

"Wow." I was amazed that my father would share that much of himself with me.

"I don't know what took that pain away," he said. "I guess you could call it God. Anyway, that's the only experience I've ever had like that. I don't know if that helps you at all."

"You've helped me a lot tonight, Dad," I replied. "Thanks."

"I'm glad I could, baby," he cooed. "And next time you call, don't ask me such hard questions!"

I laughed and hung up the phone. For the first time in my life, I understood why I always stopped following my spiritual interests as soon as I started living with a partner.

The following week, Gladys called me at work, chattering like a rabid blue jay.

"I'm going to do this!" she proclaimed. "I don't care if I get ex-communicated from the Church."

"Slow down, Gladys," I replied, grinning. "What happened?"

"I've found a new spiritual group," she squealed excitedly. "It's a New Age channeling group and is it ever powerful."

"A channeling group?" I asked as I loaded my computer printer and started printing out pension reports. "Is that where they channel disembodied spirits?"

"I'm not exactly sure what it is," Gladys admitted. "But Ardythe said this group is a bunch of people from Spiritual Science who got fed up with the Church and formed their own group."

"Are they using the teachings?" I asked.

"Oh, no, no, nothing like that." Gladys sounded annoyed. She always sounded annoyed when she didn't know how to explain something. "This group is different. They have a crystal pyramid they use to channel healing energies. I think it's just what I need to cure my back problems."

Instantly an image of a huge pyramid carved out of quartz crystal popped into my mind.

"Wow," I said. "That sounds interesting."

"We're going tonight. Do you want to come?"

"I can't tonight," I lied. I hated making quick decisions. "You go check it out and tell me what it's like."

I hung up the phone. Eddie Priggs walked into my office. He was a Napoleonic fellow in charge of the blood drive. He grinned at me.

"Can I get you to give blood this year?"

"Eddie," I moaned. "You know how much I hate needles."

"Oh, come on. Everybody hates needles." He gave me a pitiful look. "I'm having a horrible time getting volunteers." He placed a large calendar with blocks of times and dates in front of me. "Now when can I put you down?"

My eyes fell instantly on Wednesday morning at ten o'clock. There emblazoned on the line was Bonnie's name. My heart stopped.

"How about Friday at nine?" Eddie suggested. "That's when payroll is going over."

"Wednesday at ten," I mumbled, my eyes glazed over.

"Or Thursday at two," Eddie continued. "Accounts payable is going then."

I cleared my throat. "I'll take Wednesday morning at ten." I wrote my name in below Bonnie's.

Eddie looked confused. "Oh. Okay." He folded the papers and left.

I leaned back in my chair and lit a cigarette. How strange Fate is. The slivers of opportunities that appear out of nowhere. I had no idea what I wanted to say to her. But at least we would be alone together for half an hour. My mind reeled with possibilities. I walked down the hall to the bathroom.

As I opened the stall door, an idea crashed into me. A psychic's voice rumbled in my mind. You will meet a man named Arthur. He will ask you to go on a boat trip, a business trip to Italy. If you go with him, you will see things you never dreamed of.

"Oh, my God," I gasped out loud. The room reeled slightly. Wait. Wait a minute. Bonnie's not a man. So, psychic's often mistake men and women. They read energy not body form. But the name Bonnie is nothing like Arthur. I mean, sure, the boat thing could be loosely construed to be 'Fantasy Cruise.' It did go on actual cruises. And this season's cruise was to Italy. But Arthur. That didn't make any sense.

As I flushed the toilet and zipped my pants, I felt thunderstruck again. Roxanne, the producer you were directed to by the old story editor was Arthur Stone. You see, the psychic was talking about this whole situation with Bonnie.

Suddenly I understood why Bonnie kept appearing in my universe. It was useless to run away from it. We were supposed to meet. Something magnificent and magical would happen. It was Destiny.

I was horrified. My heart rate accelerated and I began to hyperventilate. Oh, come on, I argued with myself. That's not necessarily what that psychic meant. Besides, what about free will?

But there was no shaking this feeling. It anchored within the center of me like doom. My dreams intensified, erupting into my daytime consciousness with the ferocity of a fated lover. I could no longer contain my desire. By the following Wednesday, I was a complete wreck.

I sat in my office at nine a.m. Good, God, what the hell am I going to say to her? Hi, Bonnie, we were meant to be together? Come on!

Nine-thirty. Sweating. Can't breathe. How the hell can I talk to her if I can't even breathe? Okay, calm down. Now look, you don't have to talk to her. Write her a note. Just tell her how you feel. That's all. Get out of your head. Write what's in your heart.

I took a few deep breaths. Then I got a piece of paper and a pen. I shut my eyes for a few moments. The words sprang up from deep inside of me.

Bonnie, you have ignited a fire deep in my soul. I thought it had died for eternity. (Please let me know if you feel the same way.) But when I met you, you sent a spark of magic into me. You are a beautiful being.

At ten o'clock, I pounced out of my chair and dashed down to the parking lot. Bonnie was beelining it to Stage 2. She walked like an Olympic speed walker.

"Jesus, Bonnie," I muttered. I walked quickly but not so quickly that anyone would suspect I was after her. I entered Stage 2 and walked to the Red Cross entry area. A nurse smiled at me, found my name on the list and handed me a clipboard with a questionnaire on it.

I took the clipboard and walked over to the folding chairs. Bonnie was engrossed in her questionnaire, her pen scribbling across the page like a skate blade over ice.

"Geez, I guess they let anybody give blood."

Bonnie paused for a moment and glanced up at me. "Oh, hi." Then she buried her head in her questionnaire again.

"Do you mind if I sit here?" I asked.

"Huh? No, no." Bonnie looked back at her paper. "I'm sorry. I really can't talk. I've got to get out of here fast. We're on a story deadline."

"Oh," I nodded. The back nine that I was shut out of. Oh, well, don't be bitter, Roxanne, I told myself. You're day will come.

"How's the show going?" I asked Bonnie as I lay on the gurney perpendicular to her. The nurse had affixed the needles and blood bags to both of our arms at the same time. We would be stuck together for the next ten minutes.

"Fine," Bonnie muttered.

"Mmn." I grunted. Well, this is boring. "So where were you born, Bonnie?"

"Minneapolis, Minnesota."

"Really? Did you grow up there?"

"Yep."

"When did you move to California?"

"When I was twenty-two."

Hmn. She's thirty-five now. So that was fifteen years ago. Well, at least I'm learning something about her. "Which place do you like better?"

"Mmn. California, I suppose." Her voice softened. "Although I do miss the snow at Christmas. And ice fishing."

"Ice fishing? What's ice fishing?"

"You cut a hole in the ice and you fish."

"Really?" I was truly amazed. "There are fish under the ice?"

"Mmnhmn."

"Aren't you afraid the ice will break?"

Bonnie laughed. "No. The lakes freeze very hard. The temperatures drop to thirty below."

"Oh, my God," I gasped. "I was raised in California. In the San Fernando Valley. We don't get frozen lakes there."

We chatted on a bit awkwardly. Whenever there was a long silence, I would think of another question to ask. Finally, the nurse returned. She checked Bonnie's blood bag.

"Well, you're finished," the nurse stated as she deftly removed the needle from Bonnie's arm, put a cotton ball on the hole and bent Bonnie's arm up. "Just hold this like this for a few minutes. Then get up slowly. I want you to go sit at that table over there for ten minutes. Drink some juice and have some cookies. It will restore your blood sugar balance."

The nurse turned her attention to me. "Hmn. You're bleeding slowly. You'll need to stay here a little bit longer."

Great, I thought. I even bleed slowly. I hope she doesn't just bolt out of here before I can give her the note.

Bonnie stood up after a couple of minutes and walked over to the refreshment table. I lay bleeding on the gurney, waiting for the nurse to free me. After a few more minutes that felt like eternity, the nurse returned, smiling.

"There we go," she grinned as she removed the needle from my arm and put the cotton ball in place. "Now, go slowly and be sure to eat lots of cookies."

"Lots," I grunted and grinned. I rested for another minute, then I went to the cookie table. Bonnie was sipping orange juice. I sat down and reached for a container of orange juice. I opened it and took a sip. Glancing about the sound stage, I ascertained that we were alone. The moment was propitious. I reached into the pocket of my jeans and pulled out the note.

"Could you please read this now?" I asked quietly as I pushed the folded paper in front of her.

Her blue eyes glanced at me then at the note. She carefully unfolded it. Silently her eyes perused the words on the page. I watched her face. It was motionless. The note fell from her hands. I took it back. Her torso looked like a tall ivory tower. Slowly, it gracefully toppled over as she buried her head in her arms on top of the table.

My heart filled with joy.

She turned her head to look at me. "This isn't fair," she moaned softly, her eyes sparkling sensuously at me. "I can't say anything."

A wide grin spread across my face. "I know," I replied quietly. We drank in one another's presence for one moment of eternity. Then a fat man plopped down across from us at the table.

"These aren't the good cookies," he grumbled. "Last time they were here, they had Oreos."

"Oh," I nodded.

Bonnie buried her head back into her arms for a moment, composing herself. Then she drew herself up to her full sitting height. She sipped her orange juice. I sipped mine. The fat man complained about the declining state of the unions in Hollywood.

"If we go through another strike like the one in '80, we're all doomed," he pontificated.

Bonnie stood up. She looked down at me. "I'll stop by your office before I go home tonight," she said simply. "We can talk then."

"Thanks," I replied.

She turned and walked across the sound stage to the exit. My eyes followed her until she disappeared.

Well, at least you've gotten her attention, I told myself when I got back to my office. She's actually going to talk to you.

As the afternoon sunset glowed pink behind the Writer's Building, my nerves grew frayed. She's not coming, I told myself. She's just going to duck out without talking to me. Come on, Roxanne, give her time. It's only five-thirty. She's got a lot of work to do.

The phone rang.

Oh, my God, it's her.

Well, answer it, stupid.

"Hello?"

"Roxanne?"

"Yes."

"Hi, it's Bonnie." Her voice rolled through me like warm honey. "I'm getting ready to leave now. Can I come over?"

"Yes. I'm in Formosa 210."

"I'll be over in a few minutes."

"Great."

I hung up the phone. My palms were sweating. My heart raced. I got out of my chair and paced around the office. Images of me making love with Bonnie on the desk rose in my mind.

"Oh, my god, she's coming over," I said out loud. "What am I gonna do?"

I closed the blinds and straightened up my desk. Walking over to the filing cabinet, I realized I was hyperventilating. Good god, get a hold of yourself, girl!

I took several deep breaths and sat back down at my desk. A gentle knock rapped at the door.

"Come in," I said loudly.

The door opened. Bonnie stepped into the room. She was wearing workout clothes and carrying a gym bag. She had on a pair of long, thin, blue parachute pants over her gym shorts. Her blue eyes blazed fireworks as she strode majestically across the room to the spare desk opposite mine. She sat down.

"Well, my ego has been doing cartwheels all day," she said grinning.

"Oh," I replied. My stomach felt like lead. My mind went blank. *She doesn't want you*, a voice in my head intoned cynically. I smiled at her.

"I was very touched by what you said," Bonnie began.

"You've had a very deep impact on me," I replied.

"I'm flattered," she beamed. She looked radiant, like a goddess rising from the sea. Her voice crashed against me like waves breaking on the sand. I could not hear the words. I could only see the radiance in her eyes.

"And would you—?" I began, searching to discover where her interests lay.

She physically sank back in her chair, shaking her head, a five-year-old girl, speechless, scared and attracted all at once. "I couldn't," she whispered.

My heart felt heavy. "Oh," I nodded solemnly.

She bounced gleefully out of her chair. "But I must hug you," she proclaimed joyously.

I stood up in leadened-eyed despair.

She threw her arms around me, drawing me in tight against her chest. I held on. My breath quickened, coming in short, panting gasps. After a minute, she pulled slightly back to look at my face without letting go of my body. She was quite comfortable holding me.

"Are you okay?" she asked quizzically.

"Yeah," I murmured, trying to control my body. I gazed up into her eyes. She did not retreat. My lips met hers gently, without probing. Don't use your tongue, a voice inside my head instructed. She needs to know she can trust you. Then suddenly I felt her tongue quickly flicking against my lips, testing me. My body surged with sexual energy. My hands tightened in her back. I pressed my lips harder against hers, keeping my mouth closed but letting her know I felt her desire.

There was a knock at the door. We sprung apart. Beverly from Payroll poked her head in the room. Bonnie and I looked business like. Beverly looked guilty.

"I'm sorry to interrupt but do you have the current residual costs for foreign runs on the 'Carville' pilot?"

"Sure, Bev," I replied. "Can I get them to you in half an hour?"

"No problem," Beverly smiled. She looked like she had interrupted a love affair. "Actually, it can wait until morning. No rush."

"Thanks," I smiled. Beverly left, closing the door. I turned to Bonnie. My heart pounded with love and desire and now confusion began to rise. "Can I have your home address?" I asked. Fear flashed on her face. "In case I want to send you a Christmas card."

She relaxed. "Okay. But that's all."

"I promise."

I scribbled down the numbers. I didn't know why I wanted her address. I just knew I needed to ask.

"I really should go now," Bonnie said, picking up her gym bag. "Gotta get to the gym."

"Have a good workout," I said as I watched her walk out the door. The door closed. I collapsed in my chair. My head reeled. She loves me, I told myself. Why else would she hug me like that and that kiss? She didn't have to let me kiss her. And she used her tongue. Why would she do that if she didn't have feelings for me? Oh, my god. She's probably just scared. That's all. She's probably never been with a woman before. That's okay. We can take it slow.

The fantasies intensified, tormenting me all day long, a barrage of sexual imagery playing quietly in the background of my mind. At work, I had hours of free time because I had so efficiently designed the computer programs that I could do the job of six people easily with time left over to daydream.

At home, I was growing more and more distant from Carly. Her babyish mannerisms that once touched my heart now curdled my stomach. On Thursday that week, I told Carly it was over. I did not tell her there was another woman. I then went upstairs and wrote Bonnie a four-page letter explaining that I was breaking up with my partner. I put the letter in the glove compartment of my car for safekeeping. I didn't know when or if I would ever give it to Bonnie.

Gladys called me excitedly over the weekend. "You have to come to this channeling meeting," she insisted. "It's more powerful than any Church practices."

Here she goes again, I thought. Gladys is on her racehorse again.

"Minerva will be speaking about the Church. You've got to go."

"Okay, Gladys," I submitted. "I'll go." I had learned over the years that it was better to just go along with Gladys when she was this adamant. The penalty for refusal was worse than death.

So on a Friday evening at the beginning of September, I drove into Hollywood to hear Minerva, a disembodied spirit from Venus. The channeling was interesting if uneventful. I don't know what I was expecting. At the end, a handsome, sandy-blonde haired man with sparkling blue eyes stood before the gathering.

"Hi," he said, his low voice gently rumbling through me. "I'm Geoffrey. I have a full-sized crystal pyramid at my home that I am making available for meditation for a small fee. If anyone is interested, please see me before you leave."

On Saturday afternoon, I drove to Van Nuys. Not the greatest location for spiritual enlightenment but, hey, what the hell. It was a hot September afternoon. I parked across the street and ran to the front door of Geoffrey's house.

Geoffrey opened the door. As I walked into the living room, I was stunned to see a six-foot tall copper wire pyramid comprising the bulk of space in the room.

"Wow," I muttered. "I've never seen a full-sized pyramid before." Geoffrey grinned. "I thought it was made out of quartz crystal."

"Oh, no," Geoffrey replied. "It's called a crystal pyramid because we use a twenty pound quartz crystal in each of the four corners on the bottom and a smaller crystal in the top of the pyramid to generate power."

"Oh," I nodded, noting the crystal clusters inside the pyramid.

"Minerva gave the exact dimensions, the gauge of the

wires and exactly how far apart the wires were supposed to be. It's based on alchemy."

"Really?" I studied the structure. "How do you get into it?"

"This side pulls forward," Geoffrey demonstrated. "Then you just climb in and lay down." A full mattress covered with a blanket and pillows lay inside.

"Oh, yeah," Geoffrey nodded. "It's great for dreaming." He pointed inside. "Well, unless you have questions, why don't you climb in and check it out."

"Okay." I grinned. I managed to get inside without crashing into the sides or breaking anything. I had to kneel down so Geoffrey could close the door. I stared at him from inside this copper cage. "So now what do I do?"

Geoffrey smiled. "Have you meditated before?"

"Yes, a long time ago."

"Well, some people like to sit up and others prefer to lay down. You should keep your head to the door though. We positioned it along the North/South polar axis to maximize the energy."

"Okay. I think I remember how to do this." I stretched out on the mattress and shut my eyes. Man, this New Age stuff is a lot more technical than when I studied metaphysics when I was twelve. It feels good though, I thought.

"Would you like to have some music playing?"

"Oh, yes!" I opened my eyes and smiled at him. He's so sweet, I thought. I felt so comfortable with him. He put an instrumental tape on the stereo and quietly left the room.

Soft music filled the air. I closed my eyes and tried to control my breathing, following an exercise I had learned with Carly in Terrap. My body relaxed. Then I asked a question of my Higher Self.

Can you tell me more about Bonnie?

I waited for a response. Suddenly a ball of energy like the sun appeared in my mind. I felt my body spasm as the sun was eclipsed by another stellar body. Then a series of images flashed through me, each image jolted me as I tried to resist the magnetic pull they exerted on me. The image/feelings showed me that I would drive down Sherman Way, then I would go to Bonnie's house, I would give her flowers, drink two beers and kiss her. Then my mind went black. There were no words with this.

What the hell was that? I demanded to know as I felt myself loosing complete control. What are you trying to tell me? To go to her house? I can't do that. She told me to leave her alone. She'd be really mad at me if I invaded her privacy. Besides, how do I know if she's even going to be home?

The blackness simply remained calmly in my head. That still silent voice. I knew I was doomed.

Oh, God, I moaned to myself. This was worse than the booming primal voice with Natasha. At least then I got direct verbal commandments. Now all I had gotten were silent images imbued with a sense of urgency and eminence. I knew I had to do this. But it unnerved me that I did not know why.

Okay, I told myself, I'll go to her house but I'm telling you, she's not going to be there.

The remainder of the mediation was uneventful and relaxing. Geoffrey returned after an hour and helped me out of the pyramid and introduced me to his wife who was working in the kitchen. Janet was an attractive woman in her mid-thirties with long, silky brown hair. She was a registered nurse. Her energy was soft but tough. We discussed the benefits of sleeping in a pyramid. Geoffrey offered to give me the name of the pyramid maker.

"Ohh," I sighed, hearing the price tag. "That's a bit out of my league right now. Guess I'll just have to keep coming back here."

"Come as often as you like," Geoffrey smiled. "I'll be offering crystal balancing to cleanse your chakrahs. I'll be getting a crystal balancing chair next week."

"Great," I replied. I turned to Janet. "Thank you so much for allowing me into your home."

"Oh, sure," Janet nodded.

As I picked up my purse, I turned again to Janet. "You wouldn't happen to know where there's a flower shop nearby, would you?"

"Sure," Janet nodded. "There's a Conroy's on Sherman Way and White Oak."

"Sherman Way?" I repeated as a soft sensation filled my stomach.

"And White Oak. Is it on your way?"

"Yes," I said softly. "It's absolutely on my way."

I drove down Sherman Way to Conroy's and pulled in. I had no idea what flowers to get her. There was nothing specific in the meditation. What about roses, I asked myself silently. Women love roses. I stared at the red roses, waiting for a sign. They looked lifeless. Mmn. Not the roses. My eyes wandered over the flowers in the refrigerated section. The blue irises sparkled at me. Oh, yes, I thought, irises. I picked out six. But they need something more. Something . . . some brilliant yellow flowers blazed out at me. Freesias. Mmn. I've never heard of them before. But man, are they pretty. I pulled out three freesias and placed them against the irises. Perfect. I took the flowers to the counter and had the clerk wrap them with baby's-breath and cellophane.

Returning to my car, I communed with my silent voice. Hmn. Well, okay, you were right about the flowers. But I don't know about the rest of this. I pulled out of the parking lot and continued driving.

My stomach growled at me. I stopped at a sandwich shop on the way and bought a roast beef and provolone sandwich on sourdough bread. I took it with me to Bonnie's.

Pulling up across the street, I stared at the house.

"She's not home," I said matter-of-factly.

Then wait, came the reply. For at least an hour.

My heart stopped. Oh, god, I thought. Oh, all right. I'm only doing this to show you that I'm willing to cooperate.

I took out my sandwich and began eating it. The neighborhood was quiet. Upscale but not too chichi. The sandwich tasted good. How interesting that I told Carly I was going out and that I didn't know what time I would be home, I thought. Did I know I was going to do this? Oh, my god, I've got that letter I wrote to Bonnie last night. It's in the glove compartment. Well, that doesn't mean anything. I couldn't leave something like that lying around at home and I haven't had time to mail it. Oh. Well, fine. I can just leave it in her mailbox when I leave. And I am going to go home if she doesn't show up by six.

I glanced at my watch. It was five-thirty. I'd been there for half and hour.

For god's sake, Roxanne. She could be gone for the weekend. She could be out at a friend's house. She may not come home for hours. She probably won't come home at all. Just give it up. This is just some delusion you're having. You manufactured the whole thing because you want her to love you but she doesn't. She's straight as a board. Let it go, for Christ's sake. You're acting like an idiot.

I felt very small and stupid. I nervously glanced at my watch. Five forty-five. Okay. Fifteen more minutes and I'm out of here. That's it. I don't want her to come home. This whole thing scares the shit out of me. What the hell am I going to say to her if she does come home? She'll think I'm nuts.

I shut my eyes, trying to block out the voices warring inside my head. Just when I was starting to relax, a jolt of energy shot through my body. I sat up and looked at my watch. Five fifty-nine.

"Well, there you go!" I said gleefully as I started my engine.

The white VW Bug convertible sailed silently into the driveway with the top down. Bonnie's tall taut body leapt from the driver's seat. She reached for her tennis bag in the backseat and walked casually into her house.

I choked, cutting my car engine. Oh, my god. She's home. Oh, my god. I can't do this. My heart pounded like thundering horse hooves in my chest. Perspiration beaded on my forehead. Oh, my god. Well, I better do this now and get it over with.

Mustering all my courage, I grabbed the flowers and the letter, got out of my car, locked the door and walked across the street, up her driveway and up the two steps to her front door. I took a deep breath and rang the doorbell.

A few minutes passed.

What? I thought, annoyed. Is she in the shower already?

The door opened. Bonnie's big blue eyes stared at me in surprise. "Hello," she said.

"Hi," I replied. Then she saw the flowers and a smile filled her face. Tremendous relief flooded into my heart. "These are for you." I handed her the bouquet.

"Come in," she said opening the door wider.

I stepped inside. She looked around outside to be sure no one had seen me. Then she closed the door.

"They're beautiful," she said. "I think I even have a vase."

I followed her into the kitchen. She glanced nervously at me as I leaned against the counter. I watched as she dug through the cupboard below the sink.

"I thought so," she smiled victoriously as she stood up clasping a large glass vase in her hand. "One of the things I managed to salvage from my breakup with Tim."

"How long were you together?"

"Fifteen years." She unwrapped the flowers and filled the vase with water.

"That's a long time," I said quietly. "I've never made it past the five year mark."

Bonnie put the flowers in the vase. "They're lovely. Thank you."

"You're welcome."

"Well," Bonnie stated matter-of-factly, "would you like something to drink?" She opened the refrigerator door. "I have beer, ice tea, Diet Coke and some apple juice that looks pretty bad."

At the word 'beer,' my heart beamed with joy. The vision was right. "Beer," I replied.

"Heineken, Bud Light or Michelob?"

"Michelob." Why not be decadent, I thought.

"And I'll have a Bud," Bonnie said as she pulled the beers out of the refrigerator. "Would you like a glass?"

"No." I took the bottle and twisted off the top.

We walked back into the living room.

"This is for you," I said handing her the letter. She sat in a rocking chair near the couch. I sat down on the couch and sipped my beer while I watched her read. The first paragraph explained that I had just ended my relationship with Carly. Bonnie stopped reading and stared at me.

"I hope you're not leaving her because of me," she said.

"No," I replied seriously. "It's been coming for quite awhile."

"Good." Bonnie continued reading. The remainder of the letter spoke about my undying love for her, how I wanted to be friends with her and thanked her for listening to my story ideas. It was actually quite infantile. But it was extremely well written.

"Well," Bonnie said when she finished reading. "That's quite a letter." She took a swig of her beer.

I swigged my beer, waiting for her response.

"As I said in the kitchen," she began, "I just ended a fifteen year relationship. I'm trying to put my life back together. And quite honestly, I don't have any room in my life for any more friends. I'm booked up as it is."

"Oh," I sighed deeply and sipped my beer. "I guess that answers that then." I picked at the label on my beer bottle. I felt small and insignificant.

"How long have you two been together?" Bonnie asked, breaking the silence.

"We've been together for two years but we've known one another for four." I didn't like talking about Carly. "We're very different. I didn't realize that until just recently. It just isn't working." I chugged down the last bits of my beer.

"Would you like another beer?" Bonnie asked eagerly.

I was surprised. I assumed she'd want to get rid of me quickly. "Sure," I said. "One more beer then I'll go."

Bonnie brought out two beers from the kitchen. She handed me one and opened the other for herself. "What the hell," she said brazenly. "I had a good workout today."

"What'd you do? Tennis?"

"Three sets of tennis and two games of basketball," she replied excitedly, dribbling an imaginary ball. She was quite the jock.

I smiled from my sedentary seat on the couch. "Sounds like fun."

"Oh, I need it after writing all day. I put on six pounds since I started this show," she moaned.

"You look great," I said sincerely. Straight women were always obsessed with how much their bodies weighed. It was annoying.

"You want to see the house?" Bonnie asked. "We're remodeling so it's kind of a mess but I think it's going to look pretty good when we finish."

"Sure," I said rising. I wanted to be supportive. I followed her to the hall door.

"This is my bedroom," she said as she stood inside a small bedroom. I stood behind her. The room was a mess. Clothes haphazardly strewn on the hardwood floor. The bed was unmade, the blankets on the floor, the sheet crumpled in a heap on the side. An image of Bonnie sprawled out naked in the heat flashed through my mind. We both stared silently at the bed.

"Oh," I said as I backed out of the room into the hallway. She followed me. "That's the bathroom. And this will be my office." She opened the door to the other room in the house. "My brother is helping me paint this one. He can tell you what a perfectionist I am."

She took me out into the backyard and showed me where she wanted to put a tennis court. I felt poor and worthless as I stood there. That's not a nice way to feel, my mother's voice admonished me.

"That's great," I said, wanting to be supportive. But deep inside me burned a steady resentment. "You've worked hard to achieve this," I said. I said the words but the anger in me did not believe the words. I felt locked out, abandoned, like Bonnie lived in a completely different world that I would never be part of. I felt sick to my stomach. I blocked these thoughts out of my mind. We returned to the living room.

"Have you finished the back nine?" I asked.

"Pretty much," Bonnie replied as she rearranged some magazines on the coffee table.

"How's it look?"

"Considering it's the final season, I think we've done a good job."

"You must have a lot of friends," I offered. "Hundreds of writers clamoring at your door to pitch ideas."

"Yeah. Well, they either love us or they hate us," Bonnie grimaced. "We only have a limited number of slots for freelancers to fill. We have to make sure that we get our scripts in and done first. Otherwise we don't get those residuals. After all, we have to protect ourselves."

My stomach turned. I knew how much money Bonnie made each week as a story editor. Two thousand dollars a week. True, story editors did not receive residuals as story editors. According to the Writers Guild, only the writers who received screen credit received residuals. So there you are, my mother's voice rambled in my head. The poor thing needs those residuals to live on later. My anger fired. Bullshit. She gets ten thousand dollars for each script she writes plus the hundred thousand for her contract. Isn't a hundred thousand dollars enough for her to survive on? That's triple what I make in a year. And what about all those impoverished writers struggling to get one script sold a year while trying to raise kids and pay the bills by being waitresses? Who the hell is this woman?

"But we've got it under control," Bonnie continued. "We'll be writing the final episode. The captain falls in love and proposes to a woman who owns her own trucking company. It's a two-hour finale. The wedding takes place in the second hour."

Everything in me froze. My mind blanked out. Dimly in the dark recesses of my being, I could hear a little girl crying. Leadened thoughts struggled to surface in my mind. Wasn't that my idea? Didn't I pitch an idea that the captain fell in love and proposed to a woman? Shouldn't we at least get story monies? No, no, no, this is different, droned another voice in my head. Bonnie wouldn't steal your idea. The woman in yours was a lesbian. The woman in hers is a truck driver. Huh? My mind could not compute any of this. Maybe you're right, I told the voice. Maybe it was different. Besides what proof did we have? She was a professional writer. I was just a residual paymaster.

I felt sick to my stomach. And then all those feelings just disappeared, as if nothing had ever happened. I slugged down the last remains of my beer. I took the bottle into the kitchen and left it on the sink. I walked back to the living room.

"Well, I'm going to the bathroom and then I'm leaving," I announced.

"Oh . . . okay," Bonnie said softly.

I locked the door in the bathroom and sat down on the toilet. My head was feeling the beers. Well, I'm glad I came. It's obvious that she doesn't care about me. But I learned a lot.

I pulled my pants up, flushed the toilet, washed my hands and took a deep breath as I opened the door to leave.

As I stepped into the living room, my body filled with an intense magnetic energy. Music filled the room. I froze. Why the hell did she put music on?

Bonnie jumped back from the stereo. "Bruce Springsteen," she said shyly.

The sensual energy in the room overwhelmed me. My mind went blank. I could not control myself. My body moved slowly towards her, drawn by some powerful unseen magnetic force. Bonnie's body looked frozen too, anchored to a spot in the wooden floor. It was if we were puppets in some bizarre play that transcended either one of us.

As I reached her, my head shook slowly back and forth, my mouth opened, trying to say 'I can't stop' but no words came forth. As I put my arms gently around her, my head moved toward her lips. Her eyes darted down guiltily as she turned her head away. My lips connected with the delicate arch of her neck, brushing against her skin, softly kissing her, moving up her neck, a sensuous warm energy swirling between us as I lost consciousness.

I woke up with a start inside my head. Confused. Disoriented. Where am I? I thought groggily. Suddenly I became aware of my mouth. A wonderful warm sensation of my tongue pressing rhythmically against another warm pulsing tongue that pressed passionately back. Wonderful ecstasy swirling in my mouth, down my shoulders into my arms. Her body rocked against mine, swaying gently, surrendering to sensation. Oh, my god! a voice inside me screamed. I'm kissing Bonnie! We're standing in her living room. Oh, my god. All my sensations stopped. My body became an alien shell that my consciousness was inhabiting. I felt like a klutz. What am I supposed to do now? What do I do with my hands?

Her body continued to rock against mine.

Well, you better do something, I told myself. Otherwise,

she'll think you're an idiot. I moved my hands up her back, slowly coming up her sides, hoping that this was erotic, desperately wanting to please her, completely clueless about how to seduce her.

"I should take a shower," she mumbled softly as we paused for a moment.

She wants me, I thought. My passion swelled. My confidence returned. I smiled at her innocence and shook my head silently as I began kissing her again.

"I'm all dirty and sweaty," she mumbled shyly, her blue eyes staring at me in wonder.

"I don't care," I whispered hazily as our mouths moved again into that blissful motion.

She pulled back slightly, leaning her back against the firm support of my arms. She grinned at me impishly. "I'm lousy to live with," she teased.

My body jolted. Words tumbled out of my mouth before I even knew what I was saying. "Oh, I don't want to live with you," my voice replied directly. "I just ended a two-year relationship. I can't live with anybody right now."

Her huge dilated pupils instantly shrank to pinheads as her radiant blue eyes turned to ice.

We kissed again for a moment. Then she pushed me away.

"We can't do this," Bonnie said sweetly but firmly. "We mustn't do this again."

Now see what you've done, I berated myself. The chance of a lifetime. You were about to realize your dream and you have to blow it by telling the truth. I felt lost and confused.

Bonnie gently pushed me to the door.

"Now, no more flowers or presents," she instructed me. "This could only happen this once."

"Okay," I nodded like a five-year-old wanting to please her mother. I walked out the door. Bonnie closed it behind me. I stepped into the darkness of the night. A feeling of exhilaration filled me. She loves me! She really loves me, I thought.

* * *

A week later, I took Carly to Geoffrey's. I wanted to see if she would be interested in the pyramid or the crystal balancing. She wasn't.

"This is just crap," Carly snapped in the car on the way home.

"You didn't like it?" That didn't surprise me. "Didn't you feel anything?"

"No," she grumbled. "Look, can we have a joint session with my therapist to see if we can work this out?"

"Okay," I replied, knowing in my heart that it was over.

Clarice stared at me as I sat on the couch. "Would you be willing to mother Carly for a few months until she gets on her feet?" Clarice asked sweetly. "She left her support base in Boston two years ago to be with you and she's feeling very vulnerable right now. She has no friends. Could you do that for her?"

My stomach filled with nausea. "Mother her?" I whispered.

"Just for a few months until she gets reoriented."

Carly stared at me like an innocent two-year-old.

My face turned ashen. I shook my head. "I can't," I said honestly. I felt like I'd been mothering her for two years. I couldn't do it anymore. My body filled with panic. I wanted to bolt out the door.

Carly looked crest fallen.

My mother came over for dinner that evening. She sat politely through dinner then verbally ravaged me when I walked her out to her car.

"It's these New Age people, isn't it?" Mom said with the finality of an omniscient god. "They've gotten hold of you, haven't they?" She looked over the top of her glasses, eyeing me in a cobra gaze.

"No, Mom, it's not. Carly and I, we're just not coming from the same place anymore," I stammered, trying to look adult.

"Well, if you ask me, Carly is the best thing that's every happened to you. I don't approve of this homosexual thing. The Bible strictly forbids it. But I know that Jesus has you in his heart. I pray for you every day. But this New Age stuff, it's Satanic. That's all there is to it."

"Mom, you don't understand," I whined. "Carly and I have been having problems for a long time. It's just not working anymore."

"Well, fine. Do what you want. You always do anyway. But if you ask me, you're being very selfish. Carly's a nice Jewish girl. The Jews are the Chosen People, you know. They don't need Jesus. They've already got a covenant with God. But you, you need Jesus. I want you to think about that!"

"Okay, Mom," I nodded as she climbed into her car. "I know Jesus loves me."

"I'll pray for you," Mom cooed sweetly as she started her car. "You're my little baby doll. I don't want anything bad to happen to your soul."

"Just give me over to Jesus, Mom," I said wearily. I knew that Jesus would be a lot more unconditional than my mother even if I did not accept the tenants of the Born Again Christians that my mother had so readily embraced over the past few years.

"I have already," she declared. "And He showed me that you were safe."

"Well, good, Mom. You have a safe drive home." I patted her hand on the windowsill, stuck my head in the car and gave her a kiss on the cheek.

As her Buick Skylark rumbled down the hill, I gazed up at the pitch-black sky. A coyote howled in the distance. I breathed a deep breath of country air.

After a few weeks of me sleeping on the couch and Carly stomping around the house, angrily beating a bataka against the walls and the furniture, the relationship ended. Carly moved out to a house on Skyline Drive on the hilltop opposite our house.

As I sat alone in the sanctuary of my living room, I prayed to God in deep earnestness.

"God, please send me a partner who shares my spiritual quest. I cannot go through another relationship with a partner who does not have the same need for spiritual growth."

* * *

The worst part about breaking up was explaining my failure to all of my friends. When Carly and I broke up, I went over to Trevor and Neil's house in the Hollywood hills. Trevor and Neil had been together for two years. I had never seen Trevor happier. He had finally found the man of his dreams. They had bought a house with a terrific view of the Hollywood sign.

Neil was a practicing psychologist. He was a handsome, red-haired queen who believed in living in the here and now. His direct manner had alienated some of Trevor's long time friends including Priscilla. She could not tolerate his honesty and he would not bow to her playing the victim all the time. Carly and I had maintained a close friendship with both Trevor and Neil. Neil jokingly named us the Butterballs and said that he and Trevor were the Dumplings. We would meet for dinner and play Scrabble and talk. Neil was Jewish and he was from New York. I had hoped that he and Carly would get along because they had these things in common. But Carly always criticized my friends whenever we were alone at home. She was never happy with anything.

So as the relationship disintegrated, I told myself that I

didn't need to talk to Trevor or Neil because they were both of our friends and they shouldn't have to take sides. But the truth was I didn't want to have to discuss my feelings about Bonnie. Neil was not a spiritual fellow. Besides, he'd probably think I was a sexual pervert.

"Why didn't you tell us you two were having problems?" Neil reprimanded me as he handed me a beer.

I leaned over the counter bar separating the kitchen from the dining room. "Oh, Neil, I was just too humiliated," I said. "I thought I could figure it out by myself."

"Roxanne," Neil said in his most doctorial tone, "we're your family. You can always come to us with your problems."

"Okay," I nodded guiltily.

"So, what happened?"

"Oh, god," I moaned. "I just woke up one morning and realized that I was acting out my parents' relationship. My father was the scientific skeptic and my mother was the spiritual seeker. My father just kind of went along with things to placate Mom. Well, that's kind of what's been going on with Carly and me. She's not spiritually oriented and I've finally realized that that is really important to me. It just wasn't working."

"What else?" Neil asked pointedly.

"That's not enough?" I ducked the question.

"What about sex?" Neil asked.

I stared at him. I was so shocked that he asked me that directly that I started laughing. "Fuck you, Neil," I grinned, amazed at his perceptive abilities and secretly pleased and relieved that he was dragging the truth out of me.

Neil grinned back at me, knowing he had nailed me. He just stared at me and waited.

I threw my hands over my face. "Oh, god," I moaned. "Oh, alright. It's blondes, Neil. It's these goddamn crazy blondes. They appear in my life and I just fall apart."

Trevor's eyes widened, shocked at my confession.

Neil howled with laughter. "That's okay, honey. Now all you have to do is find a blonde who is spiritually oriented."

My heart relaxed. He didn't think I was a sex maniac. I lit a cigarette and enjoyed the rest of the evening.

And Neil was right. There was someone preparing to enter my life. She was waiting just around the corner—a wild and sexy blonde with a deep hunger for spiritual growth. She would rock my world completely apart.

AN EXCLUSIVE LOOK AHEAD TO PART TWO

(SYNOPSIS)

SYNCHRONICITIES

(1985-1995)

(SYNOPSIS)

SYNCHRONICITIES

(1985-1995)

There is an old Buddhist adage that says you should not seek enlightenment unless you are like a man with his hair on fire. You must be willing to do whatever it takes to find the lake that will quench the fire.

Nadia was my fire. We met at Isadora's New Age channeling group. Of course, Nadia rebuffed me at the start and I walked away mad. But Destiny was stronger than both of us.

Isadora believed the time had come for the sacred teachings of the Native Americans to be shared with the white man. I immediately joined her evening classes. It was in this group that I learned that some Native American tribes honored homosexuals. They believed that homosexuals were born with two souls instead of just one. At last, I had found a spiritual teaching that embraced my sexuality instead of condemning it.

During the public channeling group, Minerva talked extensively about the impending Harmonic Convergence. The Harmonic Convergence was an extremely rare moment in time when all of the planets in the solar system would line up with the Earth and the Sun. The combined gravitational pull was thought to be strong enough to cause a polar shift. This theory was given credence by some ancient Mayan calendars that predicted the event. According to Native American teachings, star brothers had been visiting the earth since life began here. It was also predicted that when this cataclysm occurred, our space brothers would help to evacuate the planet.

Unbeknownst to the public group, there was also an Inner Circle made up of 13 practitioners whom Minerva was training to become advanced healers. They would become the spiritual leaders after the catastrophes of the Harmonic Convergence. The Inner Circle quietly began using a naturally derived power substance in ritual ceremonies to accelerate their own spiritual growth. Geoffrey conducted the ceremonies at his house in Van Nuys.

After awhile, Geoffrey decided to offer the Spice to select people in the public group. After much deliberation, I decided to accept his invitation to participate in one of the processing ceremonies. During my first experience using a power substance in a ritual circumstance, I actually contacted my Higher Self. She was the most beautiful and the most loving being I had ever seen.

During my second experience with the power substance, only two of us took the power substance. Dottie, a strong willed sixty-year-old woman, demanded to have the full dosage. Geoffrey reluctantly gave her a whole pill. She did not wait for Geoffrey to pray over the power substance. I silently prayed with mine before ingesting it. Dottie decided to lie down on the couch in the den. Geoffrey and I entered the pyramid in his living room. We began to meditate together. Immediately, tears began to stream down my face as images of a horrific massacre filled my mind. "My people," I sobbed quietly, "my people. They killed my people." As these images of murderous pillaging flowed through me, Dottie began screaming in horrible pain. It was as if she were channeling the physical pain and I was channeling the imagery of this shared past life memory.

When the pain had left her body, Dottie told me that she did not know what the pain was about. She had simply felt it and she had seen tremendous amounts of blood. I told her about the images that had come through me. I had been the High Priestess in a peaceful, agrarian matriarchal village. Strange men on horseback descended from the mountains around us. They had battle-axes and swords. At first they were peaceful. I fell in love with their leader— a beautiful blonde-haired man with deep blue eyes. I realized immediately that that man had reincarnated as Bonnie in my present lifetime. Ultimately, the man and his followers massacred my people and laid my city to ruins. Dottie then told me about a book called *When God Was A Woman*. She told me it would answer most of my questions about the matriarchy. She also told me that I would be writing a book about this for my people, that they needed so much to hear what I had to say to them. At the time, I did not know what she was talking about. It was the end of 1985. I had no plans of writing a book. I was a screenwriter.

* * *

In 1986, the spirit of Death swept across my life. It began with my adopted gay Uncle Ken. He had been living in San Francisco for several years. We did not know that he was HIV positive or that it had developed into full blown AIDS. His roommate called Uncle Rob when Ken began screaming that the numbers in his checkbook were scrambling in his brain. We flew up immediately to be with him.

It was my first experience in an AIDS ward. I walked down the hallway, knowing that every man on the floor was condemned to death. There was no cure for the 'gay plague.' And the Reagan Administration cared little if all of the faggots in America died torturous deaths. Uncle Ken was nearly comatose. We were able to talk briefly with him before he slipped back into unconsciousness. The doctor told us that he did not have long to live. There was nothing we could do. The doctor recommended that we go home. And we were all so numb and so uncomfortable with death and this horrible disease that we did just that. We left Uncle Ken to die. I left an amethyst quartz cluster on the bed stand next to him. Amethyst was thought to help balance the spirit and to aid it in making an easy transition.

Two weeks later, I was meditating in a hot bath with candles lighting my bathroom. I had the strongest sensation that Uncle Ken had just died. I did a special meditation for him. My sister called me the next morning to let me know that he had died in the night.

* * *

In February, Geoffrey wanted to have his birthday party at my house in Topanga Canyon. I was elated. At last, I would be included in the Inner Circle. The group of thirteen would be spending the weekend at my house. We would do the power substance on Saturday night. To my surprise and delight, Nadia appeared on my doorstep. She was part of the Inner Circle. Now I knew this would be a weekend to remember.

I thought Geoffrey wanted this to be a spiritual retreat. I was wrong. Geoffrey wanted to party. He decided to drop Acid while the rest of us were doing the Spice and getting stoned. I watched as my spiritual leaders toppled from the imaginary pedestals I had put them on. By midnight, the energy in the house threatened to blow out the entire canyon. I was terrified that my landlord would appear with the sheriff to evict me. I managed to maintain my composure throughout that long night, knowing that everyone would leave in the morning. Nadia and I never got a chance to talk.

In the morning, the Medicine Man asked to take me up to Big Rock to show me where my power place was. We went for a long hike. I felt very klutzy and uncoordinated in comparison to his easy gait. He located my power spot on top of the mountain. We meditated there for a while. Then we began to descend. That was when the Medicine Man got lost. I could not believe that the man who could commune with the birds and understand the chirp of the cricket could get lost when my house was within visual range of the power spot. It took us two hours to get back to my home.

When we arrived, we discovered that the rest of the group had taken another dosage of the power substance. I was terrified. I felt like these people were never going to leave, that I had lost complete control of my home. I was afraid they would hate me if I asked them to leave by three o'clock in the afternoon. But at two-thirty, they all cleaned up the house. By three o'clock, they were gone.

After they left, I collapsed on my couch and sobbed. I was terrified that this group would never let go of the drugs. I wanted so much to be part of a family that really accepted me but I did not believe in taking drugs to achieve enlightenment. I called out to God for help. The answer came immediately. I would do the power substance a total of six times. This cycle would end in the Spring.

In March, some women in the larger group were complaining that Geoffrey was making inappropriate sexual advances toward them during the power substance ceremonies. The men were complaining that the group was becoming known as a drug group and that we needed to rethink the use of the power substance. Everyone decided to confront Geoffrey at the group retreat in Idyllwild during March.

But Geoffrey eluded all of us. Isadora's grandfather

had died in New Mexico. Geoffrey insisted on driving Isadora to the funeral. The Idyllwild retreat took place without the primary leaders. It was at this retreat, where Nadia and I finally got to talk. She was having problems with a man she was dating. Our union would have to wait for a while.

In the beginning of April, I had a very vivid dream in which a beautiful, powerful whale breeched out of the ocean and deliberately committed suicide on the beach. The next morning, I received a phone call from Isadora. It was feared that Geoffrey had driven up to Big Rock and committed suicide the night before. I was stunned. Isadora, Geoffrey's wife and several other group members came out to my house. Isadora called the Sheriff's office and reported her suspicions. They sent a squad car out to my house and a helicopter to explore the surrounding canyon area. It did not take them long to locate his body. They airlifted his body out. Two of the men went with the sheriffs to identify the body.

Geoffrey's death signaled the end of the group. Minerva, the entity channeled by Isadora, recommended that the group disband and move to one of the states in the four corners area of the United States. They would be safe there when the poles shifted in August during the Harmonic Convergence. Minerva was adding a caveat to her predictions. If enough souls raised their vibrational frequencies, the catastrophe would be averted and a new level of spiritual consciousness would be available to the whole of humanity.

In April, my mother's mother died. Lenore had been a horribly abusive woman her entire life, filled with negativity and hate. My mother went back to Ohio to help her brothers clean out the filthy, roach-infested house. When Mom returned at the beginning of June, she told me that she had discovered something very strange in Grandma's belongings. Love letters written to Lenore by her own father.

He had been a traveling salesman. He wrote love letters to his daughter, treating her as if she were his wife. Mom and I both realized that it was concrete evidence that Lenore had been incested.

Gladys celebrated her 75th birthday on May 24th. I threw her a big party at my house. Nadia had just arrived back in town. She had been in Seattle to be with her father when he died. Nadia came to the party. And she never went home. We began a nine-year relationship that night, a relationship that would change both of us deeply and dramatically for eternity.

In June, Neil called me at work. He sounded agitated. He needed to come to my office. When he got there, he told me that his T-cell count had dropped tremendously and showed no signs of recovering. He wanted me to be the executrix of his estate. He did not want to worry Trevor with the details. He asked if I could secretly meet him on my lunch hour the following week to go over his estate. Of course I would.

The following week, Neil called me and told me to just forget about what he had said. Trevor had taken him to a clinic in San Diego and he had gotten all kinds of natural herbs to help him. He needed to keep a positive attitude. I told him that I was very happy for him. He canceled our meeting. I hung up the phone knowing that he did not have much longer to live.

A week later, Nadia and I had just turned out the lights in my bedroom and gotten all snuggled down in bed when I heard three loud, long wraps on the outside wall of my bedroom. I gasped and bolted up. I asked Nadia if she had heard the wraps. She told me they sounded like death. I totally agreed. It was death wrapping at our house. I checked outside for any hints of wind or other natural phenomenon. There was nothing but stillness. I did not know who death had come for.

The following afternoon at work, the Senior Vice

President of Accounting came into my office. He never did that. Interestingly the question he asked me could only be answered by Trevor. Trevor had left HGP two years before. I told the Vice President that I would gladly call Trevor and see if he could help us.

Trevor got on the phone with me and burst into tears. He had taken Neil into the hospital the night before. The doctors did not give Neil more than a few days to live. I told Trevor I would meet him at the hospital. Then I realized that I had to call my mother to cancel a business dinner that I had set up with her.

When I told my mother I would be unable to come to dinner, she said 'I know you can't come.' I asked her how she knew. "At two o'clock this afternoon," Mom told me, "my mother appeared in the living room. She looked at me and said 'I love you, Alice' and then she disappeared. I've been drinking wine ever since." I would have been drinking too if my dead mother had appeared in my living room.

When I reached the hospital, Neil had been going in and out of a coma for several hours. His eyes were beginning to roll back and forth uncontrollably. We were able to talk briefly. I told him about Nadia, that she was a masseuse. He laughed and called me a sex addict.

The next day, I felt compelled to call funeral homes to get prices on burial services. Neil was Jewish. He would have to be buried within twenty-four hours of death unless the next day was a holiday or the Sabbath. It was 1986. Most mortuaries refused to accept bodies that had died of AIDS. I was able to locate a Jewish mortuary willing to take Neil.

That night, I met Carly at the hospital. I had told Nadia about Neil's dying but she did not feel that it was appropriate for her to be there. I agreed. It was as if Carly and I were finishing some unstated business from our past relationship.

Neil's death was one of the most spiritual experiences

of my life. By Tuesday night, he was fully comatose. One of his Jewish male friends ran out and found a rabbinical student who could come and read the Last Rites for him. She told all of us that his spirit was still present and that we all needed to finish our business with him. After we each spent time alone talking to Neil, the rabbinical student read from the Torah. As she read, we all heard a low, moaning voice that became louder as she continued. The voice sounded like it was rising up from the grave. When she finished reading, the moaning voice ceased. It was very weird.

A small group of us stayed with Neil throughout that night in a prayer vigil. By two o'clock in the morning, Johnny and the rabbinical student had devised a method of communicating with Neil. Neil could not control his eye movements or his eyelids. He could not control his hands or feet. But he could control his breath. He could exhale deeply if he was answering 'yes' or just keep his breathing steady if the answer was 'no.' It was remarkable. He had been able to tell Trevor about a check that he wanted Trevor to cash. The check was located in the upper left hand corner of Neil's desk at home. The rabbinical student worked with Neil to try to help him finish his business so he could let go more easily. We all took turns going into talk with Neil using this new method of communication.

Before my turn came, I had found a private bathroom where I was able to do a short meditation. I called on Neil's Higher Self to please join with us in helping Neil make the transition to the other side. I became very aware of a massive energy emanating emerald green. Emerald green was Neil's favorite color. His Higher Self wanted me to make Neil aware that he was there with him.

When I went to talk with Neil, I told him that I was a little nervous about discussing spiritual matters with him because Neil had always been a very pragmatic psychologist. I asked Neil if his mother was there with him.

She had died five years before of cancer. He exhaled deeply. Yes, she was. Then I asked Neil to take a look around at his surroundings. Was someone else there with him? Neil's breathing remained steady for a minute or two. Then suddenly he exhaled with such ferocity that I jumped and gasped. Yes, there was someone there with him. And he was very big. My body was covered with goose bumps. For as many spiritual experiences that I had had, I was also filled with perennial doubt. I was always surprised by the reality of Spirit.

Neil finally passed just after six a.m. on the morning of Thursday, July 3rd. Since Friday was July 4th and Saturday was the Jewish Sabbath, Neil would not be buried until Sunday. That gave all of his relatives in New York the opportunity to attend the funeral services.

A couple weeks after Neil's death, I was driving Nadia back to her apartment in Marina del Rey. We were driving along Pacific Coast Highway. I periodically glanced at the ocean as I listened to Nadia talk about her past. Her voice droned on like a monotonous weather forecaster. She was telling me how sexually obsessed her father had been while she was growing up. When she reached the part where she had walked in on her father performing oral sex on her sister, I heard Neil's voice very distinctly inside my mind. "Tell her that he's an asshole," Neil instructed me. I silently argued with him, explaining that I didn't know her well enough to call her father an asshole. Neil insisted that I do just that. Finally I conceded. "I hate to have to tell you this, darling," I began diplomatically, "but your father was an asshole." The words hit Nadia like a bucket of ice-cold water. She looked stunned. She had told this story to all of her male lovers in the past and no one had ever said that. They all just kept quiet. By the time we reached her apartment, Nadia was fuming. Her anger had woken up. It was wonderful.

Nadia was not only beautiful; she was brilliant. We

shared remarkably similar pasts as well as a passionate desire to grow spiritually. We had both been in the Spiritual Science Church and we had both recently left the Church. We devoured New Age metaphysics with the voracity of starved tigers. Because of that determination to grow, our individual worlds began to shatter. In March of 1987, I left my job at HGP to pursue my writing career.

In April, Nadia took me to a channeling session with a wonderful woman named Beatrice Virgil. Beatrice channeled a spirit called Myrna. I had been to many channels and psychics in my life. Myrna was the only spirit who reached into my heart and touched my soul. She understood who I was on a deep soul level. She told us that we were two PhDs in tension and that we needed to learn to relax.

By June 1987, Nadia had become very ill. Regardless of all the meditation and reprogramming exercises we tried, Nadia felt like her life force was being drained from her body. She began limping in her right knee. I did not know what to do to help her. Through a series of synchronicities, a New Age script that I had written connected us to a woman who could heal Nadia's cancer. I had given the script to Vance, a UPM on an HGP show. He was very interested in how I knew so much about crystals. He knew a woman who could program crystals. She had saved his wife's life. His wife had a cancerous tumor the size of a baseball on her left wrist. Medical doctors had given up on her. Vance was at his wits end when a fellow he worked with took them to meet Maya, a healer in San Diego. She was able to channel freezing energy that killed the tumor. The doctors were stunned. They could not explain it.

Maya was the only real healer I ever met in my life. When I took Nadia to see her, Nadia began to cry as Maya channeled energy into her. The energy turned freezing cold. Nadia's worst fears were realized—the lower half of her body was filled with cancer. I heard a chorus of angels singing 'Hallelujah!' At last, we had found the answer to what was killing Nadia and with that we were given the healer who could cure her.

Nadia recovered. But by the end of the year, she had fallen into another depression. She went to see Beatrice. Myrna told Nadia that she had to make a choice in her soul again. Nadia had to decide if she wanted to live or to die. If she wanted to live, she needed to get some therapeutic help. Beatrice was beginning a therapy practice and offered to work with Nadia. Nadia discussed the whole situation with me. I wanted her to live. I hoped she would be willing to do the therapy. In January 1988, she began seeing Beatrice.

Nadia insisted on playing the tapes of her sessions to me. As I listened to her sessions, I began to notice a startling similarity between our family's behavior patterns. A few months into her therapeutic work, Nadia came home and announced that Beatrice wanted her to quit individual therapy and begin group therapy with someone else. I thought that Nadia must have misunderstood Beatrice but Nadia insisted that she had not. Nadia began going to incest survivor groups. She began reading books about incest recovery. She wanted me to read everything that she read. I could not. I felt physically ill whenever I began to read any of the materials.

While Nadia's personal growth was expanding, my writing career floundered. I did not have the networking skills necessary to survive in Hollywood.

In April 1989, I began having severe debilitating anxiety attacks. I could not eat. I could not sleep. I could not drink water. My stomach felt like a ball of fire burned in it incessantly and my body felt like I was being electrocuted. I kept telling Nadia that I would be fine in a day or two. After a watching me suffer for a week, Nadia called Beatrice and then shoved the phone in my face. As soon as I heard Beatrice's voice on the phone, I began to relax and to cry. She felt so safe.

When I walked into Beatrice's apartment and sat down

for our first therapy session, she asked me how I was feeling. Instantly I heard a little girl's voice coming out of my mouth. "They won't believe me!" she said emphatically. "They won't believe me!" Beatrice leaned forward. "Who won't believe you?" "My family!" I heard the little girl exclaim. "What is it that they won't believe?" Beatrice asked. Instantly the little girl energy vanished, leaving only me staring at Beatrice. "I don't know," I said in my normal voice. Beatrice leaned forward again. "Do you realize that you were just talking like a little girl?" "Yeah," I nodded. "I guess she finally felt safe enough to come out." And so began my eleven year journey of therapy and spiritual work with Beatrice.

It was because of those anxiety attacks and because Nadia insisted that I talk with Beatrice that I began having therapy with my greatest spiritual teacher. Beatrice had been practicing different forms of Buddhist and Eastern meditation for twenty years. She was also returning to graduate school to begin work on a PhD in clinical psychology. Beatrice began to teach me how to relax and to sit with my own energies in an open-hearted way. In our eleven years of work together, Beatrice would teach me how to come home to the real world of love inside of me. The anxiety attacks were caused by suppressed memories of childhood incest. The journey to heal from the incest was also my doorway into awakening my own soul.

It was also in April 1989 when I got my first job writing a feature film. Vance was co-producing a low budget feature with a group of Chinese producers. They had gone through six writers and still needed a decent shooting script. I auditioned my work to them and they hired me to write a Karate Kid type of film. I was exhilarated. Then they hired the director. I discovered that he was actively involved in the Spiritual Science Church. He destroyed my script when he shot it. But I got paid and I got a screen credit.

My therapy with Beatrice opened a doorway deep into

my soul. Within a month, I told her about a dream I had. I was sitting by a frozen lake. It had been winter in my soul. But Spring was coming and the lake would thaw once more.

In another dream, a little blonde-haired girl went happily to bed one night. When she awoke in the morning, she was buried under rubble. Confused and frightened, the little girl managed to dig her way out from under the debris. Then she saw that her entire town had been bombed during the night. Both of her parents were dead. Panic stricken, the little girl ran frantically to the only safe place she could think of—her grandmother's house. The terrified little girl ran so hard and so fast that she couldn't see. Suddenly she smashed into something so hard that it knocked her body backwards onto the ground. Stunned and breathless, the little girl opened her eyes to see two shiny, black knee-high boots standing in front of her. As her eyes followed the boots upward, she saw the tall body of a Nazi soldier smiling down at her. The Nazi reached down and pulled her up. The dream ended with the little girl walking off with the Nazi. There was an uncomfortable feeling that the little girl was going to be used for sexual experimentations.

A month later, I had an incest memory come forward. I was resting on my bed at home one afternoon. Just as my body was really relaxing into sleep, an image arose in me. The image was of a woman standing in a doorway. She was backlit so I could not see her face. But I clearly recognized the silhouette. Terror jolted my stiffened body an inch up off the bed. It was Lenore. I was so scared that I could not even tell Beatrice about it for two months. I ran from this image. I did everything possible to block it out of my mind and my life. I argued with God, begging to please, please, please don't make it incest. I could handle anything else. But please, please, please, not that.

By August, I could bear it no more. My work on the film had ended. I told Beatrice about the memory. We discussed my fears. She suggested doing a light level of regression to help release the energy. The following week, we did the regression. It was the most real memory of my childhood that I had ever experienced. I was two months old. I could feel my little baby body doing push-ups in the crib I was laying in. The room was very dark. It was humid. I could hear a television set on in the other room. I was very content. Then the door opened. My grandmother's silhouette filled the doorway. Terror filled my body. Lenore approached my crib. She lifted me out of the crib and sat down in a chair. Then she pulled her breast out and offered it to my mouth. I began sucking her. She began masturbating herself. Because her breast had no milk, I began to cry. Lenore became very angry. She began masturbating me to try to silence me. I cried more. Her anger intensified. Suddenly a black ball of energy came out of her and shot into my heart with severe intensity. The black ball said 'I'm bad.'

By this point in the regression, I was in severe anxiety and physical pain. I could not stay long in this place. Beatrice brought me out of the regression. She told me that it was very good that I had seen the black ball in its energy form. That was a more direct way of contacting it. She told me that we would come back to this place again and again to help it heal. I was exhausted. I told Nadia what had happened but I did not give her the details. I did not want anyone ridiculing or challenging my experience. I just knew that this was my memory, my experience. I did not have to understand it completely.

As I continued my work with Beatrice, my dream life became very active and quite vivid. Some of my dreams were nightmares involving unseen spirits terrorizing me in bathrooms. But many other dreams involved intricate story lines with complex characters. These dreams were rich with symbolic subtexts. My soul had finally found a very real way to communicate with me. For me to understand these communications, I had to relax and learn this new language of symbolic landscapes and emotional colors. What was I trying to tell myself?

By the beginning of December, Nadia and I were running out of money. Beatrice had stopped channeling. Hers was not a casual decision. She had reached a deeper level in her own healing and had realized that channeling was no longer an appropriate thing for her to do because it encouraged the clients to grasp onto something outside of themselves instead of encouraging them to go within to find the answers they were looking for.

Nadia and I, on the other hand, were not interested in going within to find our answers. We were too scared about making a mistake. We wanted a psychic to tell us what to do. So we went to see Charles. Charles channeled Clarence, a wonderful old spirit who had been in human form in several lifetimes so he could empathize with our insecurities. Charles told me that he saw bright lights around Paramount Studios and that my friends at Paramount would just scoop me up into a job. But the truth was I had no friends at Paramount. Interestingly, though, a friend of mine from HGP gave me the name of an industry temp agency. When I went to the temp agency, I accidentally ended up in the owner's office. He saw my resume and sent me that day to a two-day job in Production Finance at Paramount Studios! They liked me so much, they made a permanent job position for me.

In the meantime, my therapy continued. And I still had to interact with my family. It was at my father's sixty-third birthday party in mid-December when a huge chunk of my inner iceberg fell off inside of me. Two days before the party, I had had a nightmare. I was standing in a bathroom, staring at myself in the mirror. Suddenly my face turned into my father's face in the mirror. Then his face became the ghoulish face of a devil and it shot out of the mirror and into my real face. I woke up screaming.

The party was at my stepsister's house. Dad had been

drinking wine at the party all afternoon. As usual, he was obnoxious and arrogant. My stepsister's five-year-old daughter, Kate, pulled at my sleeve and asked me to pick her up. I scooped her up in my arms. We went back into her bedroom to watch Susan's children play with Kate's toys. Kate seemed very withdrawn as she sat in my lap and clung to me. I asked her if it was okay if the other children played with her toys. She mumbled 'yes.' Then my father appeared in the doorway. He was drunk. He was holding a video camera, telling us to all to smile and slurring his words with a sexual energy as he spoke. Something inside me snapped. Dad left the doorway. I took Kate to her mother. Then I found Nadia and told her that we had to get out of there. It was four o'clock in the afternoon.

By ten o'clock that night, Nadia and I were safe at home, watching the news. We were sitting on the couch downstairs. Nadia started to put her arms around my shoulder. My body leapt off the couch as I screamed "DON'T TOUCH ME!" I bolted upstairs as I screamed to be left alone. I ran into the den, slammed the door and fell onto the floor in a heap. I felt horribly exposed and vulnerable. I was sobbing uncontrollably. I grabbed a blanket off the couch and hid under it as I lay rocking and crying in a fetal position on the floor in the dark. Waves of energy passed through me as I sobbed uncontrollably for an hour. I could hear myself muttering over and over 'Evidence. I need evidence.' Finally, after an hour of being washed in waves of nonverbal emotion, I felt a gentle peace rise up inside of me. "You have enough evidence," the voice said to me. "This doesn't have to happen to anyone else ever again." I stopped crying and sat up. I knew what I had to do.

From eleven o'clock that night until three o'clock in the morning, I wrote a twenty-three-page letter to my stepsister exposing my father as an alcoholic and as a sexual perpetrator. I warned her to protect her little girl, Kate. I broke the conspiracy of silence in my family.

The letter sparked the family to have an alcoholic intervention with my father. After immense pressure, he agreed to go into a rehab program. The rehab center could only deal with the alcohol issues. They would not deal with the incest issues. But while he was in this rehab center, my father remembered being molested by an older teenage boy when my father was eleven years old.

My sister Susan also went into therapy for her own incest issues. She had gone through her entire college career getting her bachelor's and master's degrees in psychology and she had never dealt with her own incest issues. That was the power of her denial.

The alcohol rehab group encouraged family participation. The first family group was held in March. I was determined to go. Nadia agreed to pick me up at Paramount Studios at five p.m. and we would drive together to the meeting. By four o'clock that afternoon, my body was emitting the worst smelling stench I had ever experienced. At first, I did not understand what it was since I had bathed and used deodorant as usual that morning. Then I recalled that Maya had smelled the same stench coming from Nadia during their healing work. Maya explained that it was the stench of fear stored in the cells. Part of the healing was the releasing of that stench. My office mate did not appreciate the smell. When I got to Nadia's car, I asked her if she had a sweatshirt in the back. At first she did not believe me, but as soon as the first breeze wafted my body odor towards her nose, she gagged and threw a clean sweatshirt at me.

A month later, just before going to another family session with my father, I was driving home on the Santa Monica freeway heading west. When I reached Lincoln Boulevard, I began feeling a strange energy pulsating across my chest. I was alone in the car. My first fear was that I was having a heart attack. I could hear Beatrice inside me reminding me to just relax and let the energy be whatever it was. I stayed in my breath and watched. My chest felt like it was expanding. It felt like my shirt was going to rip apart like "The Incredible Hulk." Then the energy focused and compressed into a laser type beam that targeted a specific spot in my left armpit. The energy vanished from my chest, leaving a deep burning sensation in my armpit. When I got home, I called to Nadia and ran into the bathroom. I told her what had happened as I took off my blouse. We both looked under my left arm. There in the pit was a huge, angry boil. I had felt its formation as I was driving on the freeway. My body had stored the anger I had not been able to express about my father and the incest and it was now releasing some of it in a very non-violent way. Beatrice pointed out to me that I should be grateful for my body's ability to have held so much pain with such grace and dignity. It could have manifested itself as cancer.

In December 1990, Susan shared some of her journal writing with me. When I heard her words, something inside of me snapped. Suddenly I knew that my father had molested me too. I wrote him a short terse note telling him "I know now that you fucked me when I was a little girl." I cut off all communication with him. I had no specific memory but I had no real memories of my childhood anyway. Trusting my sense memory was just another step toward accepting my own inner truth.

Beatrice suggested that I include drawing in my meditation work with my inner child. I was already realizing that the person my inner child was most afraid of was me. I was the one who had not believed her. I made a commitment to that little girl inside of me. I told her that I would believe anything that she said or drew. I would not edit any of it. I wanted her to feel safe enough to begin to trust me.

In 1991, Susan insisted that our father begin therapy

sessions with a therapist who specialized in sexual perpetrators. He only agreed when she threatened to cut him off from ever seeing his grandchildren again.

In June of 1991, Nadia and I moved to Monroe, Washington. Nadia was from Washington and desperately wanted to return there. We had the opportunity to buy a house on 7.6 acres of land with my friend Johnny. We knew at the outset that Johnny was HIV positive. But we all thought he was in good health. He was going to move to Washington with us and help us remodel the house. But at the last minute, Johnny backed out. When Nadia and I arrived at the property, we learned that the original contractors we had hired to remodel had panicked and reneged. They were afraid that Johnny would sue them if everything was not absolutely perfect.

We also discovered that our water main had been shut off by the county inspector. When I called him, he explained that there was a leak somewhere in the line. We would have to repair it. The water line ran six hundred feet from the road back to the house. We had to start digging it up by hand to locate the leak. To top it all off, our moving van ran into delays. Our furniture did not arrive for five days. We had to sleep on the floor.

Nadia and I struggled to handle the remodeling responsibilities but we were in way over our heads. We were fighting for our lives and fighting with each other. Nadia was useless when it came to the physical labor aspects of remodeling. Her body would short-circuit and she would begin screaming uncontrollably and storm out of the house. She refused to deal with Johnny when he would call us. She would not even listen on the extension. I felt like I had the weight of the entire house project on my shoulders. It was as if the Universe were replaying my childhood abuse in living color in order to get me to feel my pain. I was finally able to come out of deep emotional numbness and to actively feel my rage. I began screaming back at Nadia when she would enter her own rages. The forests behind our house became a healing sanctuary where I could scream and rant without disturbing anyone. Throughout this hideous ordeal, I made a very conscious choice to use my Buddhist training to help me stay awake in this pain. As my own inner pain came forward, I wrote my family a nineteen-page letter telling them what my childhood was like from my perspective. It was a very angry letter, a much needed expression of deeply buried pain.

After three months in the country, I felt like a shell of energy cracked off of me. Suddenly I could feel the energy of the earth and the trees. There was life outside of Hollywood! I began writing character sketches of everyone I loved and missed in Los Angeles. I did not know why I was writing this. I just felt like it. That was a huge step for me—to write for the sheer joy of writing with no thought of turning a profit. I had been writing scripts for so long that my writing had become black and white. But out there in the country, my wild side began to surface in my writing. The color returned to my writing. It felt wonderful.

In September, Johnny was told by his physician that he did not have much longer to live. He called me and told me that he was leaving us the house in his will. His HIV had developed into AIDS. He went home at Christmas to tell his mother that he was gay and that he was dying. He also mentioned that he had this land deal with two lesbians. The lesbians were having trouble paying the mortgage because the job market in Seattle had fallen into a depression. His mother recommended that he foreclose on us.

In January 1992, Johnny sent me a handwritten note stating that we were in default. I called him to talk about it. He was very sweet on the phone but he never addressed the default notice. He was about to hang up when I told him that we had gotten the default notice. "Oh, that," he said in a singsong voice. "You can just tear that up and throw that away." I relaxed. "Didn't you get the letter from my attorney?" Johnny asked as casually as if it were a vacation postcard. "No." "Oh, he's sending you an official notice of default." In that phone call, I knew that Johnny's AIDS had gone to his brain. I told Nadia that he had a brain tumor. We were not dealing with a rational human being. Johnny wanted to destroy us to prove to his mother that he was a good little boy.

Nadia and I fought like hell to keep our home. Because we had no money, I was prepared to go to the legal library at the County Courthouse to study how to fight foreclosure. But I was informed that foreclosure was a complicated legal procedure. A layperson would not be able to fight it. We had to have an attorney. We found a lesbian real estate attorney willing to work pro bono. It would take us four months and cost us our home before we realized that our attorney was delusional and incompetent.

During this holocaust, I began communicating with my father again. My mother insisted on contacting him, stating that he might be able to lend us the money to pay off the default. After several attempts at talking with him, my mother called me in complete frustration. She dumped the entire thing in my lap. I knew there was something wrong about this but I could not figure out what it was. It was after all my responsibility to save my own home. I called my father. He told me I needed to send him all the paperwork on the house. He would take it to a real estate agent he knew. She would be able to see if there was a way out of this. I did not like exposing my personal financial documents to my father. But I also wanted to do whatever I had to do to save my home. I decided to send him the information. He called later and became very melodramatic, siding with Johnny but telling us that if we pulled this off, we would be considered geniuses by the Fortune 500 companies. I really had no idea what he was talking about. The bottom line was he would not lend us the money to pay off the default. I felt like he had fucked me all over again.

But then something else happened. Two weeks later, my father called me and asked me if I would fly down to Los Angeles and have a meeting with him and his therapist to discuss the letter I had written to the family. My father would pay for my plane ticket and give me money to visit my own therapist while I was there.

I stood on the balcony of the master bedroom and stared out at the massive pine trees in the front driveway. I could hear the voice of a psychic from the Church of Inner Light in Los Angeles. Two years before, he had told me that my father would call me to come home. When that happened, it was very important that I go. When that memory arose inside of me, I knew that regardless of how much I hated my father, there was a deeper reason for me to go to that meeting.

The trip coincided with our new attorney's attempt to counter the default. I had to hand-carry the subpoena to L.A. Susan agreed to serve it on Johnny. When I arrived, Susan picked me up at the airport. She took me to my mother's real estate office to pick up her own children. My niece and nephews crowded around me with lots of love and hugs. My mother, on the other hand, stayed seated at her desk. I had not seen her in over a year. She acted like I was the parent and she was the child. "I have a gift for you!" she exclaimed. My heart started to soften. Then she shoved a picture of her new boyfriend into my hand. "He's a doctor!" she gurgled. I knew there was something wrong with this scenario but I was so numb I could not connect with what it was. Susan expressed my anger for me later that night. "You are about to go into open-heart surgery with your father tomorrow morning to discuss the most painful issues any daughter could ever have to face with her own father—incest—and what does your mother say? 'I have a gift for you. Here's a picture of my new boyfriend.'

I am infuriated with her." I was glad that Susan could feel her anger. I could not feel anything. I began to realize how much I disappeared inside whenever I dealt with my mother.

The next morning, I drove Susan's car to the New Hope Therapy Center where I met my father. When I saw him standing in the parking lot, I was shocked. He looked so old and so fat. His skin was stretched so tightly if a pin pricked him, he would fly around the room sputtering like a leaky balloon. We walked inside and met his therapist, Tom.

Tom began the session by thanking me for coming. He told me that I was very courageous to come to a meeting with my father and a strange man. Then he went on to say that if I wanted my father to admit penetration, we may as well stop the meeting right there because my father had no memory of penetrating me.

I stayed in my breath. The word 'penetration' reverberated inside the room with a disgusting feeling of nausea. I began to question why I had agreed to come into this place with two strange men. But as I stayed in my breath and trusted myself, I was able to respond. I told Tom and my father that I really didn't care if Dad ever remembered incesting me. Of course he wouldn't remember. He was drunk all the time I was growing up. It was also well documented that both the perpetrator and the victim disassociate during the abuse so that neither one of them may remember anything. I was very proud of myself during that session. I was able to stay awake and to hear my heart in the face of the most terrifying energies I would ever encounter. Tom was the polar opposite to Beatrice. I was used to a nurturing feminine energy supporting me in my therapy. Tom was a very analytical male who was not there to nurture me. He was my father's therapist so his loyalty was to him. Tom was also a Born

Again Christian who did not think that homosexuality was a gift from God.

By the end of the session, I could hear my inner child jumping up and down inside of me, telling me to show my father the pictures she had drawn as part of my own therapeutic process. I explained to both men that we would probably never agree on the details of what took place in my childhood. But I wanted to share with my father the impact and the impression that he left on me when I was a child. I took out the first picture. It was a drawing of me as a little girl. It was full of black and red slashes and swear words. There was a lot of self-hatred in that picture. Then I pulled out a picture my little girl had drawn of my father. It was labeled "A Portrait of Daddy." Tom took one look at it and looked revolted. He handed the picture to my father. The drawing was of a fat, naked man who had penises for arms, penises for legs, an erect penis coming out of his crotch, a penis for a tongue, penises coming out of his ears, a penis coming out of his butt and a chain of penises around his neck. My father howled like a wounded animal and threw the paper on the floor. "No! No!" he screamed. "It's too hideous! I can't look at it!" His body was wracked with pain. He looked like Jabba the Hut from "Star Wars." As I watched my father howling and crying, I realized how lucky I was to have had my anxiety attacks when I was thirty-four. If I had not begun my own healing process then, I could easily have ended up just like my father when I was sixty-five. All of the unfelt pain of his entire life had been stuffed, packed and compressed into every cell in his body. He was so tight that when he cried, no tears could fall from his eyes. Tom told him "This is the impression you gave to your daughter of what it was to be a man." As my father howled in pain, I felt a huge weight lift off of me like a wave. It moved back to my father where it rightfully belonged. I felt a deep sense of release. It was an amazing shift of energy. My father told me he was sorry for the pain he had caused me. I was surprised that his apology did not have more of an affect on me. Then I realized that his apology could not heal the wounds inside of me. Only my love and nurturing of my inner child could accomplish that.

I returned to Susan's house. She had agreed to drive me up to Los Angeles where she would hand-deliver the court subpoena to Johnny. When we arrived at Johnny's, I told Susan to park down the street. She got out of the car and walked back to his house. I got into the driver's seat and kept the engine running. Within a few minutes, Susan was dashing towards the car. She leapt in and ordered me to "Go! Go! Go!" I whizzed out down the street and around the corner. She told me that Johnny's brother answered the door. He went to get Johnny. When Johnny came to the door, Susan was shocked. He looked very healthy. She was expecting him to be skin and bones. He was very pleasant. She asked him his name and then handed him the piece of paper. He smiled and said 'Thank you' as if she had given him a Christmas card.

We turned onto Olympic Boulevard and came to a stoplight. I felt an energy rising out of the pavement around us. Suddenly a bag lady near Susan's side of the car began screaming at another bag lady. "How could you give me this letter!!!" the woman screamed as she waved a piece of paper at the other woman. "How could you give me this letter?!!" Susan's eyes widened in horror. She turned to me in fear. "Let's get the hell out of here!" she said. The light turned green. I gunned the engine. We took off to relative safety. I felt like Johnny's rage had come right up out of the earth around us as soon as he read the letter.

I returned to Washington in time to attend the court hearing. Nadia refused to go with me. I had never really been involved in our judicial system. I had always been taught that our system was the best in the world and that it held truth and justice as the highest values. I soon learned that I had been living in a delusion. I was not allowed to speak at this hearing. This was a pre-trial hearing where only the attorneys were allowed to present their cases. The judge would decide if the case warranted going to trial. What I witnessed from my gagged seat in the back of the courtroom were puppets acting out melodramatically. Johnny's attorney told outright lies, becoming more and more bombastic as the lies got bolder and bigger. Our attorney did nothing to counter the lies. He did only enough to cover his own legal butt. The judge ruled against us. We would not go to trial. We lost the house. We had twenty days to move before the sheriff would come to throw us out on the street.

We were forced to move into a slum house in Everett. Nadia's sister owned it. Her current tenants just happened to be moving out. We needed a house with a fenced yard for our three dogs and two cats. When Nadia first took me by the house before we moved in, I had the sinking feeling inside of me that I was going to die in that house. I felt like it was my Grandmother Lenore's house in Ohio.

The Everett house was a hundred years old. It was jacked up off its foundation because the foundation was crumbling and needed repair. It had been jacked up for so long that the floors inside had bowed and all the door jams had bent into strange shapes. Winds coming off the Puget Sound swept easily through the cracks in the doors and walls. Whenever the washing machine in the basement went into a spin cycle, the kitchen above it would shake. The walls were infested with mice. The house stunk of mice urine and feces. It was a hideous place. Oddly, because it had originally been a beautiful Victorian house, the interior felt very peaceful, even elegant. But drug dealers surrounded us on both sides of the house.

Nadia found work as a file clerk at the local hospital. I was an over-qualified accountant in a depressed market economy. I could not find work. Johnny had forced me into bankruptcy. Nadia's raging fits increased substantially. The tiniest things triggered her tirades. She would storm upstairs and trash a room. I would hide downstairs in the basement with the dogs. I felt trapped and totally financially dependent on this mad woman even though I was contributing my unemployment to our family. I fell into a deep depression for a year and a half.

I began having phone sessions with Beatrice. She had begun practicing at a psychology clinic and could give us sessions for as little as ten dollars an hour. She was a lifesaver. We were able to continue our work together. Even in this desolate and violent environment, I could connect with the Love in Beatrice's heart and learn how to develop that Love in my own heart.

Johnny died of a brain tumor in October. The doctors actually found two brain tumors in the autopsy. I had been correct in my assessment of his mental health. My real friend Johnny would not have behaved the way that maniac did when he foreclosed on us. We had owned the house together in joint tenancy. If Nadia and I had been able to pay off the default and to resume the mortgage payments, we would have owned the property outright upon Johnny's death. That was a hard one for me to let go of. I felt like that house represented all of the security I had never had in my own childhood. All of my security had been ripped away from me again.

My father flew me down to L.A. two more times before December to have several more sessions with Tom. The sessions also included Susan and finally my mother. Tom recommended that my father and I communicate with one another once a month if we wanted to build a new relationship. I tried to do that for a few months. The phone calls were cordial. But within twenty-four hours, I would erupt into rage and then be an emotional basket case for three more days. Once I saw this pattern emerging, I told my father that I needed to withdraw again. I told him he could write to me but I would not promise to write him back. He told me that he wanted to do whatever was best for me now. He chose not to write to me. All communications between us ceased.

Three months later, I walked Nadia out to her car one night and waved goodbye as she drove off to work at the hospital. As I walked back towards the front door, my body felt very relaxed. Suddenly the idea of 'stupid' came up in me. I thought that was odd. But I could hear Beatrice inside of me gently asking what 'stupid' was. I decided to deeply honor this feeling guest. I went into the house, lit some candles and settled onto the couch to meditate with my friend 'stupid.' As I relaxed back into my breath, I asked myself gently "So what's 'stupid'?" Immediately I felt a ball of energy in my head. The feeling of the ball was that it was a white, viscous substance that started in my head then rolled down my throat into my stomach where it turned into icky, squiggly worms.

I burst into tears as a very vivid memory played out inside of me. I was five years old. I woke up one night at two or three in the morning. I got up to go to the bathroom. I pushed the door open. My father was holding his penis over the toilet. He looked really mad. He was drunk. "What are you looking at?" he growled at me.

I got so scared that I split apart. Suddenly I was sitting way high up in the branches of the tree outside in our front yard. A huge, formless, feminine beingness surrounded me in the tree. She took me away to a dark place, a place where I could hear muffled voices and see shadowy forms but this was not a place of form. It was a place of formlessness. My soul had taken me there to protect the core of my personality from the potentially psychotic effects of the abuse.

Back in the bathroom, I was sitting on the edge of the bathtub. My father was shoving his penis into my mouth. I couldn't scream. I split apart again. A part of me I called

Astro Boy flew up to the ceiling and looked down at the strange little girl being molested on the bathtub. That would never happen to Astro Boy.

The door to Mom's bedroom was open. I saw her wake up. She sat up in bed and saw what Dad was doing to me. Then I saw her split apart. By the time her body reached the bathroom door, she was no longer my mother. She had become Robot Mommy. Dad pulled away from me. Robot Mommy walked past him without even noticing him. She scolded me for making such a mess. There was a lot of blood in the bathtub. I did not know if that blood was symbolic that I had lost my life that night or if there actually was blood in the bathtub.

The next morning, I woke up and walked into the kitchen. Mom was scrambling eggs. Dad was reading the paper. Everything looked normal. Dad saw me and said, "Come over here and give me a hug." My body froze. I looked at Mom. She said, "Give your father a hug." Everything twisted around inside of me. It felt horrible. Then it all went black.

I wept openly for my little five-year-old girl who had endured such horror with such courage. I was so ashamed of the memory that I could only share it with Beatrice. I could not even share it with Nadia. I decided that I did not need to tell anyone what had happened. It was nobody's business but my own. I did not need anyone else's validation for me to know that this was the truth inside of me.

In January of 1994, I called my friend Vance in Los Angeles. He had been working with a moneyman named Mr. Z. Mr. Z was doing a series of videotapes designed to teach children about the American space program. He had developed some cute cartoon characters to teach the children. I wrote a spec script for Mr. Z. He loved it. He promised to hire me to write the pilot and thirteen episodes. He even sent me a brand new fax machine to help me communicate with him. This project kept me going for four months. Mr. Z kept stringing all of us along until finally one day, he dropped Vance and hired another producer.

At the same time, I got a job offer to be the payroll accountant on a film called "Mad Love." I had to decide if I should take the payroll job or hang on for the writing job. I was finally able to talk with the new producer. Mr. Z had not told her that I was attached to the project. She had told him to stop paying me any monies. She was going to take the project in a different direction. I was dumped.

I was forced back into payroll. I had to accept a greatly reduced salary for my qualifications because I was now considered a cheap local hire. I had to take the job because I had to support my family.

As I sat in my ninth story office in downtown Seattle, I stared out the windows. If I had been able to open them, I would have ended up splattered on the sidewalk down below. Beatrice was working with me in phone sessions. She made me promise that I would talk with her first before I acted on any suicidal impulses. I promised. I did not know why God was tormenting me so much, why every time it looked like I was going to get a break, my face got shoved back down into the mud. That was how it felt to me. Beatrice kept telling me that things would get better, that I needed to keep working with my breath.

"Mad Love" was the story of a teenage boy who fell in love with a manic/depressive girl. Thinking he could save her, he ran away with her only to find that she needed more than he was able to give her. During the first week, there was a crew screening of a film the director had won a prestigious award for. The producer's assistant convinced me to go see the film when he realized that I was an incest survivor. The film was called 'Safe.' The director was Antonia Bird. The film was about homeless teenagers living in the streets of London. It was gritty and brutally real. I felt like all of my internal pain was projected onto the movie screen.

At the cast and crew bonding party, I met Antonia and told her how much I admired her film. When I told her that I was an incest survivor, her eyes bugged out, she grabbed my arm and said "Oh, my God! Why the film must have been absolute torture for you!" I was happy to know that she could empathize with my pain. I told her that I was also a writer and that I wanted to do a script about incest. She said that she too wanted to explore that subject matter in more depth. "When there's a quiet time on the set, we need to talk about it," Antonia told me sincerely. I laughed. "There's never a quiet time on the set."

The shoot was long and hard. Including travel time, I spent fourteen hours a day working. My payroll skills were rusty and my nerves were raw. Whenever I made a mistake, I felt like killing myself. When I would come home at night, Nadia would say "I don't know how you can work so many hours. I couldn't do that." And then she would tell me to fix my own dinner because she had already eaten and didn't know when I would be home. I got no real nurturing support from her.

The film went on location for two weeks in New Mexico. It was my first time ever on location with a film and the first time I had ever been away from Nadia in eight years. The experience helped build my self-confidence. We returned to Seattle and wrapped the show in September. I felt like I had lost my family. I told myself that this was a temporary work stoppage and that I should use this time off to write. The character sketches I had begun writing two years before had evolved into the beginnings of a book about my life. I realized that my book was an integral part of my healing process. It was about this time when I realized that my dreams about becoming a wealthy screenwriter were just delusions. I told Nadia not to hold her breath. She had banked her life on my success as a screenwriter. It was not going to work that way. I finally let go of the delusion and accepted that I was just another struggling writer who did film accounting to pay her rent. I felt liberated. Nadia was not pleased.

In November, I got a phone call from California. Judy was a first assistant accountant on a feature film called "Seven." She had been given my resume two years before when she lived in Texas and was working with Oliver Stone. She had filed it away. Now she needed to hire a construction accountant. My resume had fallen out of her file onto her desk. Would I be interested in the job?

My mind instantly struggled to figure out where I would live in L.A. and how I could manage this but a stronger sensation filled my stomach. 'Take it!' it ordered. "I'll take it!" I shouted into the phone. It took the rest of the week for me to locate a place to stay. As a last resort, I called Dottie in Pasadena. It just happened that my old pal Carl was moving to Colorado for four months and wanted someone to sublet his apartment while he was gone. I was his angel and he was mine. His roommate Chad and I talked on the phone to firm up the deal.

I told Nadia to quit her job at the hospital. She had injured her hands by doing too much repetitive filing. She said she would never be able to return to massage work again. She needed time to heal and to focus on what career she wanted to pursue. I would be making enough money to support both of us.

As I surveyed my den, trying to decide what to take with me for the next four months, a voice within me stated quite clearly and calmly "Take whatever you are going to take now because you are never coming back here." I was so shocked and confused and ashamed that I could not discuss this with Nadia. I told myself that I could be mistaken. I needed more time to see if we could heal our relationship.

When I got to L.A., I called the Production Office as soon as I got moved into Carl's apartment. I was actually renting an open loft with its own small bathroom. There was no privacy. I did not care. I just needed a place to crash from work. My boss asked me to start the next day.

My first night with my new roommate was spent getting to know one another. Chad was a handsome, dark haired, gay man who loved to get stoned. Chad played the piano at the Beverly Wilshire Hotel. He was a composer. He had worked with some pretty famous singers. But he had never been able to break out of the piano bar closet that L.A. had him locked in.

I reported to Warner Hollywood Studios at nine o'clock the following morning. I had not been on this lot since I left Harold Glass Productions in 1987. I felt like I had come home. The Production Office was upstairs in the Formosa Building on the same floor where my old residual office had been. I wandered outside to the iron bridge that linked the Formosa Building to the Editorial Building. My eyes casually perused the environment to see what had changed in my seven-year absence. Not much. My gaze just naturally fell on the little metal nameplates outside each door. Suddenly I realized that I recognized the names on those plates. These were the editors from "Mad Love." And if the editors were working there, then Antonia must have an office on the lot. That meant I would finally be able to talk with her about doing a script on incest. This was a genuine miracle in my book.

I excitedly told Chad about this sequence of events that evening. Chad was very happy for me. When he learned that I was an incest survivor and that I wanted to write a script about it, Chad screamed, "We've already done it! And it's a musical!" Only a gay man could get away with that line. Even with that, I thought the guy was nuts. A musical about incest? Get real. Chad explained that he had worked with a non-profit group called Stop Gap. Stop Gap helped abused children deal with their pain by creating dramatic plays or musicals to express their feelings. Chad had been a musical director for the organization for many years. One of the musicals that he wrote the music for dealt with incest. It was performed publicly to community accolades. I told Chad that I would like to read it. If it was presentable, I would show it to Antonia.

I made a point of stopping in to see Antonia every other day. I was trying to learn how to network. I was trying to become friends with her. That was not an easy task. Antonia was very busy editing two different films. One was "Mad Love." The other was a film about a gay priest. She was very busy.

Chad invited me to attend his annual Christmas party. He told me that he knew of two lesbians who would be attending—Victoria and Kerrie. Victoria was the founder of Stop Gap. I was very interested in talking with her about the incest play that she and Chad had mounted.

Nadia was not doing very well at home. Whenever I called, she was always in a crisis. Chad began hinting that I should leave her. I did not appreciate his hints especially since I was trying to salvage the relationship.

The Christmas party arrived. And I was finally able to meet Victoria. She was British. I told her that I had read the play and that I liked it. Then I launched into a lengthy speech about this director that I had worked with on my last film. She was a brilliant British woman named Antonia Bird. As I continued lauding Antonia, Victoria got a very peculiar look on her face. "Antonia Bird?" she muttered. "Antonia Bird. I believe I may have gone to school with her." "What?!" I sputtered. "Are you sure? Isn't Bird a fairly common name in England?" "No, actually, it's not." "Oh." "Was her father an actor?" "I believe he was." "She was always a bit stocky." "She still is." "She had shoulder length brown hair with bangs." "She still does." "And she would be my age." Well, we won't reveal her age. After all, Antonia does work in Hollywood where image is everything. Victoria proceeded to tell me things about the school that she attended with Antonia. She said she would love to meet her again. So many years had past since their days at Wellesley. Victoria told me that the school had been haunted by a ghost named 'Hensley.' I was excited to be able to reunite them if indeed it was the same Antonia Bird.

The next Monday, I ran into the main editing room. I had no idea at the time that Antonia was in the midst of a heated fight with her editor. It was after all a British fight. Antonia turned to me. "Does the name Hensley mean anything to you?" I asked. "No," Antonia snapped. "Why? Should it?" I held my position firmly refusing to be cowed by her acerbic tone. "Did you ever attend a girl's school called Wellesley?" "Yes, I did," Antonia replied. Then she gasped. "How did you know that?" "Do you remember a girl named Victoria Byrne?" I proceeded to tell her the entire story. Antonia was very impressed. Antonia had been terribly abused at that girls' school. She had been teased and humiliated by most of the girls because her father was an actor. The abuse had been so severe that Antonia had suffered with nightmares for years. She had only stopped having the nightmares a few months ago. She thought that could mean that she was ready to confront her past. She had always secretly dreamed of becoming a famous director and then returning to a school reunion to flaunt her success in everyone's face. This would not be so dramatic or vengeful but it would allow her closure on that part of her life. Antonia recognized the depth of the situation. But instead of including me in their possible reunion, she waved her hand at me like she was the Queen and said, "Just leave her phone number on my desk."

I was insulted. It was because of me that Antonia would be able to resolve her childhood pain. I was part of this scenario and I was not going to be treated like some servant. I told her boyfriend to tell her that. I would not give her Victoria's phone number. I would make the arrangements. When I saw Antonia the following week, she radically changed her demeanor with me, treating me like a friend and not a hired hand. Antonia and I went over her calendar. She would not have time for a dinner until the middle of February. I set the date up with Victoria.

New Years arrived. I flew home to Seattle to spend the long weekend with Nadia. It was disastrous. I was exhausted from working in production. I just wanted to sleep in Nadia's arms. She would have none of it. She wanted to go for a drive up the coast. I caved into her demands. We only drove a few miles when we had an explosive argument in the car. Nadia turned the car around and we returned home. She stormed about, raging at me the way she had always done for the last nine years. She stormed upstairs to her office and slammed the door. I waited for a while then I went into see her. She was sitting in the chair at her desk. I sat down on the small couch by the door. Nadia whirled on me. "I don't know why you even bothered to come back!" she sneered. The voice coming out of her sounded like my Grandma Lenore. The hair on the back of my neck stood up. "Honey, I live here," I reminded her gently. "I'm just working in L.A. to support our family." "Don't give me that crap!" she shouted. "You never should have come back here!" I felt like I was talking to the Devil. I wanted to run screaming from the house. But I had nowhere else to go until I left for the airport on Monday afternoon. I knew then that my inner voice had been correct. I was not going to be coming back here again.

When I returned to Los Angeles, I once again clutched at the idea of salvaging the relationship with Nadia. I was hoping that her taking six months off to heal would turn our relationship around.

In February, I drove Antonia down to Long Beach to meet Victoria. As we drove, I asked Antonia how she and her boyfriend managed to sustain a relationship when she was traveling so much of the year. She said it was difficult but doable. I asked her if she ever wondered if she and her boyfriend were in a relationship. She said 'no.' She had never wondered that. I knew then that my marriage was disintegrating because I was always wondering if Nadia and I even had a relationship anymore.

Dinner with Victoria and Kerrie went wonderfully. Antonia impressed both of them with her wit and charm and tales of filmmaking. Victoria impressed Antonia with her accomplishments in using drama as a tool to heal abused children. It was interesting that both women went into the arts and that both women focused on helping abused children in their work. We all had a wonderful time. I drove them back to their house and waited for Antonia to say her goodbyes. From the time I met Antonia, I had hoped that what had drawn us together was that we would do a script together about incest. But now as I sat in the car, I could feel that whatever the energy was that had tied me to Antonia, it had just released in this reunion. I felt humbled inside. Antonia climbed back into my car. "Weird," she said. "It's all just too weird."

On my fortieth birthday, I invited Antonia to my birthday party. She told me she would attend. She was in the middle of her editing session, when she got up and told her assistant editors "We all have to go to Roxanne's birthday party for an hour." It meant the world to me that she did that. And it greatly impressed all of my friends that a real live award-winning Hollywood director would show up at my birthday party! I will always love her for that.

I finished working on "Seven" at the end of March. I immediately got a job on a film called "Nickel and Dime." On April 3rd, I was on location in St. Louis. I did not return to Washington. In St. Louis, I had a bachelor apartment of my own, complete with a kitchen and cable t.v. I would work fourteen hours then go home, work out, have dinner and relax. I was in heaven. After nine years of incessant talking with Nadia, I had finally found the sanctity of solitude. That was when I really began to see that I could not go back to the relationship the way that it was.

"Nickel and Dime" was a road picture starring Bill Murray and a wonderful elephant named Tai. There were actually two female elephants on the shoot. Tai and Kitty. Kitty was the stand-in elephant. They brought a magic and a mysticism to an otherwise tedious location show. Everywhere we went, it rained and the sets flooded. It became almost comical. I was supposed to go to Denver to help with the accounting there but at the last minute, I was sent to Moab, Utah.

Moab looked like the womb of the earth. Its rocks and mesas were blood red. I was reborn in Moab. That's where I met Sally. Sally worked on the show. She spent a lot of time at the construction site. She liked to tease me a lot. Sally was just plain fun. Fun, fair, honest and caring. That was Sally. I fell madly in love with her. There was a very real chemistry between us. It was so real that many of the people on the show thought we were having an affair. We weren't. Not physically anyway. But we certainly were emotionally. But then straight women are like that. By the end of the picture, I realized that Sally had acted as a huge catalyst for me to wake up and realize that my relationship with Nadia was finally over. I was not willing to put any more energy into repairing it. I asked Nadia to fly down to L.A. so that we could have some sessions with Beatrice.

On August 22, 1995 in a joint therapy session with Beatrice, I ended the relationship. When Beatrice asked Nadia if she understood what had just happened, Nadia said 'She woke up and I didn't.' Beatrice concurred. I woke up from the pattern we were habitually living in and, once awake, I could not return to that pattern. I had to leave. I gave up everything I had ever dreamed of and destroyed all of Nadia's dreams in the process.

The break up was very volatile. Nadia insisted that I had abandoned her and the dogs and the cats. I continued to financially support Nadia for another year because she had supported me when I was unemployed. I wanted to leave this relationship with as much balance and love as I could.

I had no idea where I was going. I just knew I could not go backwards. I had to keep moving forward in my spiritual growth and trust this new part of me that was developing its own inner strength.

AN EVEN MORE EXCLUSIVE LOOK AHEAD TO PART THREE

(SYNOPSIS)

SOFT HEART

(1995-2000)

(SYNOPSIS)

SOFT HEART

(1995-2000)

"You have broken a very deep, habitual pattern of pain in your soul," Beatrice reminded me over and over. "This is not some small thing. It will take you time to adjust to a new way of relating to your life. You're doing really, really well." She told me that a lot.

I had broken a deep soul pattern of reaching to the outside and attaching myself to someone or something outside of myself. In Buddhism, it was called 'grasping.' It was also know as 'the hungry ghost.' In psychology, the movement was called enmeshment.

Everything in me ached. For me, internal transformation was a painstaking process. I was like an alcoholic coming off booze. The urge to return to the pattern of dysfunction was massive. For months, I felt tremendous guilt at leaving Nadia. As I breathed with the guilt, it gradually transformed into anger.

I was angry at Beatrice. I was angry at God. I was angry at Nadia. I was angry at my soul. I had worked so hard and been such a good, good student of this Buddhist teaching. Where were my rewards? Was this all I deserved? A broken marriage? A failed writing career? Bankrupt and living like a college student in a loft for Christ's sake? What the hell was this about? If this was what it meant to be enlightened, then I wanted no part of it.

It took all of her skill for Beatrice to keep me from just bolting completely out of therapy and out of our spiritual work together. She could not guarantee that my life would be a bed of roses. But she could promise me that if I continued to practice bringing my breath to my pain that my healing would deepen.

In my heart, I knew she was correct. Coming home meant coming home to whatever energies were present inside of me. The truth was when I woke up internally, I awoke to an ocean of pain inside of me. Guilt, depression, failure, a complete sense of loss of control, sadness, fear and anxiety. There was nowhere to go to escape it. I had to learn to love all of this or I would die again.

"The pain comes from our own resistance," Beatrice reminded me. "I want you to soften even more toward these feelings. Invite them into your dinner table to feast with you. Let them have a real home in you. If you feel guilty, relax and let yourself feel guilty."

In my work with Beatrice, I began to deeply understand that real internal transformation was not about the shoot 'em up 'Star Wars' imagery that we had all been fed in the movies. Being a spiritual warrior had nothing to do with building up my armor and strengthening my shields. It was exactly the opposite. Deep internal transformation would occur because of the very mundane act of sitting and bringing my breath to my own pain in any moment of time. As usual, my surrounding environment provided me with exactly what my soul needed to deepen its healing growth.

I was living in the loft of a one-bedroom apartment controlled by an amiable anal-retentive Southerner. Quentin Beauregard III had a soft heart in some areas but he was also capable of extreme vitriol if someone disagreed with him when he was drinking or when his arthritis was paining him. In my world at that moment, Quentin was the smiling

Nazi from one of my nightmares, which arose during my incest therapy a couple years before. Now that I was actively living with this energy, I could focus on bringing my breath to it. This would actually heal that same energy inside of myself.

Instead of fighting the environment I was living in, I worked daily to relax and to accept it as a gift from my soul. I knew that this and this alone would allow the painful energies to transform into Love.

In January, I got called to work on 'One Fine Day,' starring Michelle Pfeiffer and a burgeoning young television star named George Clooney. It sounded like fun. I would be working with some of the men I had worked with before. I accepted immediately. I found out later that there was another reason for me to be on this particular film. The film would shoot primarily in Los Angeles. Then it would go to New York for three weeks. My heart stopped when I heard the name of a New York crewmember—Sally Murray.

So I would have to face this one again. The only woman I had ever proposed to. Why was I so ashamed to fall in love with a woman who would not love me back? What was that about? Intellectually, I could hypothesize until the cows came home. The truth was every time I heard Sally's name, my heart ached. It just ached.

My first encounter with Sally occurred on a very rainy afternoon in February when I ran up the Production Office stairs, fully expecting to see Angie sitting at her desk as I was shaking my coat out. And there she was. Angie sitting at her desk.

Then suddenly my entire field of vision collapsed and a new reality presented itself. It was not Angie sitting at her desk. It was Sally Murray standing at Angie's desk and talking on the phone. Angie was nowhere to be seen.

I was so shocked that my body involuntarily leapt a foot backwards while my head shook back and forth with such a ferocity of disbelief that I could hear my skin slapping against my teeth as my arms flew up protectively around my head.

Sally looked like a little girl. Her face was scrunched up as she held the phone to her ear and mouthed the word 'hello' to me. I stared at her in shock. She turned her back to me. I paused for a moment then I angrily decided that I was not going to wait around for her. I stomped down to the payroll department and dropped off my paperwork. My blood raced with a general sense of anxiety. When I stepped back into the hallway, Sally had disappeared.

I was intrigued by what had transpired. It was the first time I had ever been so conscious of seeing that my visual field was actually made up of my expectations. The reality was so radically different from my expectation that the field blew up in front of me. It just dropped and a whole new image was there.

When I returned to the Production office that evening, a similar event occurred. There was a table filled with in-boxes, call sheets and other reports outside the Production Office. Sally's temporary desk was directly across from that table. Sally was on the phone. My body stopped. I had to put a cost report for the Production Designer in his in-box. I could not go home without delivering that report.

I stayed back in my breath as I walked to the table. My back was to Sally. I could hear her voice as she talked on the phone. I put the cost report in the envelope. I could not move. My mind told me to at least pretend like I was looking at papers on the table otherwise I would look like an idiot. My hands fumbled with some of the papers. My heart was melting inside my body. I could not stay angry with this woman. I could feel the energy all around me softening. I slowly turned around. Sally was sitting in the corner. A white light surrounded her. She gazed at me with such deep love in her eyes. I could feel the love emanating from deep within my own heart. It was as if we were sharing a mystical moment together in another dimension.

And then the world returned. I turned back to the table. As I turned to leave, Sally was sitting in an unlit chair next to her desk. She did not look at me as I left. I heard her telling the caller that she would be leaving for New York the next day.

I did not see her again for the duration of the show.

When I remembered the moment later that evening, I realized that the Sally illuminated in the light of Love was sitting in a different corner than the Sally talking on the phone. Was I projecting these images in some form of anxiety driven hallucination? Or was it my own soul smiling at me, saying 'I love you even when you are in tremendous pain. I love you even when she cannot.' Or was I actually connecting with Sally on a much deeper soul level, that place where heart transmissions were sent and received with the ease of a deeply felt sigh. I did not know how to rationally explain the experience. I only knew that I had that experience.

* * *

During the shoot, my father called me and invited me to spend a Sunday with him at the Pomona Computer Fair. I sat deeply with that one. It was too soon to trust him. He was still capable of being a heartless asshole. I decided that it would be a good experience for me to stay present with his energy so that I could know that I had changed. The day went by without mishap. But the next morning, I awoke with an abscessed tooth. I learned from the periodontist that an abscess was like a boil inside my mouth.

Fascinating. I had just spent the day practicing mindfulness while I was with my father. Was my mouth releasing the anger and fear that it had stored when he shoved his penis in my mouth when I was five years old?

It reminded me of the boil I had gotten under my arm when I was seeing Dad at the Vista family therapy group. I also remembered Nadia telling me that on an emotional level, the teeth represented our family.

* * *

I finished work on 'One Fine Day' on April 5th. On Tuesday April 17th, I flew to Seattle to pack up as many remnants of my past as I could. When I arrived at the house, our dog Katie plodded off the front porch to greet me. Her chubby body waddled toward me, tail wagging wildly, tongue panting a smile. I was so glad to see her and to feel her love again.

Nadia answered the door. It was an awkward greeting filled with unspoken pain for both of us. The house was its usual mess. Amy, my black Great Dane/Lab climbed off the couch to greet me. As I hugged her, my heart ached with the knowledge that I would only be with her a short while.

Nadia went into the kitchen to get me a glass of water. I sat down in the rocking chair in the living room. There were two dinner trays standing next to the television set. Each tray was jammed with unopened bottles of different types of vitamins and herbs. Nadia's hypochondria had gotten worse. Nadia returned and sat on the couch in front of the windows. She glanced at the dinner trays and smiled. I had a flash of fear that I was sitting with a madwoman. I stayed in my breath. We talked briefly, trying to avoid volatile subjects.

When I finally went upstairs to begin packing up my office, Nadia sat on the couch downstairs and watched television. Amy followed me upstairs and lay down on the bed in the master bedroom where she could watch me as I worked in my office. She followed me around the house wherever I went. She was my protector.

My office looked like it had been ransacked. It was horrible. It had been eight months since we broke up. Still I could feel the rage that Nadia had poured into the room. She had torn my writing notebooks off their bookshelves on the wall and hurled them helter-skelter onto the floor. Manuscripts had been ripped apart and heaved into a huge box of trash. My heart hurt and my stomach ached. She would have killed me if I had broken up with her in that house.

I focused on the job of packing as much as I could as quickly as I could. Nadia demanded that I spend at least two months cleaning out the house. I choked. Her self-righteousness rendered me speechless. She really did not care about me at all. She had no gratitude for the monthly support checks I had sent to her. She refused to recognize any of my contributions to our family. In her mind, she had cast me as the ultimate villain and she was the manipulating victim demanding eternal and endless restitution. I prayed to God to help me get out of this place. We were both sitting on kegs of emotional dynamite. I was terrified that if I stood up to her, we would both erupt into physical violence.

My body was already erupting with a very heavy menstrual flow. My period had started a week prior to my arrival in Seattle and it showed no signs of stopping.

On Wednesday, I saw my acupuncturist, Joy. She was so sweet and gentle with me. She told me to rest and to avoid exercise and absolutely to avoid lifting anything. That would be difficult since my sole reason for being there was to pack up my life.

When I returned to the house, Nadia said she would help me carry boxes downstairs when I was ready to move them. I continued packing, determined to get my writings and my files sent home. The work seemed endless. I knew I would be able to pack up my office within a week. But the idea of trying to clean out the basement overwhelmed me.

Then as if in response to my prayer, I got a call from

Budapest. Jim Davidson, the production accountant on 'Evita,' was in Budapest wrapping up that show. 20th Century Fox wanted him to start working on a film called 'Volcano' as soon as he returned to the States. Fox had highly recommended me for the position of Construction Accountant.

My mind reeled. Everyone in Hollywood knew 'Volcano' would be hell. But compared to bleeding to death with Nadia, 'Volcano' was a genuine gift from God. This was my way out.

After four more acupuncture appointments, Joy was shocked that my period was still flowing like a freight train. She knew of an herb that could stop the flow. But she cautioned that sometimes the herb had the opposite effect. I did not know what to do. I just knew I had to get the hell out of Seattle and away from Nadia.

When I left on Tuesday, I burst into tears as I hugged Amy and Justine goodbye. I promised them that I would come back for them.

"Oh, right," Nadia intoned sarcastically.

I wanted to kill her. She was so heartless. I wrote her a check for three hundred dollars to cover the cost of mailing the boxes because I did not have time to take them to UPS. I had a feeling I was throwing the money away. But there was nothing else I could do. Nadia did not send the boxes. She claimed she spent the money on dog food.

* * *

As I dragged my beleaguered butt off the airplane and down the ramp, I saw Carl's cherubic face beaming at me from the crowded waiting area in L.A.X.

"I parked in a very special place," Carl explained as we collected my baggage. "They're filming here today. We'll get to walk past the set on our way to my car. I wanted you to feel at home."

The parking lot was jammed with studio trucks and trailers. I noticed the wardrobe trailer door was open. Suddenly I spotted a familiar face inside. This was the Bill Murray film I had worked on the previous year. They were doing re-shoots. A crewmember directed me to Bill's trailer. My elephant friend Tai was already gone for the night.

Carl and I walked over to the deluxe mobile home trailer. The lights were out. I knocked on the door and waited a moment. Then I knocked again. The door slowly opened. An old man peered out from around the door. "Is Bill in there?" I asked. The man looked scared. I immediately realized that he was under orders to not give out any information to strangers. I reached into my purse and pulled out a partially used blue pack of American Spirit cigarettes. "Could you give these to him and tell him that Roxanne just came by to say 'Hi.' He'll understand." I smiled as the man took the cigarettes, nodded and closed the door.

Carl and I walked slowly away from the trailer. Carl kept looking back. Suddenly Carl said, "The trailer door is opening!" I turned around.

Bill Murray came out of the trailer and looked around for me. Life doesn't get much better than that. I loved that guy. He had such a good heart. We talked a little bit about the reshoot. I told him I was starting work on a film called 'Volcano.' They still hadn't cast the lead. Maybe he should go up for it. It would make a great comedy—a volcano erupts in the La Brea Tar Pits. We all laughed. I silently thanked the Universe for these dear souls. What a wonderful gift to get after such a difficult time in Washington.

* * *

I began work on 'Volcano' on Wednesday April 24th. I was still bleeding heavily. By two o'clock, I was so weak, I nearly fainted. I could not will my body to stop bleeding.

Basically, I needed rest. Realizing that this could cost me my job, I went into the UPM's office and I told him the truth. I was gay and recently divorced and my period was bleeding uncontrollably. I would probably need a week to recover. He told me to go home and rest and come back when I was better. I was so shocked, I almost kissed him.

Dr. Cheri was a very attractive blonde in her early thirties. She was the first female gynecologist that I had ever seen. In my youth, I had had some very explicit sexual fantasies about female gynecologists. Consequently, I could not be sure if I was merely projecting my fantasies on this woman or if she in fact was showing more than a clinical interest in examining me. I would probably never know. She put me on birth control pills to regulate the bleeding. The bleeding slowed to half when I began the pill.

* * *

They say that God never gives you more than you can handle. I had also noticed that She tended to send in angels during the hardest times. When I returned to work, my support angel came in the form of a tall, lanky, slightly balding production accountant named Jim Davidson.

Jim swore by acupuncture. It had saved his life after a severe car accident when medical doctors had told him he would never walk again. Jim insisted that I leave work every other day at three o'clock in the afternoon to see my acupuncturist and then go straight home and rest. I will be forever grateful to God for putting that sweet man in my life right when I needed him and for making him my boss.

There was also no mistake in my universe that I was working on a film about a volcano erupting out of the La Brea Tar Pits when my body was erupting with blood. I was the volcano. My body was releasing incest energies it had been forced to hold onto during my childhood. The bleeding was also teaching me to soften even more toward myself with my breath.

But by the sixth week, I started freaking out. It felt like the bleeding would never end. The feeling of panic and drowning must have been similar to how I felt as a little girl growing up with the incest energy permeating my house day after day, month after month, year after year. It too must have felt like it would never end. How horrifying for a little child. I brought my breath to this pain in me and softened towards it.

Dr. Cheri told me that it might take several months for the bleeding to return to normal. That was unacceptable.

I told Kazu that the bleeding had to stop. He had to locate the Chinese herbs that could treat this. He looked guilty and finally confessed that he was afraid that I had polyps in my uterus. Many years before, his old girlfriend began bleeding and it would not stop. He did everything he knew to make the bleeding stop but he could not. Her gynecologist discovered she had polyps in her uterus. She had to be scraped out for the bleeding to stop. I agreed to get a sonogram. When the test came back normal, Kazu located the Chinese herbs for me.

I called Dr. Cheri to get her approval on taking the herbs with the birth control pills. She refused because she did not know what was in the herbs. When I faxed her the ingredients, she never responded. I felt completely abandoned. I would have to make my own decision about taking the herbs.

That night, I woke up at three in the morning with a deep movement of energy. I burst into tears. There was a secret inside of me that I needed to voice to my family for my body to fully heal. I had to tell my family about what happened in the bathroom when I was five years old. My body was releasing the incest on a very deep cellular level. I needed to help it by voicing that memory. I did not need to protect my parents anymore. I began writing the letter that morning.

The next day, Kazu's secretary told me that there was a medical doctor at the Chinese herb company. He told her that the herbs were not counterproductive with birth control pills. That was all the clearance I needed. I began taking the herbs as a tea. I felt immediate relief. The bleeding slowed tremendously.

When I finished writing the letter to my family, I called each one of them from the privacy of my bathroom. I explained to each one that I had been bleeding heavily for eight weeks. I had written them a letter explaining a painful childhood memory that I had kept secret. But now that my body was attempting to let it go, I needed to send them the letter. They did not even have to read it. I just needed to send it. Then the bleeding would stop. They each told me to go ahead and send the letter. They just wanted me to heal.

When I began the herbs and writing the letter, the bleeding stopped for hours at a time. On the day that I mailed the letters, I only had one spot all day. I felt a deep sense of release and exhilaration. I felt confident now that between the herbs, the birth control pills and the acupuncture, I would be fine. I knew in my heart that sending the letters was instrumental in this physical healing. Kazu agreed that I could cut down to one session a week.

The timing was impeccable. The bleeding came under control right when my office moved to a trailer in the McDonnell/Douglas parking lot in Torrance. We would build a quarter mile long stretch of Wilshire Boulevard from Fairfax to Curson at eighty percent to scale in that parking lot. According to the Construction Coordinator, this would be the largest outdoor set in the history of Hollywood. And it would even include a replication of the La Brea Tar Pits. The original sixteen-week build schedule was gradually eaten down to twelve weeks because we were racing

'Dante's Peak' to the box office. I began working six and seven days a week. The crew size mushroomed to three hundred and fifty. We were a literal army trying to build the pyramids and the pharaohs kept pushing up the finish date.

By August 19th, the Wilshire Boulevard set was near completion. The Company would begin shooting there in a few days. Other crewmembers were inviting their families out to see this amazing accomplishment. My mother and sister had already been out to visit during the build. The only one who had not seen it was my father. My heart nudged me to call him.

I argued with myself. Did I really want to subject myself to his heartless criticisms at this point in my life? On the other hand, if we ever did heal our relationship, I would regret not having shared this with him. I would certainly never work on another film like this again. It was a once in a lifetime experience. My heart told me that I was capable of sharing this with my father without needing his validation. I invited him to come out for lunch on Wednesday.

"So this is what you do for a living?" he asked. I had been working in show business for seventeen years and my father had no idea what the hell I did for a living. Amazing. He watched as greens men in crane buckets were lifted twenty feet into the air to put prongs on the tops of palm trees. "And I thought only God could make a tree," Dad joked. He was awestruck. The size of the set was overwhelming. People got lost on that set. I introduced him to my crew in the Construction trailer.

Then we went to lunch at Millie's Restaurant. At the end of lunch, he said "Well, I better get you back. I don't want you to get in trouble with your boss."

I smiled. "You remember those people I introduced you to, Dad? They work for me. I'm their boss."

His eyes got wide. "Oh." He drove me back to the set.

Before I got out of the car, my father turned to me and said, "I'm proud of you."

I wanted to cry. Regardless of how much abuse he had heaped on me growing up, he was still my father. I had not realized how much it meant to me that he was proud of me until the words actually came out of his mouth. In that moment, I realized that for my entire life, I never thought I mattered to him and in my rage at that, I had decided that he did not matter to me. Neither idea was true. When all the pain stripped away, we did matter to one another. We just did not know what to do with that idea yet.

* * *

By the end of 1996, I knew that sooner or later, I would have to start dating again. On November 9th, I bravely went to Girl Bar alone. I had never been to Girl Bar. It was packed full of the most mouth-wateringly beautiful women I had ever seen in one place before. This was definitely not the Palms. There were even Go-Go Dancers gyrating on top of the bars. I wasn't sure if I should be offended or titillated. I was both.

I quickly learned that God had a sense of humor because the first woman to talk to me looked like my sister and her name was Nadia. There was no way that I could date her. I chatted with a variety of women throughout the evening and I went home with three phone numbers. But I was too scared to call any of them.

My first official attempt at a date began on November 24th. Quentin and I walked up to the House of Blues for a special Girl Bar event. Quentin moved through the crowd with the grace and skill of a professional schmoozer. He introduced me to some gay guys. They introduced me to some lesbians. Of course, I was attracted to a woman who was already involved. Then another woman named Lucille came over to me. We began talking. I couldn't hear her over all the noise and I was getting tired. So I invited her to dinner, thinking that at least then we could have a conversation without shouting. Her eyes got big. She wanted me to take her to The Ivy. My stomach dropped. Quentin told me later that Lucille was a gold digger. The Ivy was one of the most expensive chichi restaurants in town.

Gold digger or not, Lucille would be my first official date in ten years. I needed the practice. We met at Cafe Med on Sunset on Friday night.

Lucille was an attractive forty-three year old blonde from Defiance, Ohio. And defiant she was. Lucille thought Life sucked and that people were horrible. She wanted to start a business with chic, expensive items for dogs—like exotic dog biscuits priced at twenty dollars apiece. She thought she could make millions by playing on the eccentricities of the Beverly Hills set. Her lover had dumped her, giving her the twenty-five thousand dollar Ford Explorer but disconnecting her mobile phone. The nerve! When Lucille finally asked me a question about me, I began to recount my woes with Nadia. As I chattered away, I noticed Lucille eyeing different women entering the restaurant. She was not listening to me at all. And I was obviously not over Nadia.

On December 9th, I took my new gay friend Vincent to the cast and crew screening of "One Fine Day." I was very glad to see everyone I knew again. Vincent kept looking around to see if George Clooney was in the audience. George was a little late but he actually came. I loved George. He was such a regular guy. He had probably already seen the film numerous times because of the Premiere and publicity junkets. But he understood how important it was to the whole crew to be able to see the film together with the cast. We were all a family and we all created this baby together.

Michael Hoffman, the director, stood at the front of the room and congratulated all of us on the wonderful job we all did. He told us that this was one of the best-edited films he had ever seen. The scenes shot in Los Angeles were indistinguishable from the scenes shot in New York. "As a matter of fact, after one of the New York screenings, I heard two New Yorkers arguing over where a particular street was located in the city. I didn't have the heart to tell them that that street was actually shot in Los Angeles. That's how good this film is. You all did an incredible job. And the New York team did as well. As a matter of fact, we are honored to have a member of that team in the audience tonight. Sally Murray."

My heart stopped. Oh, my God, I thought. What's she doing here?! This is my town. She's supposed to be in New York. I scanned the audience to see where she was sitting. Then I spotted her sitting next to a well made-up blonde. A small pang of jealousy shot through me.

But the film was so wonderful that I even forgot that Sally was in the audience. Afterwards, I jumped up to go. I wanted to get the hell out of there before Sally could see me and reject me again. Then I realized that I couldn't find my umbrella. Vincent and I searched under the seats and finally located it. I raced to get out of the theatre. As we dashed out onto the street, I spotted George Clooney walking away from the crowd. "George!" I screamed loudly. He stopped and turned. I ran after him like a sex-crazed teenager. Running up to him, I threw my arms around him and pressed my ample bosom into the hardness of his chest. I don't know exactly why I was acting like this but I was distinctly aware that part of me hoped that Sally would see this and get jealous.

George seemed a bit surprised but was very polite. The director finally rescued him from Vincent and me. I knew I was acting out because of Sally. I relaxed back into my breath. We headed for my car.

Vincent needed to go to the bathroom. As I waited in the garden area of a dimly lit building, I lit a cigarette and wondered why Sally had shown up in my life again. She had every right to attend the screening. But I felt like there was unfinished business between us. Vincent returned.

As we stepped back onto the street, two women walked toward the car parked in front of us. It was Sally. I took a breath.

"Hi," she said to me, breaking the silence between us.

"Hi," I replied as my body walked past hers.

"The movie was good," she said.

I kept walking. "It looked great," I said. She was standing at the driver's door to her car. Realizing I was running away, I stopped and stayed. "This is my friend Vincent," I said.

"Hi, Vincent."

"Hi, Sally."

"This is Jennifer," she said.

I could see Jennifer. She was the attractive blonde from the theatre. I looked at Sally. But I could not see her face. There were two black rectangular boxes that covered her eyes. I knew this was some kind of internal reaction inside of me. I looked at Jennifer. No rectangles. Just eyes. Back to Sally. No eyes. Just black boxes. Mmn. Interesting. Guess I'm really mad at her. We said goodbye. Vincent and I got into my car.

Vincent turned to me. "God, now I know why you feel so strongly about Sally. She's hot."

"Yeah," I intoned. "She's hot."

"I would say that she's definitely gay," Vincent continued. "And I can see why you think she likes you. Did you see the way she was looking at you?"

I sighed deeply. "No, actually, I couldn't," I replied. "Whenever I looked at her face, I could only see black boxes in front of her eyes. I couldn't see how she was looking at me."

"Well," Vincent rolled his eyes, "she was looking at *you!*"

I sighed again. I will never understand Life. "Well, at least I know I'm not crazy and imagining it."

"Oh, no," Vincent chuckled. "She really likes you!"

"I wish she knew that."

The next day, I made an appointment with Beatrice. Between the fiasco date with Lucille and then seeing Sally again, I realized that on a soul level, I needed to forgive my mother. I understood that that would take some time. But I needed to begin focusing on that part of my healing. I wanted to have a healthy sexual relationship with another woman. I had broken the pattern of enmeshment with my mother by leaving Nadia. I hoped that by forgiving my mother on a deep emotional level, it would free me from pulling in the same type of partner in the future.

I had a session with Beatrice on Monday December 16th. A very intense pain arose in me regarding my mother. "She's not coming," I told Beatrice. The feeling was one of being stranded, lost and forlorn, waiting for my mother to turn around and join me. "She's not coming," I repeated. The same was true with Nadia. She's not coming either. Why? Why weren't they coming?

Beatrice explained to me that it was okay that my mother was not coming. We were still connected in the larger fabric of Love. This separation would allow my soul to come into me with love for all this pain.

I stayed in my breath. The pure energy of the pain was amazing. "She's not coming."

There was something profoundly deep and spiritual in that aloneness. That pain was my own lost inner child calling for her mother to come home. My greatest responsibility in my life was to answer that call and be the healthy mother that she had never had.

* * *

By the end of the year, a deep desire arose within me. I

needed to get my own apartment. It was time to be completely independent again. In February I began working on a film called "Primary Colors" starring John Travolta and Emma Thompson. I did not care about John. I wanted to meet Emma.

On March 1, 1997, I moved into my own bachelorette apartment. Freedom. What a luxurious word. It took about two months for my body to relax from the unconscious expectation that at any moment, my roommate would be walking through the door.

In my therapy, I was dealing with individuating and all that that entailed. Of course, my family patterns were activated at work so I had plenty of live energy to breath with. Crazy Alice, belligerent Fred and dysfunctional Susan were dancing around in the guise of my co-workers. But something else was afoot in the Universe. The deeper patterns of the collective unconscious were beginning to dissolve.

On April 30, 1997, I was sitting with a packed house full of lesbians at the Sports Connection when the character Ellen Morgan came out on prime time television. For lesbians everywhere, this was a bona fide miracle. Every lesbian in America watched that show. Laura Dern was magnificent as the lesbian catalyst. It gave hope to all lesbian and gay Americans that a door to equality had been soundly opened.

Two days later, on Friday May 2nd, I attended the cast and crew bonding barbeque for "Primary Colors" where I actually ran into Laura Dern. I gasped audibly. She wasn't in the cast. What was she doing here? My body immediately moved towards her. Laura had stopped to talk with someone.

I walked up to the duo and stood quietly, waiting for an appropriate moment to express my thanks to Laura. The two women talked at length. As I stood waiting, I gradually became aware that the woman Laura was talking to was none other than Emma Thompson.

Oh, God, I thought. It's Emma. Whatever shall I say? I knew exactly what to say to Laura Dern. But whenever I thought of talking to Emma, I was completely blank. So I did the only thing possible, I relaxed back into my breath and trusted that being blank was a good thing. As I stayed in my breath, I noticed that Laura's energy was nice but tight; the kind of tension that occurs when one is in their early thirties. I shifted my attention to Emma. She was an ocean, deep and mysterious. I wanted to swim in that ocean.

When the two women stopped talking, I stepped forward slightly and spoke to Laura. "I just had to tell you how much I enjoyed your performance on television the other night." I spoke quietly, not wishing to draw attention to my words.

Laura looked blank.

"On 'Ellen,'" I added softly.

I saw an actual ripple of energy in the field around the three of us, as if my words had sent a shiver through the invisible fabric of Love connecting all of us. Laura's face tensed, blanching a bit. Emma's eyes widened. They both looked shocked.

"You were just wonderful," I said.

"Thank you," Laura squeaked as she shook my hand.

Turning to Emma, I took a deep breath. "And you," my voice deepened reverentially, "my God, . . . you're . . . Emma." I said it with awe and bravado.

She bowed deeply, with great humility.

I extended my hand. She took it with genuine affection. I asked if she gave out autographed pictures. She smiled and told me that she would arrange to get one for me.

That was my first meeting with Emma.

My next encounter with Emma took place on June 30th. I was racing from Stage 27 to the Production Office when I heard my name called out urgently. I stopped and saw Emma's assistant Michael waving to me.

"Roxanne, Roxanne! Now would be the perfect time to get that autographed picture!"

I turned around immediately. He escorted me inside Emma's trailer. She was sitting at a table by the window. I managed to extricate myself from the hanging beads in the doorway. My body moved towards her instantly.

"Emma!" I cried like a long lost lover. "Do you remember me?"

"Roxanne," her sultry voice intoned as she pulled her magnificent body up to its full stature. "Of course I remember you," her British accent rolled down my spine as she quoted part of our previous conversation at the barbeque. "You said 'You shall never see me again.'" Her eyes twinkled as her voice dropped sexily. "And you looked *so sad*."

I blushed instantly and stared at my shoes. "Yes. I did," I replied shyly, embarrassed and exhilarated by her sexual tone.

We began talking about the film. She signed a very nice 3x5 color photo of her with one of her two Oscars. At some point, Emma asked me if the film was being good to me. My mind short-circuited on how to reply. Then suddenly I heard myself telling her how unfair it was that Construction was not allowed to eat off the catering truck. While it was common practice to not allow Construction to have lunch, Construction was always allowed to have breakfast. But not on this show. I told her that I had never felt so excluded on a film in my entire life.

Emma was wonderful. She told me that no one should feel that way. As we left the trailer for her to go to the set, I told her that the reason I wanted to be on this film was to get to see her.

Emma turned to me outside her trailer. She spoke loudly. "Come over for tea anytime." Her voice dropped seductively. "Just knock on the door." She put her right hand up in the air and knocked on an imaginary door. Her energy was quite playful and flirtatious.

I was so shocked and unsure of my own perceptions that I blurted out incredulously "Are you sure?"

She stared me right in the eyes. Her voice was low and sexy. "Quite."

A rush of sexual energy washed through me. "Oh. Okay." I smiled. My head nodded once. I floated off and remained in complete euphoria for the remainder of the week. Emma Thompson had invited me to tea.

When I went to my next session with Beatrice, I thought that we would spend the session discussing my feelings about Emma. But when I sat down in my seat, I realized that an energy of anger had arisen inside of me and there was no logical reason for me to be angry with Beatrice.

Beatrice was very happy to hear that. She then explained that in Buddhism, there were three states of being that we all move in and out of—aversion, grasping and ignorance. In psychology, it was termed avoidance, enmeshment and delusion.

I was able to work very actively with my own energy of aversion. Anger accompanied aversion. As I sat with my anger, I noticed a distinct feeling that I was bad and that I was being punished.

That was just part of that state, Beatrice explained. She told me to soften even more towards these feelings.

I could feel that there was a lot of power in this state. It was pretty scary.

"Yes," Beatrice confirmed. "This is where the nuclear arsenal is kept. When we can't just stay with this energy, we become it and we go off to war, thinking it's the only choice we have and we sincerely believe that we have the right to destroy other things when we are in that state."

I asked about grasping.

"That's the energy that says, 'This is it! This will save me!' or 'Gee, if I could just have that, I know I'd be okay!'" Beatrice used her hand like a hand puppet, making it into a gooseneck with an open mouth. "In Buddhism, there is an image of a person with a distended stomach, like a Biafra baby, and a mouth that is so small, a single grain of rice can't fit into it. The pain of grasping is horrible. You honestly think if you can just get enough to eat, you will be satisfied. But you can't eat anything; you just chase after people, ideas, objects, circumstances and are never fed." Ignorance was just another word for denial or keeping a bag over your head to feel safe. Beatrice suggested that I begin a series of sessions at this point since the energies were coming up so intensely.

* * *

On Monday morning, I took a decorative purple bag containing tea and biscuits and a card for Emma and secreted it beneath my desk at work. After going through twelve unsuccessful drafts of my cost report, I finally surrendered to the reality that I could not do anything until I delivered that bag to Emma.

I walked discreetly over to her trailer and knocked on her door. There was no answer. Then I noticed the worn strip of masking tape just below the doorknob. There was a message written in faded blue ink. "Knock and enter. Nude actress inside." I coughed slightly. Really. I rather liked that. I knocked again then walked inside.

Emma was nowhere to be seen. I left the bag on her desk by the window. A deep feeling of sadness filled me. My last chance to see Emma and she wasn't there. I chose to embrace my feeling rather than abandon it. I found refuge on a deserted set where I sat down and cried a little. I was just very sad. I told myself that I would let myself cry more when I got home. In the meantime, I had to finish the cost report. I returned to my desk and immersed myself in work.

It was mayhem until four o'clock. Suddenly I stopped my work. My body rose from the desk. I realized I was going to the set. Emma could be there. I walked up to Stage 23. The heat had not subsided. I waited outside the stage until the flashing red lights had turned off. Then I entered with some other people. I allowed my eyes to adjust to the darkness. Emma was not on set. I wandered over to a group of chairs occupied by extras. I watched as the crew was setting up the Control Booth for the next shot. I consciously stayed in my breath.

"Roxanne."

My body turned toward the voice. My eyes adjusted then widened to the sight of Emma approaching me. She was in full make-up, smiling seductively at me. I grinned.

"Emma."

"You brought me biscuits." Her voice was lilting, like a flattered schoolgirl.

"It was so sweet of you to open the door," I began. I instantly felt something in her energy that silenced me, a demand for privacy perhaps; I was not sure. She hugged me. We stepped apart. She stared at me and said again,

"You brought me biscuits."

The timbre of her voice told me that she'd read the note. It was a thinly veiled love note. I knew she was divorced but I was unsure if she was single. I felt exposed and shy.

"Yes," I mumbled, feeling myself tighten inside, suddenly uncertain. How was she going to respond to the note?

"I was just writing you a note," she said.

"Oh."

"I'd been looking for chocolate everywhere," she continued in a relaxed tone. "Some people had brought Mike Nichols a whole box of chocolates that he had in his trailer. I was figuring on filching the entire box when I got your biscuits. Instead, I tossed back a couple of fingers. That did the trick."

I smiled and nodded. I was quite overwhelmed and

completely speechless. I kept breathing, I felt painfully shy. The Company bustled all around us.

Emma stood with me for a moment, then walked over to the chairs in the director's circle and placed a sweater on one. I fully expected her to stay there. Instead, she returned to my side. I tried to think of something intelligent to say. I felt like an awkward teenager on a first date. I kept expecting her to leave and talk to someone else. She could easily have done so. Instead, she stayed at my side for at least five minutes while the shot was being set up.

"1st Team on set!" the First Assistant Director shouted. That meant Emma.

As she left, she stepped close to me, discreetly placed her hand under my right forearm and squeezed my arm tightly. Then she walked directly up the stairs to the set. I stood motionless, breathing, aware of my numbness, not knowing what her touch meant.

I watched her for a while then the crew filled in the Control Booth area and blocked my view. I moved toward a video playback screen in the Director's area, taking care to stay back and out of the way.

Mike Nichols sat in a chair in front of the video screen. Elaine May sat next to him, discussing the script notes. John Travolta was sitting next to Geraldo Rivera on the Audience Set. Robert Klein and Billy Bob Thorton were in the Control Booth with Emma. Michael Baulhaus was the Cinematographer. Ann Roth perused her costumes. I breathed it all in. You are witnessing genius, I told myself. The magnitude of talent on this film was unmatched in my experience. I let the energy nourish me. There was a greater force at work here.

Other people were moving around the Director's circle. After a few minutes, Mr. Nichols requested that everyone clear out. He needed space. We all fled like terrified children.

When I returned to the Construction trailer, I sat down

at my desk. I was alone in the office. I focused on my breath. A very distinct energy rose up from way down deep inside of me. It rolled through my toes, up my legs, through my stomach and lungs, up my neck and formed my face and lips into a big smile. I felt like a happy Buddha baby.

"She liked the biscuits."

* * *

My session with Beatrice on Saturday was a continuation of our work the previous week. Emma was not an issue. We were working on much deeper levels of energy.

Wednesday was the last day of shooting. The Company was at the Disney Ranch filming the Church set. I drove out to take pictures and to have lunch. It would be my last time to see Emma. I had wrapped up a box of chocolate-covered biscuits in tissue paper and red ribbon and taped my business card on top with a message telling her that she was always welcome for tea and biscuits in my home.

At some point in the morning, I had a deep realization. I was sitting at my desk, staring out my door to the sunlight hitting the gray wall of Stage 27. I became conscious of my breath and the thoughts whirling around my mind. The thoughts were about Emma—what would I say, what would she say. That one had more fear in it for me. I breathed with it. Then suddenly, I realized that it really did not matter what she said. That even if she hated me, I would not die; I was not bad. The point of this entire exercise was for me to have an experience of being able to be just who and how I was in the present and to allow the present to be the present. That was what self-love was all about—trusting my soul in each present moment.

When I drove out to the Disney Ranch, I was in such a state of inner peace and self-acceptance that magic happened. When I entered Emma's trailer and discovered her boyfriend

Greg Wise nervously smoking a cigarette, I could feel a very solid pattern of sexual energy that was stuck in the room. Everything felt dead. Emma came out of the bathroom. I stayed in my breath and let my soul dance through me as I talked with Emma and Greg. We discussed the mundane issues of the shoot. I stayed in my breath, waiting for some internal clue on when to leave and what to say.

As I began to leave, a deep energy arose within me, stopping me, causing me to turn back to Emma. It was then that my love for her came forward intensely as I shamelessly flirted with her in front of Greg. She did not reprimand me. Greg did not punch me in the face. In fact, three months later, Emma gave an Emmy Award winning performance on "Ellen" where Emma played herself as a closeted lesbian. The synchronicity was remarkable.

What I learned with my experience with Emma was that when I truly trusted my inner voice and allowed my soul to just come through me, no one ever got hurt; and, if there were energy that was stuck, that energy would transform into freedom. I could stand in front of one of the greatest actresses of our time and bare my soul without shame and no one was harmed. In fact, when Greg and Emma came out of their trailer that hot July afternoon, they both smiled at me with such brilliance that it was as if Heaven itself were shining through them to me.

That night I woke myself up at three in the morning, moaning the way I would in a nightmare. But this was not a nightmare dream. It was a lucid dream. In it, there was an angry man staring at me. He was big and burly, frightening in his stature. I walked straight up to him to confront him. Then I realized he wasn't real. Physically he was real but he wasn't alive. I even pulled the bottom lid of his left eye down and out to see if he was real. It was very odd. That was when I woke up. I realized that my greatest fear inside of me wasn't even real. It signaled very deep self-integration.

Two weeks later, I was sitting in meditation when suddenly the entire scene of Emma coming out of her trailer played out inside of me. I watched it, using my breath to support me. Suddenly I had an awakening.

"Oh, my God," I said out loud. "She wasn't leaving. I was!" The truth was right there inside of me. Emma was smiling at me. She was beaming. The love of God was radiating through her. I was the one closing down internally. I was the one who was leaving.

"Good grief," I muttered. "This is major. I've got to tell Beatrice. This really isn't even about Emma. This is about my relationship with God."

In the movement of aversion, it felt as if I was being abandoned by someone outside of me. I thought God had abandoned me. But the greater truth was that I had just closed down like an open flower closing in the face of darkness. God had not abandoned the flower. The flower was not being punished. Darkness was just another face of the Divine. It was just another energy. It had nothing to do with my self-worth or value. So that hideous pain that came with rejection was not something outside of me. It was just me scrunching down inside.

I wrote it all down then dashed off to work. It was my last week with the show. Two days later, Vincent and I decided to walk down to Hoy Wok's on Santa Monica for dinner. On the way back home, an extraordinary synchronicity occurred. I ran into Nadia's ex-boyfriend Cliff. I had not seen him in six years. He told me that Nadia had been living with her old friend Arnold for quite awhile now and that they were buying land together. They were very much in love.

My body involuntarily leapt backwards. My arms flew up into the air in sheer glee and I screamed out "I'm free!"

"You have always been free," Beatrice chided me when I recounted the entire story in our Saturday session.

That was true. We were all free souls. But we were also

trapped in delusions, bound by magnetic forces we could not see or comprehend. Dysfunctional patterns of behavior were made up of actual magnetic energy that dissolved when you brought your breath to it. The emotional bonds that tied us were just as real as barbed wire or handcuffs enslaving us to habitually repeat the patterns over and over again.

* * *

On August 30, 1997, Princess Diana died in a horrible car crash and the power structure of England changed over night. On a deep spiritual level and on a mass cultural level, a habitual pattern of victimization was broken for all of us. Diana had been perceived as the victim of the Royals for years. But in her death, all of England rebelled and threatened to overthrow the monarchy if the Queen did not acknowledge the Princess of Hearts. When the Queen Mother stood on the streets with the common man and bowed her head as Diana's coffin passed the Palace, an archetypal transformation occurred. It was no mistake that Mother Teresa died within a few days of Diana. The beautiful Princess and the Old Crone—two profound feminine archetypes had returned to the Void.

The following Saturday, I experienced my own power change. My mother spent the day and night at my apartment. She had never come to visit me. I only needed one therapy session in the middle of the day to make it through the entire experience unscathed. I deliberately directed the conversations with my mother away from volatile issues.

By late in the evening, Mom began spinning her reconstructed version of the family history. According to Mom, she was responsible for the healing in the family. Anger rose up in me. I stayed in my breath. She talked none stop for half an hour. Finally, I cut her off. I was polite but firm. I told her that my recollection was different than hers. I told her it was my twenty-three-page letter to Lucy that set off the chain of healing in the family.

Mom said "Oh, yes... That's right. You were the one who made it happen. You were responsible for the change." But her voice sounded wispy and delusional. I doubted that she would even remember saying that.

Beatrice told me that by directly contradicting my mother, I had faced the worst thing I would ever have to face in my life. I did not have to be afraid of it anymore. That was not very real to me at that point. But I realized that I had made a huge step. I also realized that I would have to do this over and over to integrate it more fully

* * *

During one of my sittings in December, I had a most bizarre experience. I could feel energy rising in my solar plexus. As usual, I stayed in my breath and let it do whatever it was going to do. The energy intensified. Then suddenly, Santa and his reindeer came flying out of my solar plexus and headed for the North Pole! There was nothing I could do but laugh. It made no logical sense to me at all. But I was willing to accept the experience as valuable without trying to make it something it wasn't.

Two weeks later, the Construction Coordinator of a film called "Jack Frost" called me to see if I would be available to work on the show. "It could become a Christmas classic," the coordinator told me. When I recalled my Santa Claus meditation experience, I knew that this really was the show I was supposed to be on.

1998 would be the year in which I dealt with healing deep patterns relating to my father. It would also be the year when the President of the United States would be impeached and nearly thrown out of office for getting a blowjob from a White House intern.

I had to sit with deeply painful energies inside of me that dealt specifically with breaking the law and for making mistakes. I broke the law when I accidentally ran a camera light as it turned from yellow to red. The camera light ticket brought up the part of me that refused to see that I broke the law. It fed immediately into the 'I'm bad' energy. It was horribly painful to sit with this energy.

But Beatrice made me. She just kept saying 'You broke the law.' She said it politely and told me that I was not bad. But no matter what justification I gave her, she responded with 'You broke the law. You're not bad. You're not evil. You just broke the law. You're okay.' She told me to say that in my sitting exercises. It would bring up deeper levels of pain regarding my own victimization that I needed to address.

Just when I thought I had everything under control at work, the I-9 accounting crisis occurred. It began with a heart-felt phone call from a twenty-something Assistant Production Office Coordinator explaining to me that all of my I-9s were wrong. They would have to be redone.

For some reason, this information rocked me to my core. In my inner world, it translated as 'For the last twenty years, you have been doing this wrong!' I believe that on a deep spiritual level, I was actually awakening to the reality that I had been living lifetime after lifetime after lifetime in a state of complete delusion. In that regard, I had victimized myself. There was no one to blame but me. My brain short-circuited and a deep painful rage emerged.

Beatrice gave me another exercise to do to work with this energy. "I make mistakes. I'm okay," she said as she demonstrated rocking back and forth in her chair. "Get really soft with this energy and say that. I make mistakes. I'm okay."

That was very transformational for me. Whenever I sat with that energy, I could feel the rage within me diminish. The rage reminded me of how my father's voice sounded when he was mad.

Those two issues held extremely deep pain for me. I had always tried so hard to be good. I had a very solid part of me that did not want to admit that I made mistakes. But by bringing me experiences that stimulated these painful parts of me, my soul was preparing me for much deeper transformation. I had to love the criminal in me before I could forgive my father for his criminal behavior.

* * *

My father called me towards the end of the shoot. He and Ruth had recently driven past our old house on Canzonet. He had driven past that house many times over the last twenty years and he had never had this reaction. "I pulled over to the side of the road and parked," my father told me. "As I looked at that house, I felt so sad. There was so much pain in that house. All I could do was cry."

I was shocked at the depth of my father's sensitivity.

"We've been having some family meetings with Tom recently," Dad told me. "I wanted to know if you would be willing to come into some of them when you finish your movie. We would like to talk about the letters you wrote. Those are the only things left that haven't been addressed."

I instantly agreed. The openness of my father's heart told me that this was very important to both of us. I would begin attending in the middle of August.

To prepare for this session, I reread my letters. I was deeply and profoundly shocked by the angry letter I had written in 1991. It was not what I remembered it to be. My perspective had changed. Did that mean that my memories were false and imaginary? No, Beatrice assured me. In 1991, I was in a lot more pain than I was now. Of course my perceptions were distorted. As I integrated my pain, my perception widened to include a larger truth—that for a child, there were no differences between the physical act of sexual incest, the physical invasiveness of uncontrolled adult sexual energies, and the experience of penetrating energy in emotional incest. For a child, they were the same. That understanding freed me from the trap of habitually needing physical evidence to prove the abuse had occurred and in needing my family's agreement on the details of my childhood. I trusted my inner soul to show me the truth.

* * *

My first family session with Tom took place on Tuesday August 11th at ten o'clock in the morning. My stomach was nervous on the drive down. I listened to Thich Nhat Hahn's tape on Love. Dad, Susan and Mom were all there when I arrived. Tom explained that we would be discussing all the dead dogs, that my letter was a catalyst and that we would also discuss my book. Mom said the only reason she was there was because of me. That led into a discussion about her relationship with Susan. The session was pretty heated.

At one point, Mom looked at Susan and said, "The only thing we have in common is the children and religion." Mom dropped that bomb and continued talking.

Suddenly Susan woke up to the insult and turned to Mom and said "That makes me angry. You're saying that I'm nothing."

Mom reacted defensively denying any wrongdoing. Tom dealt directly with Mom's insistence on always being right. Mom countered by saying that she did not think she would be coming back. I told Mom that I hoped she would come back. I deeply wanted to have a real relationship with her, not the superficial puppet relationship that we currently had. Mom said she wanted a real relationship too. But she would not make a commitment to the therapeutic process.

When Mom did not return to the sessions, Tom explained

that Alice was a classic narcissist. She refused to allow herself to be seen in a bad light. Tom was pretty hard nosed about it. In my heart, I understood that my mother was unable to stay, that the pain she experienced was very real and that she did not have the skills to sit with that pain.

In the meantime, Susan and Mom had another huge fight that nearly came to physical blows. It scared both of them so badly that Mom found a female therapist and made an emergency session for both of them. Susan told me that in that session Mom told the therapist "Roxanne had a happy childhood. She just can't remember that." Susan and I had a good laugh at that one.

On Friday, as I drove to my session with Beatrice, I noticed I was particularly impatient with other drivers. I focused on my breath. As I rounded the bend on San Vincente, a succession of thoughts arose in me.

First came an image of the family session with Tom, Mom, Dad and Susan. Susan was angrily saying to Mom "You're saying I'm nothing."

Then came Susan's statement to me of what Mom told her new therapist. "Roxanne had a happy childhood. She just can't remember it."

"She's saying I'm nothing," I said out loud. "That's what that statement really means. That I'm nothing."

"And how does it feel to be nothing, Roxanne?" I asked myself out loud.

Immediately, the image of Lenore molesting me when I was two months old arose. "Oh, my God!" I said out loud. "She was masturbating herself and she was masturbating me. She was using me like a dildoe. Oh, my God! The dream about Lenore. That wasn't Lenore!" I shouted. "That was my mother!" A deep desire to kill my mother instantly arose in me. The emotion was unmistakably powerful and alive. The term emotional incesting transformed from an intellectual concept into the vile and loathsome reality that it actually was. It was not longer cloaked in invisibility. My mother used me like a dildoe to masturbate her own ego. I meant nothing to her. I could see it with crystal clarity inside of me. It took all of my skill to stay with the feeling, park the car and run up to Beatrice's office. This was a monumental inner event.

As I told Beatrice the whole story of how I came to this realization, tears streamed easily down my face. I spoke clearly.

"I want to kill her, Beatrice. I just want to kill her. I don't care if she has a fucking psychotic break. I'm through protecting this behavior. She's used me like an emotional dildoe my entire life. I just want to kill her!" The emotion was so beautifully real, strong and unfettered by any judgments. It was the first time in my entire life when I had connected so cleanly with my anger at my mother.

"That's it," Beatrice said. "You've broken the pattern. It's over. You've done it. You're through. There's still a bit of housekeeping to do. But it's all just little pieces of rubble to be picked up. Like that dream you had of the little girl whose house had collapsed. Only now you can see that there's nothing to be afraid of. You don't have to hide from anything anymore. Good work, Roxanne. Good work."

* * *

When I tried to explain my transformational experience to Tom in the Tuesday session, he kept interrupting me. But I insisted on telling the entire story. When I finished, he looked shocked. Then, instead of congratulating me on my good work, he tried to take credit for it, claiming that he had 'lanced the wound.' I was stunned. I could not stand this man. He was too much like my mother. And that was exactly why I chose to stay in the family sessions. It did not matter if Mom was present. Tom was playing her part for me. This was a great opportunity for me to breathe with deeper levels of pain being restimulated within me.

The sessions with Tom continued for eight weeks. Each week, I would stay in my breath and respond directly to him. It was like talking to a wall. He was entrenched in his theories and could not connect with his heart. He knew how to use heart language at points—buzz words like compassion, tenderness, etc. But they were just buzz words with no real energy to back them up.

Beatrice could see how much pain I was in. She had such deep love and support for my courage as we breathed together and talked. "You are doing such a good, good job. You are healing the fabric for all of us," she told me.

I asked her to keep telling me that because there was a lot of fear in me.

After eight weeks of working with Tom, I finally reached my limit. I told him that I thought his methodology was cold-hearted and lacked compassion.

He told me that it wasn't his methodology that I was having trouble with. It was the fact that he was a man. He told me that I had never had any experience with a male authority figure who was trustworthy or tender. He was a male authority figure. He was directing us to look at certain areas of our lives. He had genuine love and caring for me as an individual. He said that he could be tough but he could also be tender. Tom recommended that I have some individual sessions so that he and I could bond together.

I wanted to puke. Tom was not my therapist and I had no need to bond with him. At that moment, I thought he was an arrogant ass who insisted on being in a position of authority because he lacked a deeper connectedness that could recognize the equality and value of all viewpoints and energies. I left the session knowing that I could not go back there.

I saw Beatrice at four o'clock on Wednesday in an emergency session. I asked her immediately if she would allow us to move the session up to her office so that I could discuss my letters with my family with her as the therapist instead of Tom.

Beatrice smiled. She told me that she would not give me an answer until our session on Friday. Instead, she wanted to focus on what had happened that brought up these feelings.

I felt like I was going to explode. "I can't go back there, Beatrice," I told her firmly. "Why not? What happens when you go there?"

"It's like I'm back in that house again," I sputtered, my jaw clenched in rage. "The house where I grew up." The raw pain that I had blocked out with such skillful finesse in childhood now reverberated in every cell of my body. I used my breath and worked with Beatrice to support these energies with unconditional love so they could finally heal.

On Friday, Beatrice told me that she could not allow us to move the therapeutic process up to her. That would only create another imbalance because Dad and Susan would feel exactly the way that I felt about them and Tom. Beatrice recommended getting a totally neutral therapist.

I knew that would not work. It would take way too long and we were at a culmination point. We had already invested eight weeks in this process.

After the session, I drove out to Ocean Park and sat in my car and smoked. I felt totally abandoned by Beatrice when I needed her the most. Logically I understood what she was saying. I knew she was right. But I also knew that it was completely wrong to continue the therapy sessions with Tom at the helm. That would be abusive to me. I never felt so alone in my life. Every direction I looked in there was simply overwhelming pain. I did the only thing I could do. I stayed in my breath and stayed with my pain, holding it in my heart, telling myself that I was not bad, that the pain was not bad either. As I sat in my breath, a powerful movement occurred: The walls of pain encasing me released.

I knew I had options. I was strong enough now to call my father and tell him the truth in my heart. I was not going to go back to Tom.

I spent another four hours at home, sitting with all of my feelings and fears. Finally, I called my father at nine o'clock. I calmly explained to him that I would not be going back to the sessions. He gasped in shock. I took a deep breath and spoke from my heart. I reminded Dad that the original reason I agreed to come to the sessions was to discuss my letters. Eight weeks had passed and we still had not discussed my letters. Dad agreed that that was too long to wait. I told him that when I wrote that letter in 1991, I was a different person. I was in tremendous pain and in tremendous anger. The letter implied that he had molested Susan and I on a regular basis for years. I told Dad that I knew now in my heart that that was not actually the case. There were instances of sexual abuse. But the energy in that house was so sexualized all the time that it felt like constant abuse.

We touched on the idea of False Memory Syndrome—the backlash movement that arose when Oprah Winfrey made incest a household word. My father had jumped on the False Memory Syndrome as his way of shirking any responsibility for my painful memories. To his credit, Tom argued that while False Memory Syndrome had validity, the syndrome itself had its roots in some form of childhood abuse. The mind did not fabricate those types of traumatic memories for no reason whatsoever.

"Are you saying that you never did anything sexual to me?" I asked my father tersely on the phone. "No, no," he cried like a little boy, "That's not what I'm saying. I—I don't want to talk about this without a therapist." I was glad to hear him squirm. To me, it meant that on some level, he did know that he had molested me.

Dad finally told me that he was worried about how I portrayed him in my book. "I'm willing to take the blame for the things that I did. Believe me, I was an asshole when you were growing up." His voice softened to that of a little boy's. "Just don't be heaping stuff on me that I didn't do."

* * *

I finally called Susan the following afternoon. She was much tougher on me than Dad had been. When I told her I would not be returning to the sessions, Susan burst into tears.

"Oh, please, don't do this to me!" she cried. "Mom always abandoned us. Please don't be like her."

I could feel her pain in me. But I was so comfortable with all of my feelings, that her pain did not hurt me because I did not resist any of my feelings. "I know it looks like I'm acting like Mom but I'm not leaving because I hate Tom. It's just time for me to go." I told her the same things that I told Dad.

Susan did not agree with me. I smiled. It was really okay with me if she did not agree. I assured her that while I had to leave the family in the past in order to survive, I was not leaving the family at all at this point. I agreed to attend one last meeting with Tom so we could all have closure.

On Monday night, I did a long sitting to prepare for the session with Tom in the morning. Deep feelings arose. I could see how much Tom's methodology was like my mother's gargantuan narcissism. I had not wanted to return to Tom because I did not want Tom to take credit for my awakening. I wanted my father to know that I had come to this place on my own and that it had taken me years of hard work to achieve this freedom and awareness. When I realized that as a child, I literally had no place in my entire world to go to escape Big Mama Alice's emotional incesting or Dad's sexually abusive energy, I sat down and wept for little Roxanne. As my heart opened deeply for my wounded inner child, I experienced internal transformation. By forgiving my little girl for being a vulnerable child who was powerless in the face of her abusive parents, I freed myself from the limitations of my own self-hatred.

After that, Tom was just a guy with an opinion.

September 29th became known as the Day of Transcendence in my family. On that day, I was more real than I had ever been in my life. For me, the meeting was very natural, filled with deep, open emotions of love and compassion, joy and exuberance. I told Tom exactly how I felt about all the sessions and why I was leaving.

The most profound moment came for me when I said to my father, "Even the 1996 letter, Dad. I don't know if what happened in the bathroom happened in the way that I remember it. I don't know if it even happened—"

He leaned towards me with such an open heart and said, "I don't know if it happened, Roxanne. The drinking, the blackouts. I just don't know." He was so open and defenseless.

"I don't know if it happened either, Dad. But even if there is a tiny possibility that it did, I want you to be able to—" I stopped as I stared into his eyes and realized that I was about to acknowledge my father's death. "I want you to be able to die with a clear conscience. Please do not carry this with you in your soul."

I did not care if anyone understood what I was saying. This sentiment came from deep in my soul and transmitted directly to my father's soul. I felt like Jesus saying to Judas 'It's okay if you betrayed me. It's part of a much bigger whole picture. I love you.' On a much deeper soul level, even the incest was an illusion, just a wave on the ocean. That understanding in no way diminished the horror of the incest or the responsibilities of my parents. That realization came from a much larger place in my soul.

As my father and I hugged one another and sobbed in relief, I felt a shackle of energy binding us in our ankles release. This was deeply significant.

When I got home that afternoon, I felt very strange. My mind felt sort of like gauzy cotton, unfocused, expanded. The idea of orgasms came up. Then I realized that this was probably how people felt when they'd won an Oscar. I called Susan and left a message for her to call me back. In the interim, I noticed some little thoughts of fear pass through, wondering if this experience was real, had anyone else felt the same thing or were Dad and Susan going to return to the way that they had been before and just sort of forget about me.

Then the news began coming in. Susan called first.

"Something happened in there today, Roxanne. We've all had meetings with Tom in the past. We've talked about things and Tom has said things and we've all cried. But today, it was different. I don't know what happened in there today, if it was something mystical or magical or what. But something dynamic was unleashed in there today."

"Yeah, it did," I said, amazed at my sister's openness. "On a very deep level. I have goose bumps."

"It's like birth," Susan said.

"It is like birth," I agreed. "We're three separate people now."

We talked longer. At the end, she said "Please thank Beatrice for all of us. Thank her for all the work she has done to help you with this. I know that God has used her as an instrument in your life and that she is a very important part of your life."

My heart felt very warm. This was a big deal for Susan to step through her Christian fears about other religions and to thank the woman who taught me Buddhist meditation and mindfulness. "Thank you, Susan. I will tell her that."

My father called me the next morning to share a letter he had written about what he experienced in that session. He was still riding a wave of ecstasy from the experience.

He had tried to explain what happened to Ruth when he had gotten home but could not find the words. But this letter managed to capture some of it. For my father, the session on September 29th was a spiritual experience with his two daughters. "In the period of one hour, it seemed that our brain chemistries fused with each others and we became 'one.'"

It was phenomenal. Both my father and my sister had had transcendent experiences when I became real. This wasn't an intellectual experience. This was real.

I called Beatrice on Wednesday and asked if we could have an hour and a half session on Friday. "A miracle happened," I cried.

Dad called me on Thursday and told me that he was continuing to have some very different experiences. Since Tuesday, when he walked around the house in the middle of the night, he had been getting the distinct feeling that a spirit was going to manifest right in front of him. "I just hope it's not the Grim Reaper," he told me. I told him he had nothing to fear even if it was the Grim Reaper. He could just go real easily on the journey to the great beyond. He did not want to go yet.

In my session with Beatrice that Friday, I told her about everything that had happened. By the end of the session, Beatrice stared at me. She leaned forward. Her eyes began to glisten. I couldn't hear what she was saying because I suddenly realized, my God, she's crying. My teacher is crying. I had never seen Beatrice cry. I jumped up and opened my arms. "Come here!" I exclaimed.

She stood up as tears came down her face.

"You have been such a good mother to me, Beatrice," I said.

"Thank you," Beatrice said quietly as she cried. "You have come through so much pain," she said loudly with such deep understanding and conviction.

My heart cracked open as I threw my arms around her

and we both just sobbed. More than anyone else, Beatrice really did know the amount of pain that I had come through. When she said that, I felt like something very deep in the fabric released and we could both just let it all go.

She looked at me. Her face was such a beautiful glistening river. "I am so proud of you," Beatrice said. "*I love you.*" She said each word with such power and commitment that they reverberated in the very marrow of my bones and I felt the earth shake nine stories beneath my feet. "You could die today and your life would have been so meaningful. You have changed the fabric. Susan is not the warrior. You are."

I had never been loved so deeply in my entire life.

* * *

The following week was a love feast for my soul. I felt such a profound sense of freedom and joy. I would also suddenly burst into deep sobbing tears as I continued to relax inside of my soul's loving embrace.

I experientially understood the importance of allowing the entire present moment to be manifest and expressed fully in all its feelings and content both inside of me and outside of me. The result was always that more Love entered the universe and transformation occurred.

On the way to my next session with Beatrice, I brought her seven yellow roses and two deep pink roses to symbolize the nine years we had worked together. To represent her four cats, I bought four blue irises. I also brought her a nice bottle of Merlot with a little Buddha taped to the top of the bottle. Included in the gift bag was a beautiful lantern candle, two pink votive candles, four gray mice in an ornamental heart box, two kitty play balls, and a dozen home made chocolate chip cookies. Of course, there was a card and also a twenty-nine page brief history of our relationship together.

Beatrice was stunned. I had never seen her overwhelmed before. She sank back into her chair in total shock. She said she would probably keep the bottle of wine forever. I knew she might have thought I was leaving therapy. I explained that this was a completion celebration that I wanted to thank her for all of her love and support and teaching over the years. She was my spiritual mother. I was individuating. But I assured her that we still had lots of work to do together.

Two weeks later Beatrice called to cancel our session. She had been assaulted while on her morning walk. I was horrified. When I saw her in session the following week, she told me again that even the worst things in Life were gifts from our souls. The man who had attacked her had actually saved her life. Because of the attack, Beatrice had gone to a doctor. During the doctor's exam, they discovered that Beatrice had breast cancer.

Now I was stunned. My worst nightmare was sitting right in front of me in the form of the woman I loved more than anything else in the world. My deepest fear had always been that if I ever became real, my mother would die. It would kill her if I were really alive. Now here I was individuating from my spiritual mother and she was literally dying in front of me. It was horrifying and yet profoundly perfect in its manifestation. The only way that I could heal this deep-seated fear was to have it manifest in my life. I also knew that Life was not a one-sided proposition. Beatrice had her own reasons for contracting breast cancer. I did not know what movement was occurring in her soul but I trusted that the cancer really was the gift that she kept calling it.

* * *

When Buddha sat under the Bodhi tree on the day of his enlightenment, Maya sent powerful armies to heave spears and to shoot arrows at him. But all of their weapons turned into flowers as they entered Buddha's field of energy.

The army was not an external band of men. The army was Buddha's own internal fears and judgments rising up to test his ability to face any energy no matter how scary or ugly or painful with an open soft heart of unconditional acceptance. That open heart transformed the arrows, the perception of punishment, into flowers, into gifts of wonder and beauty.

My sessions with Beatrice became very weird and strained for me as I struggled to stay in my breath, to stay awake, to have a gentle, soft heart with myself and to simultaneously allow my worst fears to come forward through Beatrice. I could not tell where my projections left off and reality began. Every time I tried to talk to Beatrice about the cancer, she would deflect my questions. No matter what I did, there seemed to be a dense wall of energy between us severely distorting our communications. I knew this was part of my own pattern. I knew that the best thing I could do was to stay real and bring my breath to my pain. Somehow this was part of my individuating process. I did not have to understand it. In December, we stopped having sessions because she was beginning chemotherapy.

* * *

1999 began with my biological mother demanding to have therapy immediately. Alice was a two year old having a tantrum. She was jealous that I was having a real relationship with my father. She was not going to be outdone.

I told her that I would love to have therapy with her but I would not be available until the beginning of September. I was starting a film in two weeks and there was no way that I could go into that place of pain for more healing when I was in production. I suggested that Mom try getting therapy with Susan in the interim. Interestingly, Susan was having therapy with her husband and would not be available until March or April. The diva would have to wait.

When I began working on a film called "Galaxy Quest" in the middle of January, I noticed that something was missing inside of me. An energy of fear. It had always been part of my internal background landscape whenever I was working with large groups of redneck men. Now it was gone. I knew this related directly to Tuesday September 29th, the Day of Transformation. I had no idea then that what took place there would actually affect my ability to work in construction. But it was true. The deep fear of needing to protect myself from men had disappeared. Now there was just the room, my computer equipment and different men coming in and out doing their usual mundane routine stuff. My fear always felt like an energy outside of me, encasing me. But the larger truth was that my fear was an internal judgment that had dissolved when the pattern with my father released. This was real freedom.

While 1998 had definitely been the year of dealing with my patterns with my father, 1999 would be the year of facing my patterns with my mother. On a deep spiritual level, I seemed to be trying to resolve these painful habitual patterns by the end of the millennium.

I called Beatrice in January to try to arrange sessions with my new work schedule. She was very bitchy to me on the phone. I had hoped that the month off would have given her time to come back to normal. But she sounded worse than ever. Her bitchiness scared me to death. She was my rock. She was my stability. Now she was falling apart. I knew that as my therapist, it was inappropriate for her to talk to me that way. But I also knew that she was my friend, that she was fighting for her life and that I would not abandon her after all the support she had given me. I stayed in my breath and allowed her to become a complete bitch. We managed to schedule a phone session for Friday.

By Friday, I was very tense. I fully expected that Beatrice would apologize to me about her behavior on Tuesday night.

Instead of apologizing, she raised my rate! The tension between us was palpable.

I didn't know what to do. It wasn't supposed to be this way between us.

I closed my eyes as I dropped back into my breath. My bed felt very supportive and safe. My body felt like it was going to crack apart. I could not believe that after ten years of good hard work together, we would end our journey on this note of combativeness. I felt very, very sad. We sat in silence for fifteen minutes. I wanted to hang up the phone, to just get the hell out of there and never go back. I stayed in breath. It was very hard. But I stayed. Finally I spoke.

"I can't talk to you anymore, Beatrice," I said quietly. "I feel like I can't come back here anymore." Tears filled my eyes. "Every other part of my life is fine right now. The only problem I have in my life right now is you." I felt a weight lift off my body.

"Good," Beatrice said tersely. "Then I'm doing my job."

We didn't have much time left to talk. But I felt like the curse had been broken, that I had finally been able to speak directly to her while she was being a bitch.

"You're doing really well, Roxanne," Beatrice acknowledged before hanging up. "I know how hard it was for you to say that."

It was monumentally hard because I was directly breaking a life long pattern of avoiding direct confrontation with female authority figures. The astounding part was that I needed Beatrice to be dying for this pattern to really come up inside of me. I would not have been able to heal it that deeply under any other circumstance.

The following Friday, I had a session in Beatrice's office. She was more like the old Beatrice. I could relax again. I told her most of my feelings about how weird she had been acting and how scary it was for me. I explained my deep fear that if I became real, my mother would die. Then just when I began individuating, Beatrice got cancer.

Beatrice nodded. "And in addition to what you have said, I can tell you that my cancer has a very definite purpose in my life that has nothing to do with you. When I was eighteen, I went to India. I met a very spiritual, psychic man. He gave me a life reading. He predicted that at this age in my life, I would be fighting for my life. So you see, my soul has been preparing for this experience. It's not a punishment. It's a gift."

I nodded.

"I want you to be strong in the Love and to be strong about living your life in your way. I want you to be separate from me. I want you to succeed." Beatrice stared at me intensely. Her heartfelt conviction made me weep. "It's not a betrayal, Roxanne. You will help me the most by doing that. So write your book."

I blew my nose and wiped my eyes as we both laughed. "I so need to hear this, Beatrice," I cried. "My mother was never capable of saying those things to me. She couldn't tell me that it was okay for me to be separate and successful because she thought she would die without me."

"You won't betray me by becoming separate. You will strengthen and deepen the love between us." Beatrice's deep brown eyes bathed me with love.

"Thank you," I sniffled. "Just keep telling me that. It's food for my soul."

* * *

In March, I received a letter in the mail from my mother. As I unfolded the actual letter, my stomach felt nauseous. It read like a bad tabloid headline. Spread across the top of the letter in capitalized bold-faced type and underlined were the words "THE MISSING PIECE TO MY PUZZLE! MY NIGHTMARE IS FINALLY OVER!" I felt like vomiting. Oh, my God, I thought. My mother really is crazy.

In the letter, Alice blamed my father for absolutely everything including her own inability to notice that her husband of twenty years was sexually abusing her children. She insisted that she had been victimized along with her children. At the end of the letter, she gave a token apology for 'whatever (she) may have done to hurt you girls.' But she took no real responsibility for anything.

The following night, I was watching a Frasier rerun. At first I began laughing hysterically. Then I broke into deep heaving sobs. I was so embarrassed and ashamed about my mother's mental illness. Part of me realized that if my mother was that way, then I must be that way too to some degree because she was the role model I grew up with.

* * *

At work, the space ship began to melt. The heat from the lights was so intense that the vacuform on the walls began buckling and warping. It was a hideous and costly mistake. I was also dealing with a narcissistic boss who was becoming progressively worse as the show became more difficult. The construction crew shot to over a hundred and twenty. I began working Saturdays. I had not done that many estimates and projections since I had worked on 'Volcano.' The ten hours a day, walk-in-the-park show had turned into the nightmare show from hell.

My nerves began to fray. I was worried about Beatrice. She was deep in the midst of the chemo treatments. I wanted to trust that she would be okay but part of me was terrified that I would lose her. The idea of living the remainder of my life without her presence was unbearable. Yet I knew that I might have to do just that.

I could not control Beatrice's life or death. But I could hold her in my heart and let her know how much I loved her. I sent her one musical cd a month to coincide with her chemo treatments. Each card and each gift of music came from a special place in my heart. This was not about grasping or aversion. Even in her illness, Beatrice was teaching me about deeper levels of love. I had never felt such unconditional love for anyone before.

One day when she called to cancel our appointment, a question came from deep in my heart. "Are you going to make it through this?"

The response came from the depths of her soul. "Yes. Yes. Yes."

I burst into tears and wept my fear away. We talked openly for a few minutes. Her final chemo was scheduled for the following Friday. Then she would begin radiation. She was so grateful for her cancer. It was teaching her so much about Love. I was grateful that she was alive and that she wanted to stay that way.

* * *

As I continued individuating, unconscious patterns of avoidance and fear that had ruled my life in the past simply dissolved. I began acting differently in my day-to-day life. I joined a lesbian writing group. I had always avoided writers' groups because I could not bear the idea of someone else ripping apart my work.

Now I understood that my fear of being torn apart came from my mother's acerbic narcissistic attacks when I was growing up. Had I been drawn deliberately into Hollywood and into screenwriting because it contained such a familiar energy of rejection? Yes, I had. My experiences in the industry restimulated the frozen pain within me and gave me the opportunity to bring my loving breath to that deep, deep pain.

My choice of women was also intrinsically tied into my pattern of emotional abuse with my mother. This truth was hideous to look at and very hard to sit with. At two o'clock one morning, I stood in my living room and cursed my mother in a harsh whisper, telling her to go to hell, to get the fuck out of my life, that she had no control over me anymore, that it was because of her bizarre, sick enmeshing tactics that I was drawn to narcissistic cold-hearted women. I told her that I did not care anymore if she thought I was the bitch daughter from hell. I was going to tell the truth about her to the entire world.

That week, I had a phone session with Beatrice. I was able to connect with a very deep level of shame about my sexuality and to voice that shame, shame at my mother and her perversity, shame at my father and his perversity, shame at myself because I was just like them because they were my role models about sexual energy. Perverts. It was all so distorted, twisted, power-based, hungry, abusive, manipulating, ugly, nauseating. My face burned red with shame. I clenched my teeth and told Beatrice that I wanted to hang up the phone but I was determined to stay with this shame and bring my breath to it. Beatrice supported me in my shame. The energy transformed like a boil finally popping.

That Sunday I was a woman freed from years of imprisonment. I was so excited at the prospect of reading my book to my lesbian writing group that I made my special tofu pasta sauce and cooked up a huge pan full of pasta. I bought a fresh loaf of Artesian French bread on my way to the meeting. I wanted to share my inner wealth with my friends. In a very real way, I was coming out to the world. I was speaking without shame about my sexuality. It was exhilarating.

And then I hit the wall. It was higher and longer than the Great Wall of China and thicker than the densest material known to man. That great wall was my mother. I had called to let her know I would be available for therapy in September.

"I haven't made a lot of money this year. I can only afford two double sessions." Alice's energy had the intensity of a class five hurricane. "I shouldn't have to pay for all this," she snapped rapidly like a machine gun firing at my heart.

It was not the words she used that stung me. It was the vitriolic intensity of the energy beneath. She had become her own abusive mother. She could easily have said 'I'm sorry. I know I asked you to go to therapy with me. But I didn't make enough money this year and I don't have enough for more than two double sessions.' But Alice was incapable of being wrong or apologizing. Instead Alice victimized herself and shamed me.

I stayed in my breath. "Well, why don't I call you at the beginning of September when I finish the film and we can discuss when to schedule the sessions." She agreed. I hung up, stunned at her ferocity and cold-heartedness. If this was any indication of what was to come, it was little wonder why I had blanked out my entire childhood. I had spent most of my time with her.

At the beginning of September, my mother backpedaled again.

"I can only do one double session," Mom snarled at me loudly. "I just got a four hundred dollar insurance bill and I have to use the money Dave gave me to pay for that!"

Memories of Nadia rose up inside of me. Every time she had to get a job, she would throw her back out. There was always an excuse. I stayed in my breath. Screaming at my mother would not accomplish anything at this moment. "Then why don't you set up that one session and we'll just see what happens with that."

"Okay," she agreed. She had no idea how she was treating me.

When I phoned Beatrice on Friday for our session, I broke down crying.

"My mother doesn't love me," I sobbed. The devastating emotional pain of that truth seared through my heart. "Honestly, I never really believed it before but the woman is just a bitch! She is so narcissistic; she doesn't value me at all. She doesn't even know I exist!" My mind spasmed. "I—I—I—I . . ." The horror of that narcissism was so great, my throat choked and I could only sputter senselessly.

Beatrice did not minimize my feelings. Instead she held me in her breath. When I finished, Beatrice told me to practice this statement in meditation. "I will never again invest my life force into people or things outside of me." That felt good.

For the entire year, I had been working on my pattern with my mother through interactions with other people including Beatrice. Now I would have the opportunity to look the pattern in the face. Mom and I began having therapy sessions with Dr. Paul Hamilton. One session turned into five with Susan attending the final four. Mom would only pay for her third. I could not afford to pay for this therapy and my sessions with Beatrice. Susan insisted on paying for my portion.

I walked into the sessions knowing that my mother would probably never wake up. I knew that my personal objective was for me to be able to stay awake and to speak my feelings directly to my mother. It did not matter if she changed. The very act of speaking would mean that I had changed, that I was consciously breaking the pattern.

Instead of labeling Mom a narcissist, Dr. Hamilton explained that Mom had never learned how to empathize when she was a little girl because her mother had not modeled that behavior. It was as if Mom was speaking Greek and Susan and I were speaking Russian. Mom just could not understand emotional empathy. Mom asked how she could learn that language. Paul told her that coming into therapy sessions was a good start.

The sessions were extremely tough. Susan and I would alternately grasp onto any ray of hope that Mom would wake up. But Alice consistently returned to her narcissism, nesting in it like some insidious creature. Alice had to habitually keep rebuilding her image as a saint. Whenever the facts contradicted that image, Alice would simply rewrite history. It was astounding, confounding, disheartening and terribly, terribly sad. She had such potential to be a real kind-hearted human being. But she was trapped inside extremely strong delusions.

In the fourth session, it became obvious that Mom was not going to wake up at all.

I brought the discussion back to the dieting issue. It had been a major portion of my 1991 letter. From the time I was eight, Mom had gone on every fad diet around and had always insisted on taking me with her, saying 'We're going on a diet.' That was just a historical fact that our family always agreed upon.

"Do you remember the books, Mom? *Martinis and Whipped Cream, Dr. Atkins, Dr. Pritikins,* the calorie counters, the carbohydrate counters, the little postal scale we used to weigh out four ounces of tuna fish?" I asked, hoping to cajole her memory.

Mom leaned towards me on the couch, her face cold with anger. "Those were *my* dieting books," she said, her voice dripping with venom as steel daggers shot from her eyes.

I gasped. She was honestly going to lie outright to my face, to rape me again by completely invalidating my only real memories of having any relationship with her at all. She was totally willing to deny even that to protect her own image.

Mom turned to Paul. "I have *never* been emotionally invasive to my daughter."

"How do you feel right now, Roxanne," Paul asked quietly.

"Angry," I replied as the energy rolled through me. "A memory's coming up. When I was around twelve years old, Mom and I had been on a diet and we'd just finished it. It was a Sunday. We'd gone to church and on the way home, we stopped at Winchell's Donuts because they had good hamburgers and milkshakes." I was reliving the memory as I spoke. The energy and the emotions were alive in me. "We walked into the house on Canzonet and I was eating my hamburger when Dad and Susan began teasing us about eating junk food after we'd been dieting. They were always making fun of us." My body vibrated with rage. "This time I got so angry that I threw my hamburger across the room and it hit the side of the kitchen counter island. And then I ran upstairs crying." Tears streamed down my cheeks. My voice cracked as the experience replayed inside me.

My mother reached over and put her hand on top of mine. "Now, can't you just admit that you're half wrong and I'm half wrong?" she said cheerily. "You expect *me* to say that I'm wrong. Can't we just meet half way?"

"Alice," Paul said sternly.

I looked at my mother. The rage pulsed in my veins. "I want to kill you right now. I just want to kill you."

Mom looked disgruntled and sat back.

Paul turned to her. "Alice, what did you hear Roxanne saying?"

Mom made a dismissive move with her left hand. "Oh, *that*," she snapped coldly. "I've heard *that* before."

The image of my mother's hand dismissing my pain with a mere wave burned into my mind. The coldness of it. The complete lack of compassion. The absolute devaluation of my pain without a second thought. She did it with the ease that Hitler and his henchmen demonstrated when they casually slaughtered millions of human beings. It was exactly the same energy. I did not care how much abuse she had suffered growing up; she did not have the right to treat me like a piece of shit. The image of her dismissive hand would stay in my mind like a bell to wake me whenever I fell into the delusion that my mother was a saint.

We had one final session to finish with Paul.

By the end of that session, Paul asked us how we felt. Mom turned to me. "I want to know how you feel," she said quietly.

I shook my head and sighed deeply. "I'm very angry with you right now. I cannot believe how incredibly far apart we are in our memories of my childhood. I really don't want to have anything to do with you right now. And that makes me very sad."

"Well, I feel the same way," Mom said shortly.

"And there's no need to try to push away the sadness," Paul said softly. "It's okay if you need to take a time out and not talk to each other for a couple of months. I would strongly suggest that when you do get together that you avoid discussing charged issues. When you feel the need to discuss those areas, you should come back in here."

As we left the office, Mom paused in the outer office. "You know, Susan, I think that you and Dave and I should get together and pray about this."

Susan just stared at her. It was as if nothing at all had happened in five therapy sessions. Mom had forgotten all of it and had returned to her original controlling position.

"I don't think that's a good idea, Mom," Susan replied. "Paul just told us we should not be discussing these issues outside of therapy. So if you want to have prayer sessions about this with me then we better just turn around right now and go talk to Paul about it."

"No, no," Mom shook her head, completely annoyed. "Just forget it."

The next day, Mom called Susan and continued to

pressure her. She ranted on for several minutes before Susan cut her off.

Susan sighed deeply as she and I sat on the living room couch. "Mom thinks that Satan has a hold of our family and that Satan had a hold of the therapy sessions. She wants to pray with me about it. I told her no. That she could pray with other people about it if she wanted to." Susan sighed again and shook her head. She looked really sad. "I want to apologize to you, Roxanne," she began. "For years, Mom and I have prayed to cast the homosexuality out of you."

I snorted. "What?"

Susan looked ashamed. "I am deeply sorry. When we drove out to your house in Topanga Canyon, we would pray all the way up to cast Satan out of your house and your life."

That felt icky. I made a face.

Susan acknowledged my grimace. "I am so sorry. I have become so much more aware of how Mom uses Christianity to further her own illness. I still believe in the Bible. But I don't agree with how Mom is using it to prop up her own image. It's just not right."

Well, hallelujah! I felt like screaming. At last the truth was coming out about how people really felt in my family. The insanity of putting on the nicey-nice masks and pretending had come to an end. At least it had between my big sister and me. And that was all that really mattered right now anyway.

From a place deep within me, I realized that I really needed to write lesbian books, books about my life, books about healing from this deep pattern of pain in our collective souls.

I drove home. I was emotionally and physically exhausted. I cried a lot on Thursday. I had not realized how deeply I had longed for a healthy family when I was a little girl. I had gripped onto the idea that my family was good, that my mother was Donna Reed and nothing could shake that loose. I had to cling to that delusion or I would have gone insane in that house where there was no real nurturing love and only perpetually pulsing perverted sexual energies.

When I told Beatrice what had transpired, she had a very interesting response.

"Your mother is a brick," Beatrice said firmly. "And maybe it's good that she is a brick right now because it will act as a very solid boundary that will continue to impel you to stay inside of yourself, to find your self-worth in the only true place—within you. So in a very odd way, on a much deeper level of awareness, she is doing a deeply loving thing." Beatrice studied my face. It was obvious that I was having a hard time digesting this. "That in no way diminishes the abuse, Roxanne."

"I know . . . It's just really hard."

"It's *very* hard," Beatrice nodded.

That was October 22nd. This was going to take a long time for me to digest. I had to allow myself to grieve the death of my own delusional relationship with my mother.

The holidays came and went. I did not see my mother at all. I was grateful that she did not attend our family holiday gatherings. We e-mailed one another briefly. I had no idea what to do with this situation. So I did nothing, trusting my soul and the larger Love to provide me with right action.

Deep feelings of failure with my mother transformed into a deeper understanding that everything really was okay. My mother had been the false god in my life, subconsciously ruling my choices. Now that delusional edifice had collapsed like the Berlin Wall. I did not know where my life was going. And that was all right.

I spent New Year's Eve day watching Peter Jennings follow the change of the millennium as the sun crossed the time lines around the world. It was a magnificent, globally unifying experience even if not everyone agreed that the year 2000 was the actual change of the millennium. I felt a deep hope for humanity as a whole.

I spent New Year's Eve night at a party with my gay male friends that nearly got cancelled because a major pattern of dysfunction in Vincent's life was beginning to collapse. It seemed that we were all growing together as the millennium changed.

After New Year's Day, I went on a 'coffee date' with a woman I had been strongly drawn to at a lesbian Christmas party. Mary was an attractive brunette in her early forties who worked in women's politics. I was surprised that Mary brought a friend to our 'date.' We all went to lunch at a casual seafood restaurant. I steered the conversation into family histories. Mary had been physically beaten by her drunken father when she was a child. She had never had any therapy. When I asked her how she dealt with her own anger, she looked like a terrified five-year-old. She was an emotional time bomb waiting to explode. This was not going to work. After lunch, I politely said goodbye and wandered alone down the Santa Monica Promenade.

I felt such a sense of freedom as I strolled down the promenade and watched some of the street performers. I had been able to stay awake with Mary. I could see her patterns without judging them. I could just see them. That gave me tremendous freedom. I could turn and walk away without any guilt or self-hatred. What an amazing experience. It really was a gift from my soul

Now I knew that I would be able to find another healthy integrated woman to have a relationship with. It did not matter when. I could trust it would happen at just the right time for me. In the meantime, I had a book to write. And I could feel the whole universe opening up to support me and to give me the time I needed to finish that book.

What a wonderful way to start out a new millennium.

With love and peace in my heart at long last.

It did not mean the rest of my life would be easy. It just meant that I would be more able to swim in the ocean of my Life. I could count on the fact that I would fall asleep again. But I could also trust that I would wake up again too.

FORGIVENESS
(2003)

We are our parents whether we like it or not. They are in our blood, in the marrow of our bones. They are the ones who mirrored to us. And if we don't own them, then they will own us.

True freedom can only come with forgiveness—not of the acts that they committed against us but of the sicknesses they could not heal in themselves, the patterns of illness that had been their heritage from their parents, the legacy they bestowed upon us.

Forgiveness does not mean we have to like them or even talk to them again.

You cannot cheat your soul and feign forgiveness for your abusers by merely spouting words and putting on a pretty face. Forgiveness comes when the heart cracks open and real warmth and compassion flows out—first for your own wounded inner child, then for the wounded child in your abuser. Then true transmutation occurs. The patterns dissolve and you are born anew.

It is the only way I know of to break the chain of the disease.

ACKNOWLEDGEMENTS

When I began writing this trilogy back in 1992, I felt lost and all alone. As I consider whom to thank now, I am blessed with a treasure trove of such good, kind, generous and loving friends.

First, foremost and always—Dr. JoAnne Golden and her "kids." You are such a part of this trilogy. It could not have happened without you.

I want to thank my lesbian writing group, The Spirit's Quill, for sustaining me for four years. The original 12 boiled down to the Fabulous Four. Reva, Kimberley and Mara—thank you for being my emotional bedrock as I made the journey toward bringing my baby into the world. They listened to six pages a month for four years and they loved all of it.

I want to thank my "Boys Club" network—Steve, Joey, Guy, Darien, Luis, Rich, Rocky, Brian, Walker. You have all been such wonderful friends. I feel like Dorothy in the Wizard of Oz and you guys are all the loving farm hands—only you're much cuter.

Eternal thanks to Carol Stanzione, my friend and neighbor. Her emotional response to reading the manuscript gave me great courage and hope. Before I even knew about Xlibris, she had a vision that I would be selling my book out of the trunk of my car—I just needed to get it bound.

Much thanks to Lisha and Scott for the wonderful cover shoot. I was a nervous wreck but you two helped me relax and have fun. And the craft service was phenomenal.

Back in 2000, when I was still out in the middle of an ocean of words and nearly ready to quit, Ben Rogers was like a lighthouse beacon for me, encouraging me to bring the book to shore and to get it published.

I want to thank my 'star brother' Steve Gaines for his loyal support and love over the last 17 years (I can't believe it has been that long!). And Jeannie Clark for being there whenever I called with publishing questions.

Kazu encouraged me for eight years by telling me stories about how long it took other authors to get published. David Brooks and Beans badgered me over the years with one incessant question: "When do I get to read that book of yours?" You don't know how many times I would remember all of that when I was completely ready to quit.

Many thanks to the wonderful professionals at Xlibris for making this first publishing experience a good one.

FINAL DEDICATION

Ultimately we all want the same things—to be happy, to feel safe, to have Love, and to develop that profound sense of inner peace and well-beingness. I hope this book contributes a little bit towards that for all beings.